Management, Society, and the Informal Economy

T0290058

Informal economic activity, defined as exchanges made by individuals and organizations in extra-legal or non-bureaucratic contexts, represents a significant and growing share of global economic activity. The informal economy brings to mind images of street vendors in markets and bazaars throughout the developing world; indeed, informal economic activity ranges from 25%–75% of economic activity, depending on the country under study. Informal activity also includes "under the table," or "off the books" business in the developed world, such as informal labor arrangements in child care, construction, or home cleaning in the United States or Western Europe.

What many fail to realize, however, is the increasing presence of informal economic activity in the developed world's largest corporations and most innovative entrepreneurial ventures, such as technology development work in Silicon Valley, open-source software agreements, or employment arrangements between "technology stars" and firms.

Management, Society, and the Informal Economy brings to light the role of the informal economy in the 21st century. The book does more than illuminate, however—it also calls for increased focus on the informal economy by management scholars. Each chapter contains a call to action as well as practical and methodological advice for scholarship on the topic.

Management, Society, and the Informal Economy contains a multi-faceted set of arguments, descriptions, and illustrations designed to convince management scholars that they should attend to the informal economy and view it as a serious and rigorous context for theorizing, empirical research, and even practical advocacy.

Paul C. Godfrey is the William and Roceil Low Professor of Business Strategy and Organizational Leadership at the Marriott School of Business, Brigham Young University, USA.

Routledge Advances in Management and Business Studies

Management, Society, and the Informal Economy

Edited by Paul C. Godfrey

Routledge
Taylor & Francis Group

LONDON AND NEW YORK

First published 2015 by Routledge

2 Park Square, Milton Park, Abingdon, Oxfordshire OX14 4RN
711 Third Avenue, New York, NY 10017

Routledge is an imprint of the Taylor & Francis Group, an informa business

First issued in paperback 2018

Library of Congress Cataloging-in-Publication Data
Management, society, and the informal economy / edited by Paul C. Godfrey.
   pages cm. — (Routledge advances in management and business studies ; 62)
   Includes bibliographical references and index.
  1. Informal sector (Economics) 2. Management. I. Godfrey, Paul C.
HD2341.M3496 2015
   330—dc23   2015010343

ISBN: 978-1-138-79706-2 (hbk)
ISBN: 978-1-138-61781-0 (pbk)

Typeset in Sabon
by Apex CoVantage, LLC

Contents

PART II
Empirical Research in the Informal Economy

Figures and Tables

FIGURES

TABLES

1 Introduction

Why the Informal Economy Matters to Management

Paul C. Godfrey

In May of 2014, 15 organizational scholars convened at the Chicago O'Hare Marriott to discuss the following question: Why should management scholars pay serious attention to informal economic activity? We came from different perspectives and all had our favorite operating theories; some approached informal activity from a Base of the Pyramid or subsistence entrepreneurship perspective, others saw informality as a pervasive feature of social and economic life in highly developed, Western economies. The group featured individuals steeped in communications theory, micro- and macro-organization theories and those fascinated by entrepreneurship or ethics in the informal economy. This book represents one outcome of that conference.

The goal of the conference, and consequently this book, was/is to open a new conversation. The conference, as good ones always do, raised more questions than it answered. An initial question turned on the importance of the notion of "illegal yet legitimate" in defining the informal economy (Webb, Tihanyi, Ireland, & Sirmon, 2009). Some substantial portion of informal economic activity fits this mold, such as informal enterprise in the developing world and "off the books" work in developed economies; however, there remains a portion of informal activity that qualifies as "legal and legitimate" but is governed by traditional or informal norms rather than the rule of law. Additionally, should we include under the rubric of informality business and work that occurs "extra-legally" where the legality of the activity is in doubt? Legal status and standing obviously matters as a dimension of informal activity, but how strictly must one construe the construct of "legality" to mark the break between formal and informal economies?

Other questions highlight the role of economic activity for the study of the informal economy. If social norms and customs govern transactions in the informal economy, how important are social relationships, formal and informal, in a picture of informal economic activity? Barnard (1938) wrote of informal organization—organization without a conscious, goal-directed purpose—as a critical element of and support for formal organization. What about friendship, kinship, or other associations that have goal-directed, conscious economic components? At what point does social informality with an economic component become informal economic activity within a social system? This question, like its predecessor, probed the boundaries of what might be considered a new construct or context for management scholars: the informal economy.

Finally, how strongly must, or should, informal economic activity remain anchored to another emergent context, the Base of the Pyramid? Much of our collective work, and motivation, stems from the prevalence of informal economic activity in poverty environments; informality constitutes a way of life for billions, and its pervasiveness and vivacity create barriers for formal organizations (commercial and philanthropic) hoping to establish operations in these markets. While informality and poverty exhibit a positive empirical correlation—and strong theoretical arguments can be marshalled to support this link—the two constructs cannot be the same because informality appears in many non-poverty environments as well. As with our other questions, a serious study of informality requires scholars to cut at the politically charged and economically relevant joints that separate prosperity from poverty. Such questions demand theoretical answers and not merely empirical mapping.

The chapters that follow take up these questions in greater detail. The editorial charge given to each author was, first, to craft a chapter that considered and illustrated some aspect of informality and its relevance for management scholarship. The second charge lay in considering the following question: What are the implications, for theory, research, and practice, of a serious and sustained scholarly effort to investigate, model, and understand informal economic activity? As you'll see throughout this work, the authors have taken that charge seriously and have produced a set of thoughtful, and thought-provoking, essays. To set the stage for their work, in the remainder of this introduction I'll take up three questions to provide some context. I'll draw on my own work (Godfrey, 2011) to answer What is informal economic activity? I'll then offer some thoughts as to why informal economic activity—and informality in general—has remained in the background of our research agenda. This will help answer Why haven't we studied informality before now? Finally, I'll take up the question Why should we study informality now?

WHAT IS THE INFORMAL ECONOMY?

Informal economic activity certainly pre-dates what we understand today as formal economic activity, economic transactions carried out by legally recognized and bureaucratically administered firms (Booth, 1993); indeed, individuals and groups engaged in exchange long before law or bureaucracy existed. In the academic world, however, the timeline has been reversed; we've studied the formal firm (often as entrepreneur) since the 18th century (Smith, 1776), but the informal economy only appeared on our scholarly radar in the middle of the last century (Hart, 1973). Development economists, sociologists, and political scientists have done most of the conceptual heavy lifting; however, management thinkers have made substantial contributions as well. Table 1.1 provides a summary of key definitions of informal economic activity from these various fields.

Table 1.1 Defining the Informal Economy (Adapted from Godfrey, 2011)

Author (s)	Year	Key Variable	Definition
Economics			
Lewis	1958[a]	Labor supply	p. 407: "The capitalist sector is that part of the economy which uses reproducible capital, and pays capitalists for the use thereof . . . The subsistence sector is by difference all that part of the economy which is not using reproducible capital . . ."
Hart	1973	Bureaucracy	p. 68: "the key variable is the degree of rationalization of work—that is to say, whether or not labor is recruited on a permanent and regular basis for fixed rewards."
Marcouiller & Young	1995	Property rights, legal protection	p. 631: "the informal sector comprises producers who avoid taxes by bypassing the procedures [government-sanctioned procedures for establishing and recording property rights and for resolving disputes], thereby foregoing any claim on the order provided by the government."
LaPorta & Schliefer	2008	Legal registration, taxation	p. 1: "unofficial economic activity . . . that conducted by unregistered firms or by registered firms but hidden from taxation."
Sociology			
Polanyi	1957	Institutional origins	p. 250: "the human economy, then, is embedded and enmeshed in institutions, economic and noneconomic. The inclusion of the non-economic is vital. For religion or government may be as important for the structure and functioning of the economy as monetary institutions or the availability of tools and machines themselves that lighten the toil of labor."
Portes, Castells, & Benton	1989	Institutional regulation	p. 12: "The informal economy is . . . characterized by one central feature: it is unregulated by the institutions of society, in a legal and social environment in which similar activities are regulated."

(*Continued*)

Table 1.1 (Continued)

Author (s)	Year	Key Variable	Definition
Venkatesh	2006	Illicit exchange and illicit activity	p. 7: "we cannot truly understand the 'shady' economy if we see it is as a dirty, lawless world of violence and disrepute, one that tarnishes an otherwise pristine sphere where everyone pays their taxes, obeys the laws, and turns to the government to solve disputes and maintain order . . . Its [the informal economy] boundaries are not so clear. Nor, for that matter, is the underground economy inhabited by a single, distinct class of citizens."
Centeno & Portes	2006	Relationship with state	p. 26–27: A final alternative definition of the informal economy would be transactions where the state neither provides protection nor receives a 'cut' . . . therefore, the relationship between the informal economy and the state is, by definition, one of inevitable conflict."
Policy/ Political Science			
De Soto	2000	Legal/ institutional basis	p. 21: "Once these newcomers to the city quit the system, they become 'extralegal.' Their only alternative is to live and work outside the official law, using their own informally binding arrangements to protect and mobilize their assets."
International Labor Organization	2002	Status of labor	p. 12: "the informal economy is seen as comprised of informal employment (without secure contracts, worker benefits, or social protection) both inside and outside informal enterprises . . . (small, unregistered or unincorporated enterprises)."
Becker (Swedish International Development Cooperation Agency	2004	Labor	p. 11: "The informal economy is largely characterized by: Low entry requirements in terms of capital and professional qualifications; a small scale of operations; skills often acquired outside of formal education; Labor intensive methods of production and adapted technology."

Zinnes	2009	Institutional capacity	p. vii: "a firm [that] operates in the informal economy [sic] is unable to take full advantage of the legal, financial, and marketing benefits that, in principle, the judicial, banking, and economic systems of its country offer."
Management			
Barnard	1938	Organization	p. 115: "by informal organization I mean the aggregate of personal contacts and interactions and associated groupings . . . informal organization is indefinite and rather structureless."
Spicer, McDermott, & Kogut	2000	Socially embedded ties	p. 639: "Informal networks of local firms . . . [characterized by] dense horizontal socioeconomic ties emerged to help managers and work teams, suppliers and customers, firms, and local party members coordinate continual adaptations to the shortage environment."
London & Hart	2004	Social embeddedness	p. 352: "In the developing world, on the other hand, it is simply too costly or complicated for many entrepreneurs to enter the formal economy . . . In the informal economy, relationships are grounded primarily on social, not legal, contracts."
Webb, Tihanyi, Ireland, & Sirmon	2009	Legality	p. 492: "We define the informal economy as the set of illegal yet legitimate (to some large groups) activities through which actors recognize and exploit opportunities."

A quick glance at Table 1.1 indicates several areas of similarity between fields of study as well as key differences. All disciplines differentiate formal from informal economic activity by reference to institutional status. Formality means to be grounded in, structured through, and sheltered by the formal institutional matrix of a larger social unit like a nation state. Marcouiller and Young (1995) and LaPorta and Schliefer (2008) use the language of law, taxation, and the regulatory institutions that govern economic relations between the state and firms or actors. From the early writings of Polanyi (1957) to the work of Alejandro Portes (Centeno & Portes, 2006), sociologists use the same regulatory institutional language to cut at the joints between formality and informality, and De Soto (2000) and Zinnes (2009) echo this conversation from a political science perspective.

The differences, while less apparent in this abbreviated table, reveal more fundamental disciplinary grounding. Economists fret over the lost productivity and wealth that they claim accompany informal organization. Sociologists count the costs to people, as individuals and social groups, attending informal organization; indeed, sociologists see oppression from above and the lack of upward mobility from below as the negative consequences of informal economic activity. Political scientists see the informality rooted in political ideologies and warn of a stable world order in which societies (and by implication the individuals living within them) exist in semi-rigid relations based on efficiency and related gains from trade (see Wallerstein, 2004 for the best articulation of these concerns).

Management scholarship, as one can read from Table 1.1, accepts the basic definition of informal economic activity as that occurring outside the rule of law; however, management researchers tend to highlight the positive effects of the socially embedded nature, and resulting governance, of informality. Barnard's (1938) early work ignored the legal dimension altogether as he modeled informality as existing in a symbiotic relationship with formal organization. Informal organization provided vitality and flexibility that energized formal organization and provided a conduit for communication and work to occur outside the defined lines of formal organization. Later scholarship (exemplified in the table by the work of Spicer, McDermott, and Kogut (2000), London and Hart (2004) and more recently in 2011, and Webb et al. (2009)) follows the Barnardian tradition by accentuating the positive aspects of informality.

I now turn to the second question I raised earlier: Why has management scholarship neglected a serious and systematic study of informal economic activity? Without offering a normative critique of our scientific endeavors, I'll suggest that we've neglected the informal economy because our most productive theories steer us away from informality, and our empirical predilections make a systemic study of the informal economy a challenging and daunting task.

WHY HAVEN'T WE STUDIED THE INFORMAL ECONOMY BEFORE?

I tread lightly in answering this question for two reasons. First, critiques of why a field has not pursued a topic viewed as essential by some scholar easily slip into a language that reeks of academic whining. As you'll see from what I argue below, the lack of interest in the informal economy should not be taken as evidence of the field's lack of collective ability to spot the "next big thing" or most "critical" dependent variable. We have solid reasons why we haven't studied informality with the intensity we've focused on its opposite. Second, much of the argument I make relies on an argument that should be classed as probable rather than certain. To provide a general outline, the neglect of the informal economy has both theoretical and empirical roots.

Theoretical Priors

The preference for formality as a method of social organization has a long history. With the Decalogue, Israel's God provided a formal, written declaration of law that supplanted generations of traditional practice (Eliade, 1978). In a more secular vein, Wieacker (1981: 257) notes that the formality of Roman law, a set of encoded statutes, laid the foundation for the Western legal (and in many ways economic) system:

> Roman law forms a constituent part of the occidental world. It formed nations and legal systems and allowed them to become aware of their own identity. It provided the basis for the rational character of the systems and the legalism of the western nations. Further, even the very principle of settling social and economic conflicts not only by force, authority or compromise, but also by the application of general conceptual rules—which is the characteristic feature of western legal thought— became possible on the basis, and perhaps only on the basis, of Roman law, or what was thought to be Roman law.

Formality, or more adequately stated formalization, moved the Western world away from the adhocracy, stagnation, and tradition that characterized the Middle Ages and toward a more rational, legalistic Enlightenment (Ertman, 1997; North & Thomas, 1976). Formalization (the reasoned agreement between parties) replaced informality (the reliance on custom and tradition) and became an engine of social progress. This theme runs through the influential works of both Durkheim (1933) and Weber (1947); indeed, the displacement of traditional forms of authority with ones grounded in rational and legal thinking represented a critical inflection point in the transition toward modernity. Formality carried a cost, however, as these scholars noted. In perhaps the first invitation to reconsider the relentless march and ultimate superiority of modernity and its reliance on formality, Weber (1958: 182) lamented the emergence of the iron cage of capitalism (formality's economic manifestation):

> No one knows who will live in this cage in the future, or whether at the end of this tremendous development entirely new prophets will arise, or there will be a great rebirth of old ideas and ideals, or, if neither, mechanized petrification embellished with a sort of convulsive self-importance. For of the last stage of this cultural development it might well be truly said: "Specialists without spirit, sensualists without heart; this nullity imagines that it has attained a level of civilization never before achieved.

In spite of Weber's concern for the negative impacts of formality, the field of management appears to have accepted the premise that formality offered a superior approach to the organization of economic life. Frederik Taylor's emphasis on "scientific management," complete with calculable time and motion mapping of work, epitomized the idea that rationality and formality trumped tradition, custom, and informality (Wren, 1994). The work of Henri Fayol and the application of industrial psychology in settings such as the Hawthorne studies added impetus and momentum to the acceptance of rationality as both the basis of organization and the best way to study and learn about them.

There were, to be certain, outliers. Barnard (1938) showed a keen appreciation for the role of flexible and informal systems as a necessary complement to formal organizational systems. His nuanced perspective on the complex interplay between formality and informality reflected two desires: first, to articulate his learning based on his own experience and, second, to develop a theory of the common features of organization. Barnard (1938: 114–115) defined informal organizations as "interactions [. . .] that occur without any specific conscious *joint* purpose . . . by informal organization I mean the aggregate of the personal contacts and interactions and the associated groupings of people." In spite of his advanced thinking about informality, he gave management scholars little to work with in terms of substantive constructs. He defines informality for what it is not. In the world in which we live, however, informal economic activity takes place with clearly defined joint purposes in mind, and informal actors often prove very deliberate in the networks of association they cultivate.

To sum up, the theoretical foundations of management and organization theory create a strong current that moves researchers toward a focus on formality. The link between formality and progress is not mere happenstance: Formality allows economic and social life to occur outside narrow spheres of personal association and shared beliefs and norms; formality facilitates scale, growth, and social units with pluralistic beliefs, norms, and values (North, 1990; Rawls & Kelly, 2001). The size and complexity of the formal economy, and the formal organizations that operate within it, provides ample space for management theorizing and research.

Empirical Challenges

The relative neglect of the informal economy, and informality in general, owes to the dual forces of a theoretical orientation that favors formality and a set of empirical challenges to cataloging and studying informal economic activity. Researchers hoping to study the informal economy face three challenges: the lack of large scale, secondary data on informal firms and activity; non-trivial barriers to the collection of primary data; and the use of a different set of empirical, qualitative techniques to systematically study informality. I'll consider each challenge in turn.

The lack of legal registration presents one criteria for informality, the lack of bureaucratic codification the other: Both elements of informality mean that few, if any, written records exist to catalog and document informal activity. The archival sources that generate secondary data about informal economic activity do not exist; therefore, large-scale, econometric studies of informal economic activity will continue to rely on data collected in the field or on expert estimates. Friedrich Schneider and Dominik Enste have compiled size estimates of the global shadow economy over the past two decades. They note that cataloging the size of the shadow economy at a national level involves either direct or indirect estimation techniques (Schneider & Enste, 2013). Direct estimation occurs through surveys or selective tax audits of firms operating in the formal economy. Indirect estimation calculates differences between national income and expenditures or between official employment statistics and the actual size of the labor force.

Both direct and indirect methods only yield estimates, and only at the national level. For management researchers, the problem is obvious: Even the best estimates contain little meaningful data at the firm, or even industry, level. The type of management scholarship that relies on large-scale data to compare different organizational types, characteristics, and performance proves difficult to find or collect. When data does exist, it will usually be limited to a specific region or time period. These facts mean that researchers often trade off precision against generality (Weick, 1979).

Data proves difficult to acquire for another reason as well: In most instances, the decision to operate informally is made consciously. Revealing facts about an informal business may invite negative consequences; both De Soto (2000) and LaPorta & Schliefer (2008) find that, in the developing world, the specter of corruption rises as firms formalize. There are advantages in flying, and staying, below the radar that make informal economic actors hesitant to provide meaningful data. Scott (2013) focuses on hidden organizations, those whose organizational mission or strategy require them to remain anonymous, a close cousin to true informality. Researchers hoping to collect primary data from informed respondents should exercise caution on two counts: caution about the risks involved in disclosure; and caution in interpreting findings, realizing that informant data may obscure or omit key details.

My own empirical work on the informal economy takes a decidedly qualitative and historical tone (Godfrey & Dyer, this volume; Madsen, Bednar, & Godfrey, 2014). Approaches that mix participant observation (a component of trust building and emic understanding), semi-structured interviews that invite subjects to situate responses within a historical continuum, and repeated interactions have yielded adequate data. Hermeneutic research, closely related to the iterative methods suggested in the grounded theory approach, allow insight and understanding about the phenomenon under study to emerge and evolve according to their own logic and timetable for both the researcher and the subjects. Aspects of informality may remain subconscious for participants until researchers bring the issues to conscious consideration and it takes time to both understand and justify why certain aspects of informality exist as they do.

To sum up, the historical and theoretical emphasis of the field of management has focused on formality in both economic activity and organizational form. The empirical challenges of studying informality give rise to another set of barriers to a systematic study of informal economic activity, if not informal organization. As I now explain, however, management scholars have much to gain by turning their collective gaze to the context and construct of informal economic activity. These gains come as this new context helps establish boundary conditions for existing theoretical paradigms and provides the opportunity to develop new theory to fit a different context. These gains help answer the question Why should we study the informal economy now?

WHY SHOULD WE STUDY IT NOW?

My colleague Dave Whetten spent much of his career helping young scholars improve their theory development capability. He taught many of us that scholars can make a theoretical contribution in one of two broad ways: We can either make a contribution *of* theory or a contribution *to* theory. A contribution of theory uses existing models and paradigms to investigate and explain new phenomena. A contribution to theory occurs when scholars deepen theoretical paradigms by showing that new constructs can explain outcomes of interest or by providing new mechanisms and causal pathways that link explanans (independent variables) with explanandum (dependent variables). Dave's model of contributions of and to theory provides a useful frame to answer the question of why the field should take up the informal economy. Informality allows us to make contributions of theory and to theory.

Contributions of Theory

The contribution of theory perspective views *informality as a new context* in which scholars can "stress test" the boundary conditions of existing theory. Candidate theories taken up in this volume include standard notions of economic rationality, transaction cost economics, contract theory, the resource-based view of strategy, and institutional theory. Importantly, the view of informality as a context means that formality and informality differ in degree, not in kind. Institutional theory illustrates this assumption most clearly; explanations of informality at the Base of the Economic Pyramid (BoP) often invoke the lack of formal institutional structures such as financial markets, property rights, or the rule of law to explain why informality exists and persists (De Soto, 2000; La Porta & Schliefer, 2008; Peng, 2003). Institutional theory, particularly the three pillars of institutions view held by Scott (2008), offers the view that in the absence of formal, regulatory institutions actors rely on common cognitive and normative institutions to govern economic activity. The formal and informal economy differ in the mix of regulatory versus cognitive/normative governance.

Justin Webb and Duane Ireland take up this topic in Chapter 2. They assert that informal activity in BoP and emerging economies takes place because institutional voids discourage entrepreneurs and others from formalizing their businesses. McMillian (2002) notes that in the absence of institutional regimes that provide infrastructure, public services, and security economic actors have little incentive to register businesses and pay taxes. Why pay for what one does not receive? Webb and Ireland accept this basic premise, but their argument goes beyond the extant notion that these weak institutions explain informality.

The title of their chapter, "Laying the foundation for a theory of informal adjustments," suggests that the standard institutional story of institutional voids may be incomplete. Webb and Ireland view both formal and informal institutions as imperfect. For example, trust and social norms, two manifestations of shared cognitive and normative institutional foundations, act as substitutes for threats of arbitration or litigation and bind parties to their obligations. Much of the literature on trust, for example, extols the virtues of trust but fails to see the inherent limitations in the construct (see Barney and Hansen (1994) and Mayer, Davis, and Schoorman (1995) for classic contributions to the trust literature). Trust, for example, provides imperfect governance in any economic situation. Webb and Ireland highlight the conditions facing actors in BoP, emerging, and developed economies: Both formal and informal methods of structuring transactions leave gaps. Further, the evolution of both sets of structures occurs in tandem; the iterative adjustment of formal and informal institutions leads to a dynamic process that means boundaries between the two sectors will always display a fluidity that allows permeability by actors across sectors.

Craig Scott and Mige Haseki study organizations using communications theory and perspectives. Their chapter, "Communication, Visibility, and the Informal Economy: A Framework for Future Research," employs these perspectives to explain the persistence of informal economic activity. While informality may be a rational choice for actors and their business at any given time, Scott and Haseki posit that organizations develop internal routines, external customer sets, and broader relationships that create value out of informality. Specifically, the lack of visibility may attract unique customer segments, suppliers, and employees. Even when institutional conditions change and invite formalization, registration, and prominence in the formal economy, actors may choose to remain anonymous and informal. Opportunities for scale and growth may not offset the advantages of informality and invisibility.

Scott and Haseki's work makes two vital contributions to an emerging study of informality. First, they bring different theoretical paradigms and perspectives. Their constructs of visibility, identity, and relevant audiences resonate with management scholars who study identity and reputation; however, a reading of this chapter provides scholars with a nuanced view with subtle differences from communications theory that has much to add to the management conversation. Their contribution is one of new theory, not merely of theory. Second, their model questions unspoken assumptions about organizational identity, image, and reputation. Successfully managing all three constructs may entail what an organization chooses not to do (in terms of transparency and visibility). That the lack of action may represent a deliberate and value creating strategy.

My work with Bill Schulze appears as Chapter 4. We expand management theory's use of the contracting process to control and coordinate transactions by importing notions of contract from both law and economics. We also employ another context, the family, and employ the archetypal family business, the ancient Greek Oikos (or household), to examine the origin of contracting. We posit three types of contracts: informal ones typified by the relations among family members in the Oikos; the formal contracts that ostensibly govern transactions in the modern, formal economy; and a hybrid relational contract that offers parties the best of both the Oikos (flexibility) and the firm (scalability).

Our work (as I see it) attempts to redraw the relationship between formality and informality. As I noted above, the weight of theory leans in the direction of the superiority of formal organization and organizing principles, the natural consequence being that informality exists as an imperfect or incomplete substitute. Formality is the figure, informality the ground. Our work takes the opposite view: Informality should be considered the figure or dominant type of economic activity while formality exists as the ground. Given the complex interplay between the search for meaning and the pursuit of gain, actors' default may be a preference for meaning but almost surely entails some type of balance between the two. Thus, we argue that informal or relational contracting represent preferred modes, with formal contracting only occurring when the preferred forms prove inadequate to the conditions of a particular exchange relationship.

My work with Robb Jensen follows next. While this chapter makes a theoretical argument, our thinking on these matters occurred within the context of a larger, empirical project that explored the growth of micro-franchising around the world (see Jensen, Godfrey, and Mealey (2013) for some of our initial empirical results). Micro-franchising, also known as a business in a box, modifies the traditional franchising model for use at the BoP (Fairbourne, Gibson, & Dyer, 2007). Our empirical interest lay in determining how different country characteristics influence the adoption of this new organizational form. The theoretical grounding drew from Transaction Cost Economics, specifically under what conditions we would expect to find hybrid forms as a vibrant and sustainable organizational form.

As our chapter shows, the logic of transaction costs transfers fairly well to the BoP environment, and we supplement transaction costs with insights from contract theory. We make no assertions about opportunism, as we see no reason why the tendency toward opportunistic behavior would be higher or lower in BoP environments vis-à-vis developed ones. Asset specificity requires some transformation due to small scale and lower levels of technology. We decompose uncertainty into the constructs of imperfect foresight and unobservability to capture nuances of markets that lack monitoring agencies common to developed economies. Our argumentation concludes with the suggestion that hybrid forms, such as franchise agreements, should be more common in BoP environments. Informality may spawn a number of different, hybrid organizational forms that might not survive in more formal settings.

Brad Skousen and Joe Mahoney invoke various streams of management and strategy theory, including the very traditional logic of micro-economic rationality, entrepreneurial motivation, family business, and institutional theory, in their essay. Based on the former's work in Brazil, Skousen and Mahoney take up a valuable question: Given the choice of participation in either the formal or informal economy, what factors might underlie the outcome of this decision? Such a question makes little sense if viewed from a perspective that sees formality as the default, always superior choice, or one that sees informality as the only option for exchange. Their question proves non-trivial for millions of economic actors in the informal economy who operate as informal sole proprietors, as the option to formalize exists in many environments.

Skousen and Mahoney weave a tight argument that reveals the underlying complexity of the decision to formalize and the degree of formality an entrepreneur might find optimal. Their work highlights the benefits and costs of business registration not merely in terms of money and time but also in terms of opportunities for advancement, an understanding of the intricacies of formal institutions, and membership in important social networks. Their conclusion that registration is not a given but rather is contingent upon a number of factors reveals important factors that contribute to the persistence of informal economic activity, particularly when formalization carries certain risks but uncertain payoffs. Informal entrepreneurs face the same types of complex decisions and contingencies that managers of large formal organizations face.

Contributions to Theory

The next five chapters constitute, loosely construed, contributions to theory in the sense that they make empirical contributions over and above traditional theory testing. None of these pieces builds upon quantitative empirical work (my chapter with Gibb Dyer falls under the heading of inductive, qualitative research), but each chapter uses systematic experiences from the field to inform and shape our understanding of the informal economy. These chapters don't build on existing theoretical foundations, but they each ask whether new constructs might be necessary when thinking about informality.

John Ginther and Anita McGahan open this section with their description and analysis of informal healthcare delivery systems around the world. Their abstract piques our interest by noting that "Healthcare in the informal economy is at once small and large." Informal healthcare delivery clearly operates outside the regulatory apparatus of state licensure, professional training, and safety standards. This illegality can lead to dire consequences in terms of individual patient outcomes but also in terms of community and public health impacts. They illustrate through case examples how critical patient and community outcomes, such as the role of accurate diagnosis in treatment, vary widely between formal and informal providers.

Informal healthcare, in many places, builds on strong cultural and historical norms that legitimate these practices; in fact, Western, formal practitioners face a burden of legitimation in many places (Stinchcombe, 1965). From community birth assistants to village witch doctors, entrenched yet informal practices and structures dominate healthcare in many countries or regions. Ginther and McGahan's work adds an urgency to the study of informality in healthcare: In an increasingly globally connected world where rare diseases are a plane ride away, we all have a stake in finding an equilibrium between traditional and modern medical practices. One area for theory development lies in the establishment, maintenance, and migration of a cooperative equilibrium between tradition and modernity.

Xiadong Yu and Garry Bruton review and critique the state of theory and understanding about informal activity in China. China matters on so many levels to the future of management research. Its huge population, cultural and political uniqueness, and increasing impact on global economic outcomes require that the country be included in most topics of interest. China's unique history, ancient and modern, mean that comparisons between China and the rest of the world certainly yield a picture worth viewing; however, comparing current to past versions of the middle kingdom often provide richer insight. Where China is today begs the question of where she has been and what the trajectory might be.

Yu and Bruton assert that 15% of economic activity in China occurs informally, which is on par with countries like Australia, slightly more than the United States, and substantially less than its neighbor to the northwest, the Russian Federation (Schneider, Buehn, & Montenegro, 2010). This brief mental picture captures the conundrum and challenge that may define the state of China: appearing simultaneously like a capitalist oriented economy while retaining a collectivist state orientation. Yu and Bruton capture this dynamic and invite scholars to consider a number of questions that might, and might not, be answerable by a set of management theories built on Western assumptions.

My work with Gibb Dyer grew out of my initial forays into understanding poverty (Godfrey, 2013). Invited by my Dean to focus more of my research on poverty, my first foray was a trip to Ghana to learn how subsistence entrepreneurs succeeded without the help of foreign NGOs or social entrepreneurs. I continued to visit the country over the next several years (in 2005, 2008, and 2009) and conducted a number of in-depth interviews while making personal observations. These trips helped me understand many dimensions of informality and the limits of both formal and informal elements in the economic lives of these Ghanaians.

I enlisted Gibb Dyer and his excellence in qualitative methods to make sense of the data and find some emergent stories. Our chapter presents some of those learnings. Our basic contribution is a brief account of the causes and consequences of semi-formality. Semi-formality represents, in many ways, an institutional condition in its own right as something like formal property ownership proved impossible, not because of the entrepreneur's poverty but because the state's poverty in adequate record keeping left large tracts of land without any titleholders. The state, however, did have institutions that provided imperfect, but adequate, substitutes for property rights. Ours may represent an empirical case that Webb and Ireland could build upon to better understand how institutions adjust.

Urs Jaeger and Vijay Sathe's chapter describes an important effort in India's efforts to eradicate poverty and more fully formalize its economy: the creation of individual identity for millions of poor Indians living in the informal economy. For people born in the industrialized West, the problem is almost incomprehensible: a segment of the population that does not exist, at least in terms of formal markers such as a birth certificate. People living in India's informal sector clearly exist, and they are known and recognized within their communities. Lacking formal identification, however, these individuals cannot move into the formal economy (the U.S. correlate is a person without a verifiable, valid work status), nor can they access public and social services that could positively impact their lives.

This chapter represents an intriguing opportunity for theory development around informality because it suggests that elements of the informal economy might differ in kind, and not merely degree, from their formal economy counterparts. Education, for example, comes in relative degrees, and moving from illiteracy to literacy happens in stages. The lack of identity, however, represents something different, not merely a poor identity or an underdeveloped one, but not one. Zero, in this case, is qualitatively different than one. Further, identity comes in a complete grant, or it comes not at all.

The identity, and identification, process may reveal other qualitative differences between the sectors that can spur theory development and testing.

Les Dlabay's work on informal finance completes the empirical portion of the book. Unfortunately, we can't print the slide deck that Dlabay shared with us at the conference. That deck told two compelling stories. The first, and the subject of his chapter, is about the incredible diversity of organizational forms that informal financial services assume. You'll get a flavor of that from his work. Second, and I wish we could include this, Dlabay showed a number of photos of informal activity in the developing world juxtaposed with the same activity occurring in his Chicago hometown--a very powerful object lesson in the pervasiveness of the informal economy.

Dlabay's work seems a fitting conclusion to the book because it raises so many questions for which we have so few answers. How did the multiplicity of organizational forms originate and evolve? There are Susu collectors, lending associations, village banks, and many other forms. What cultural, political, and religious factors of the external environment helped shape, and help sustain, these different forms? Financial services in the Islamic world take on a different structure and character due to Sharia (Quraishi, 2006); however, even among nations with Christian or indigenous belief traditions, Dlabay still sees a variety of types and forms of finance. How might contingency theory approach such diversity? Institutional theory? What about a view such as the resource-based view?

CONCLUSION

In practice, the chapters often blur the lines between contributions of and contributions to theory. The one request I made of each author team at the outset was to include a section in their chapter that considered what their data, ideas, and thinking implied for the future of management theory, both in general and in the specific realm of the informal economy. Each author, or team, has done so. Each chapter should provide you with three things: a description of a phenomena of interest in the informal economy, a reason why that matters to the field of management, and a set of theoretical lenses that ought to help us—individually and collectively—enhance our understanding of informality and informal economic activity. If you complete your reading armed to study informality, then we have accomplished our goal.

REFERENCES

Barnard, C.I. 1938. *The functions of the executive.* Cambridge, MA: Harvard University Press.
Barney, J.B., & Hansen, M.H. 1994. Trustworthiness as a source of competitive advantage. *Strategic Management Journal,* 15: 175–190.

Becker, K. F. 2004. *The informal economy: Fact finding study*. Stockholm, Sweden: Sida.

Booth, W. J. 1993. *Households: On the moral architecture of the economy*. Ithaca, NY: Cornell University Press.

Centeno, M. A., & Portes, A. 2006. The informal economy in the shadow of the state. In P. Fernandez-Kelly & J. Scheffner (Eds.), *Out of the shadows: The informal economy and political movements in Latin America*: 23–49. Princeton, N.J.: Princeton University Press.

De Soto, H. 2000. *The mystery of capital : Why capitalism triumphs in the West and fails everywhere else*. New York: Basic Books.

Durkheim, É. 1933. *The division of labor in society*. New York: Macmillan.

Eliade, M. 1978. *A history of religious ideas*. Chicago: University of Chicago Press.

Ertman, T. 1997. *Birth of the Leviathan: Building states and regimes in medieval and early modern Europe*. Cambridge University Press.

Fairbourne, J. S., Gibson, S. W., & Dyer, W. G. 2007. *MicroFranchising : Creating wealth at the bottom of the pyramid*. Cheltenham, England: Edward Elgar.

Godfrey, P. C. 2011. Toward a theory of the informal economy. *The Academy of Management Annals*, 5(1): 231–277.

Godfrey, P. C. 2013. *More than money: Five forms of capital to create wealth and eliminate poverty*. Stanford, CA: Stanford Business Books.

Hart, K. 1973. Informal income opportunities and urban employment in Ghana. *The Journal of Modern African Studies*, 11(1): 61–89.

International Labor Organization. 2002. *Women and men in the informal economy: A statistical picture*: 64. Geneva, Switzerland: International Labor Organization.

Jensen, R., Godfrey, P. C., & Mealey, C. 2013. Entry Modes at the Base of the Economic Pyramid: The Emergence of Hybrid Organizational Forms. *Academy of Management Proceedings*, 2013(1): 10214.

LaPorta, R., & Shleifer, A. 2008. *The unofficial economy and economic development*: 1–75. Working Paper Series, National Bureau of Economic Research, Washington, DC.

Lewis, W. A. 1958/2006. *The theory of economic growth*. London: Routledge.

London, T., & Hart, S. L. 2004. Reinventing strategies for emerging markets: Beyond the transnational model. *Journal of International Business Studies*, 35(5): 350–370.

London, T., & Hart, S. L. 2011. Creating a fortune with the base of the Pyramid. In T. London & S. L. Hart (Eds.), *Next generation business strategies for the base of the pyramid*: 1–18. Upper Saddle River, N.J.: FT Press.

Madsen, G. C., Bednar, J. S., & Godfrey, P. C. 2014. Africa, the informal economy, and the hermeneutic circle. In Zoogah, D. B. (Eds.), *Advancing Research Methodology in the African Context: Techniques, Methods, and Designs*: 133–166. Bingley, England: Emerald Publishing Group.

Marcouiller, D., & Young, L. 1995. The black hole of graft: The predatory state and the informal economy. *The American Economic Review*, 85(3): 630–646.

Mayer, R. C., Davis, J. H., & Schoorman, F. D. 1995. An integrative model of organizational trust. *The Academy of Management Review*, 20(3): 709–734.

McMillan, J. 2002. *Reinventing the bazaar: A natural history of markets*. New York: W.W. Norton.

North, D. C. 1990. *Institutions, institutional change and economic performance*. Cambridge University Press.

North, D. C., & Thomas, R. P. 1976. *The rise of the Western world: A new economic history*. Cambridge University Press.

Peng, M. W. 2003. Institutional transitions and strategic choices. *The Academy of Management Review*, 28(2): 275–296.

Polanyi, K. 1957. *Trade and market in the early empires; economies in history and theory.* Glencoe, IL: Free Press.

Portes, A., Castells, M., & Benton, L. A. 1989. *The informal economy : Studies in advanced and less developed countries.* Baltimore, MD: Johns Hopkins University Press.

Quraishi, A. 2006. Interpreting the Qur'an and the constitution: Similarities in the use of text, tradition, and reason in Islamic and American jurisprudence. *Cardozo Law Review*, 28: 67–122.

Rawls, J., & Kelly, E. 2001. *Justice as fairness : A restatement.* Cambridge, MA: Harvard University Press.

Schneider, F., Buehn, A., & Montenegro, C. E. 2010. New estimates for the shadow economies all over the world. *International Economic Journal*, 24(4): 443–461.

Schneider, F., & Enste, D. H. 2013. *The shadow economy: An international survey.* Cambridge University Press.

Scott, C. R. 2013. *Anonymous agencies, backstreet businesses, and covert collectives: Rethinking organizations in the 21st century.* Stanford, CA: Stanford Business Books, an imprint of Stanford University Press.

Scott, W. R. 2008. *Institutions and organizations : Ideas and interests.* Los Angeles: Sage Publications.

Smith, A. 1776. *An inquiry into the nature and causes of the wealth of nations with a life of the author: Also a view of the doctrine of Smith, compared with that of the French economists, with a method of facilitating the study of his works, from the French of M. Jariner.* Nashville, TN: Thomas Nelson.

Spicer, A., McDermott, G. A., & Kogut, B. 2000. Entrepreneurship and privatization in Central Europe: The tenuous balance between destruction and creation. *The Academy of Management Review*, 25(3): 630–649.

Stinchcombe, A. L. 1965. Social structure and organizations. In J. G. March (Eds.), *Handbook of organizations*: 142–193. Chicago: Rand McNally.

Venkatesh, S. A. 2006. *Off the books : The underground economy of the urban poor.* Cambridge, MA: Harvard University Press.

Wallerstein, I. 2004. *World-systems analysis: An introduction.* Durham: Duke University Press.

Webb, J. W., Tihanyi, L., Ireland, R. D., & Sirmon, D. G. 2009. You say illegal, I say legitimate: Entrepreneurship in the informal economy. *Academy of Management Review*, 34: 492–510.

Weber, M. 1947. *The theory of social and economic organization.* (T. Parsons, Tran.). New York: Free Press.

Weber, M. 1958/2008. *The protestant ethic and the spirit of capitalism.* Stilwell, KS: Digireads.com Publishing.

Weick, K. E. 1979. *The social psychology of organizing.* New York: Random House.

Wieacker, F. 1981. The importance of Roman law for Western civilization and Western legal thought. *Boston College International and Comparative Law Review*, 4: 257.

Wren, D. A. 1994. *The evolution of management thought.* New York: John Wiley.

Zinnes, C. 2009. *Business environment reforms and the informal economy.* Cambridge, England: Donor Committee for Enterprise Development.

Part I

Theory and the Informal Economy

2 Laying the Foundation for a Theory of Informal Adjustments

Justin W. Webb and R. Duane Ireland

The informal economy exists due to differences in how institutions define, monitor, enforce, and support what is socially acceptable (Webb, Tihanyi, Ireland, & Sirmon, 2009). Importantly, scholars have distinguished between formal and informal institutions. Formal institutions represent the codified laws, regulations, and supporting apparatuses that establish one definition of social acceptability in society. Informal institutions are concerned with a society's norms, values, and beliefs that establish a second definition of social acceptability (North, 1990). Formal and informal institutions do not always prescribe, condone, or facilitate congruent definitions of what are socially acceptable behaviors and outcomes. The informal economy then includes those activities that lead to behaviors and outcomes outside of formal institutional boundaries but remain within informal institutional boundaries (Castells & Portes, 1989; Godfrey, 2011; Webb et al., 2009).

Consistent with this notion, scholars have emphasized the distinction between legality and legitimacy (e.g., Nichter & Goldmark, 2009; Siqueira, Webb, & Bruton, 2014). More specifically, the informal economy encompasses activities that are considered illegal in regards to formal institutions but that remain legitimate in regards to informal institutions. Based on this narrower conceptualization, relevant activities include efforts by societal actors to skirt registration laws, tax laws, labor standards, environmental regulations, and property rights laws (Webb, Ireland, & Ketchen, 2014). By definition, these activities are illegal in that they violate the society's codified laws and regulations. At the same time, these activities are often rationalized as legitimate by large groups in society. Skirting registration laws is often viewed as legitimate in developing economies given burdensome registration requirements, severely limited formal employment options, and the need for individuals to meet their subsistence needs through self-employment (De Soto, 1989). Similarly, the skirting of labor standards may be rationalized as legitimate again due to burdensome policies governing overtime compensation or firings and/or significant global competition (Webb, Bruton, Tihanyi, & Ireland, 2013).

In this legal/legitimate research stream, scholars have examined the role of formal institutions in motivating and facilitating informal economy activity. The emphasis among scholars is on an understanding of how formal institutional policies and infrastructural decisions influence informality (e.g., Kistruck, Webb, Sutter, & Bailey, 2014; Portes & Haller, 2005; Williams, Windebank, Baric, & Nadin, 2013). The practical implications of this research concern how policymakers can construct policies that lead to a more attractive/desirable business environment within formal institutional boundaries while simultaneously creating a less attractive/desirable business environment outside of formal institutional boundaries.

This research stream has provided important understandings of how formal institutions influence informal economy activity. However, an understanding of formal institutions alone overlooks the importance of informal institutions in explaining why the informal economy exists and how actors within the informal economy operate, govern, and grow their activity. Our objective with this chapter is to begin laying a foundation for understanding the role of informal institutions in developing and facilitating activity within the informal economy.

THE ROLE OF INFORMAL INSTITUTIONS: ADJUSTMENTS TO FORMAL INSTITUTIONAL IMPERFECTIONS

Theory explains the how and why of relationships that exist among concepts (i.e., what). Therefore, in establishing a theory of informal adjustments, we begin first with presenting the basis of our primary conceptualization—informal adjustments. We then explain how and why informal adjustments occur. Next, we discuss other theoretical lenses that can inform a theory of informal adjustments and present various possibilities and conceptualizations for scholars as they undertake research in this vein.

Defining Informal Adjustments

Taking an economic anthropological view, Hart (1973) first introduced the notion of the informal economy. During his research in Ghana, he observed significant activity occurring outside of formal institutions. Unlike prior musings that activities occurring outside formal institutional frameworks dissolve into anarchy and anti-social behavior (e.g., Hobbes, 1991), Hart found this activity to remain structured and with the potential to create value for those engaging in such activity, leading him to label these activities as the informal economy. Very quickly, developmental economists picked up on this phenomenon (Rakowski, 1994). Noting that developing contexts are often characterized by much larger informal sectors than developed contexts, the developmental economists viewed the informal economy as undermining economic development within these contexts. Relative to the formal economy, the informal economy was believed to involve less productive economic activity that failed to contribute to development due to issues such as limited potential for growth, loss of tax revenues, and unfair competition with formal economy firms. The pertinent question for scholars and policymakers then became, "What formal institutional policies will facilitate transitions of actors operating in the informal economy to the formal economy?"

In our view, the efforts of developmental economists neglected and over-shadowed a key aspect of Hart's (1973) seminal work—that is, activities within the informal economy remain *structured* outside of formal institutions. The role of informal institutions in terms of providing structure and governance to organizational activities is a defining feature of the informal economy (Godfrey, 2011). Consistent with other scholars (e.g., Mair, Marti, & Ventresca, 2012; Peng & Heath, 1996), we contend that when formal institutions fail to structure and govern economic activity, informal institutions can serve as an alternative guiding framework. In this way, informal institutions provide a complementary framework to formal institutions, at times overlapping with and supporting formal institutions while at other times providing a different framework that can guide and facilitate activities within society when formal institutions for whatever reason fail to do so.

Our focus herein is on the phenomena that manifest when informal institutions provide an alternative framework to imperfect formal institutions. In our view, the informal economy is society's mechanism to provide for itself in legitimate ways where formal institutions have failed to do so. That is, individuals within society adjust to imperfections of formal institutions. The term *informal adjustments* refers to individuals drawing upon norms, values, and beliefs within society to facilitate, govern, and structure their economic activities instead of relying on formal laws, regulations, and supporting apparatuses to do so. Importantly, the norms, values, and beliefs can become the basis for collectively shared rules, whether implicitly held or formally codified, as well as tangible organizations and infrastructures. The informal institutions can then be formalized in a sense, but they remain separate from formal institutions and generally much more localized to, or within, a community.

Formal Institutional Imperfections and Informal Adjustments

Formal institutional voids. There are a number of reasons as to why formal institutions may imperfectly structure and govern economic activity. In developing contexts, for example, formal institutions often do not exist (Khanna & Palepu, 1997). Such formal institutional voids can include the lack of or poorly defined property rights, ambiguous and inefficiently enforced contract laws, limited enforcement and judicial apparatuses, the lack of basic utility infrastructures, and undeveloped capital and labor markets (Kistruck, Webb, Sutter, & Ireland, 2011; Webb, Kistruck, Ireland, & Ketchen, 2010). Not surprisingly, then, we see various types of informal mechanisms substituting for the lack of formal institutions. In Guatemala, for example, the lack of effectively responsive police enforcement to theft, extortion, violence, and other criminal activities led vendors in some street markets to privately order enforcement. In one market, the informal enforcement officers were known as angelos justicieros (i.e., angels of justice) (Sutter, Webb, Kistruck, & Bailey, 2013). These individuals mill around the market in plain clothes monitoring the market activity and are ready to step in to enforce when necessary. Portes and Sensenbrenner (1993) observed similar informal enforcement within Cuban ethnic enclaves in Miami, and Odegaard (2008) discussed the use of informal enforcement to ensure only informally registered vendors operated within an informal market. We have also observed the use of social auditors as informal mechanisms that serve as adjustments to the lack of efficient court systems in developing contexts. Social auditors are trusted individuals within a society who are tasked with providing unbiased decisions to resolve transactional disputes between actors (Kistruck et al., 2011). Failure of an individual to comply with the social auditor's decision may lead to social stigma or ostracism. In other cases, the lack of capital markets in developing contexts has led to various forms of informal finance (i.e., informal lending, informal insurance, etc.), and limited labor markets have led to kinship-based sharing arrangements and interhousehold transfers of assets (Kimura, 2011; Lam & Paul, 2013). Finally, the lack of contract law leads actors to instead rely more upon trust and relational norms (i.e., mutuality, flexibility, reciprocity, etc.) to facilitate their transactions.

Formal institutional inefficiencies. In addition to formal institutional voids, institutional imperfections may manifest as formal institutional inefficiencies, or resource misallocations by formal institutions (Qian & Strahan, 2007). For example, formal institutions in societies can seek to protect or maximize economic rents for elites or other social categories through redistribution of resources (Acemoglu & Robinson, 2012). Formal institutional inefficiencies can manifest as overly burdensome taxes and regulatory, registration, and licensing costs. Established corporations can lobby policymakers for higher registration costs, for example, to ensure the quality of firms within an industry (De Soto, 1989). Especially in impoverished developing contexts, however, these significant registration costs can serve as an entry barrier to new entrepreneurs (De Soto, 1989; Siqueira et al., 2014). Instead, entrepreneurs undertake activities in the informal economy, skirting these costs imposed by formal institutional inefficiencies and relying on relational norms to facilitate their activities.

Formal institutional uncertainty. Conversely, technological and sociocultural changes can outpace changes in formal institutions to accommodate new domains of economic activity (Dhanaraj & Khanna, 2011). In such cases of institutional uncertainty, discretion is left to individuals and organizations as to how to set legitimate goals and operate in socially acceptable ways (Goodrick & Salancik, 1996). For example, advancements in telecommunications, networking, and the Internet more broadly as well as in other technologies have recently enabled individuals to connect in ways that have been previously unforeseen. Airbnb is an interesting example of a venture that has exploited an opportunity facilitated by these changing environmental conditions. Airbnb is a website that allows individuals to rent out lodging. The website has come under fire from regulators as it facilitates individuals' efforts to skirt local housing, tourism, and tax regulations. Uber (in the taxi industry) and Aereo (in the TV streaming industry) are two other recent examples of ventures in the informal economy that have taken advantage of technological advancements to create new domains of economic activity that potentially skirt (or facilitate other individuals' ability to skirt) laws and regulations. Highlighting the legal/legitimacy debate, these ventures and more recently the entrepreneurs who have founded them face lawsuits questioning their legality by relevant regulatory agencies seeking to play catch-up to the technological changes; simultaneously, they have attracted significant capitalization from venture capitalists and positive response from consumers.

Formal institutional weakness and instability. Other formal institutional imperfections can also influence informality. Institutional strength reflects the authority and capacity for formal institutions to monitor and enforce their prescriptions (Estache & Wren-Lewis, 2009; Meirowitz & Tucker, 2007). Actors within society have greater opportunity to operate in the informal economy when there are weak formal institutions because the formal institutions lack the capacity to enforce what could be well-defined and efficient underlying policies (Agnew, 1993; Webb et al., 2009). Also, institutional instability reflects constant change within formal institutions over time (Levitsky & Murillo, 2009; Yue, Luo, & Ingram, 2013). When there is institutional instability, actors are asked to comply with certain laws and regulations at one point in time and asked to comply with other laws and regulations at a later point in time (Roever, 2006). Each change creates new costs and disruptions to the actors' economic activities. Unless strong institutions absolutely mandate compliance, actors are likely to rationalize that future changes in formal institutions will simply require future compliance revisions and additional costs (Garcia-Rincon, 2007). Instead of changing in accordance with institutional instability, actors will then "wait" for formal institutions to resolve themselves and meanwhile operate informally.

Each of the informal adjustments discussed previously rely on specific rules, investments, and organization made by actors. For example, informal markets can have their own rules, such as ones defining who can operate in the market, where the vendors can operate specifically within the market, and what their responsibilities to the market are (i.e., trash cleanup, market fees). The informal markets can also have their own organization of individuals who make decisions for the market. Individuals invest in and commit to these rules and organizations to provide some infrastructure to their activities. Likewise, informal lending arrangements also have their own rules, such as interest rates and other repayment terms, required collateral, and how lack of payment is resolved, among other considerations (Guirkinger, 2008). Informal lending also can have organizations, with specific roles related to the tellers, security, and moneylender, although these roles are generally less visible or obvious. In short, informal adjustments are socially construed among individuals locally (although, at times, much more broadly) when formal institutions are imperfect in facilitating desired socio-economic activities and outcomes.

RELEVANT LENSES AND RESEARCH

A number of extant lenses and bodies of research seem appropriate for informing and being informed by a theory of informal adjustments. We discuss research related to organizing rules, norms/values, structuration, and private ordering/social movements below.

Organizing Rules

Ostrom's (2005) discussion of organizing rules seems particularly relevant for understanding how actors within the informal economy organize. More specifically, Ostrom (2005) sets forth seven rules for organizing: position (i.e., specify the different positions within an organization, how many of each position, etc.); boundary (i.e., outline the requirements to serve in a particular position); choice (i.e., establish the responsibilities and constraints on an individual serving in a particular position); aggregation (i.e., define how decisions are made, especially when multiple individuals inform a decision); information (i.e., delineate how information is communicated between and across positions); payoff (i.e., describe the incentives for participating and performing); and scope (i.e., define the expected range of outcomes within a group). Ostrom's (2005) framework can help scholars understand how informal organizations, such as informal street-market associations, operate to facilitate informal economic activities and how the rules of the organizations influence their efficiency and effectiveness. However, informal institutions can also be characterized by imperfections. For example, rules underlying an informal organization can exclude certain types of individuals (i.e., boundary rules might require informal licenses or registration that some individuals cannot afford) or undermine procedural/distributive justice among individuals within the organization (i.e., aggregation rules might specify that leaders within the informal organization have authority to determine decisions without taking into account the voice of members within the organization). Examining the nature of organizing rules may help scholars understand why some informal organizations become institutionalized whereas others are more temporary.

Norms, Values, and Beliefs

Frameworks also exist that can inform understanding of how norms, values, and beliefs may influence informal economic activity. For example, Kaufmann and Dant (1992) distinguish seven different relational norms that can shape the cooperation and the risks taken within a transaction relationship: relational focus, solidarity, restraint, role integrity, conflict resolution, flexibility, and mutuality. Various categorizations of trust (e.g., contractual versus competence versus goodwill) and power (e.g., coercive versus noncoercive) are also available to understand the nature of cooperation and cohesion within relationships. Taking a relational governance perspective, scholars may seek to understand how relational norms among actors within an informal economy shape their respective transaction costs and overall performance in the absence of judicial and enforcement institutions. Certainly, intangible norms, values, and beliefs can be difficult to discern and may require creative approaches. Aharonovitz and Nyaga (2010) provide one example of such a creative approach, collecting children's stories and running content analyses to discern cultural values (e.g., risk-taking, altruism, integrity, morality, etc.) across communities.

Structuration

Structuration theory focuses on the interaction between individuals' agency and structure. In particular, social structure guides and constrains individuals' behaviors, yet individuals also have agency to behave in ways that can perpetuate or alter their existing structures or even create new structures (Giddens, 1984). Social structures are the sets of rules and resources available within a particular setting (Giddens, 1984); the rules of these social structures are communicated to and embodied by individuals via scripts, or observable patterns of behaviors and interactions among actors within a specific context (Barley & Tolbert, 1997). Individuals directly observe (or indirectly observe through education) and experience behaviors and interactions in their social structure, interpret the cause-and-effect, and undertake future behaviors based on their interpretation.

In our view, informal adjustments manifest due to imperfections in formal institutions. As a key aspect of individuals' social structure, formal institutions are imperfect in establishing the rules and/or allocating resources. The scripts provided by imperfect formal institutions are inherently flawed, and individuals then seek to either alter formal institutions or create their own alternative social structures to the formal institutions. Drawing upon a structuration lens, scholars may seek to understand how individuals draw upon informally derived scripts to guide behavior, and also how informal structures can then either alter or otherwise exist alongside formal institutions.

Private Ordering/Social Movements

Research related to social movements, collective action, collective identity, and private ordering all seem to be highly relevant to the study of informal adjustments. In particular, these frameworks can inform the factors that facilitate cohesion and cooperation within groups, bring together individuals with a common purpose, and lead those individuals to not only organize but also institutionalize routines and structures. Our own research in developing markets has uncovered significant informal activity in certain areas but limited informal activity in other areas. Historical conditions that lead to unfamiliarity among individuals and a lack of trust undermine private ordering (Sutter et al., 2013). Exacerbating the lack of trust are limited enforcement and judicial institutions that provide the opportunity for illegitimate stakeholders to step in and construct their own power structures (Kistruck et al., 2014). At the same time, critical junctures that represent a confluence of environmental conditions and societal emotions can spark collective action towards rectifying problematic politico-economic environments (Acemoglu & Robinson, 2012). A significant difference exists, though, in coming together and then staying and working together; moreover, why individuals assume responsibility for private ordering versus relying on formal institutions remains unclear.

THOUGHTS FOR FUTURE RESEARCH

Actors within societies can be creative in how they draw upon informal institutions in making adjustments for formal institutions and their imperfections. Interestingly, the informal mechanisms (i.e., informal lending arrangements) that surface in one context can be very different from the mechanisms that surface in other contexts, with the localized norms, values, and beliefs within each context idiosyncratically shaping how the informal mechanisms manifest (Kistruck et al., 2011). In the following sections, we discuss thoughts for building theory around the notion of informal adjustments.

Imperfections of Informal Institutions

Thus far, we have discussed informal institutions as adjustments to formal institutional imperfections. Numerous scholars have previously advanced the idea that informal institutions can provide alternative frameworks to formal institutions (Mair et al., 2012; Peng & Heath, 1996). However, the effectiveness of informal institutions as an alternative framework for formal institutions is unclear. To the extent that informal institutions do not provide an alternative framework for structuring and governing transactions, the informal economy may consist of less productive activities.

Like formal institutions, informal institutions can be characterized by imperfections. Informal institutions can lead to the marginalization of social categories based on a number of attributes, including gender, race, income, migrant status, and age (Bird & Shepherd, 2003; Cleaver, 2005). Such social exclusion undermines individuals' access to resource-rich networks, desirable property, and markets. For example, women in many developing contexts still cannot own property and may be excluded from basic access to credit markets (Palmer, 1991; Varley, 2007), although improvements are being made. Marginalization of social categories can create insecurity and limit the willingness of individuals to take risks in transacting and in their asset investments (Platteau & Abraham, 2002).

The tangible manifestations of informal institutions, such as informal lending and informal insurance arrangements, are often localized to specific communities (Carter & Maluccio, 2003; Woolcock, 1998). These informal mechanisms can support local entrepreneurial activity and help individuals and families absorb some losses (e.g., injury or death in a family, broken equipment) in the community where they occur. However, given their localization, informal institutions are not able to diversify their risks, and regional disasters, such as conflict, famine, flood, and health epidemics, can neuter these informal mechanisms (Carter & Maluccio, 2003).

Trust is seen as a relational lubricant supporting transactions among actors within a society. Interestingly, De Soto (2006) notes that developing contexts have much lower levels of trust. In our own conversations with local individuals in Ghana, a respondent cynically suggested that there may be too much trust, implying that individuals can instead trust that transaction partners will either let them down due to incompetence or opportunistic behavior. In a survey of microentrepreneurs in Swaziland (Bruton, Pryor, Webb, & Zahra, 2014), we actually found relatively high levels of trust; however, higher levels of trust led to lower levels of venture performance, perhaps because such trust led to the potential for opportunistic behavior in this setting that lacked efficient formal institutional mechanisms to resolve transactional disputes.

Finally, informal institutions may not serve as the only alternative framework to formal institutions. To the extent that formal institutions are imperfect, and informal institutions fail to provide sufficient cohesion, governance, and structure for socio-economic activities, illegitimate power structures can take hold (Sutter et al., 2013). Such power structures can include organized crime, militant factions, and totalitarian states that use coercive mechanisms to impose constraints and costs (i.e., taxes, extortion, etc.) on both formal and informal economic activities.

Future research. In short, we encourage scholars to examine the role of informal institutions as alternative frameworks to imperfect formal institutions, but not to presume that informal institutions are necessarily effective alternative frameworks or the only alternative frameworks to formal institutions. Scholars should examine both the advantages and limitations of informal institutions on the productivity of the informal economy. Questions to consider in this respect include the following:

- What are the different ways through which informal institutional frameworks emerge, and how does the path of emergence influence the effectiveness of informal institutions?

- How do different types of trust (i.e., competence, contractual, good-will, etc.) among actors within a society influence the effectiveness of informal institutions?
- Why do imperfections surface in informal institutions, and how can societal actors manipulate informal institutions to their own advantage?

Boundaries of Institutions

One perspective suggests that institutions are relatively static, with significant formal institutional changes occurring approximately every 10 to 100 years whereas significant informal institutional changes occur only every 100 to 1,000 years (Williamson, 2000). As a second perspective, one can point to the new laws, regulations, and supporting apparatuses that are formed on an ongoing basis in societies and, increasingly, the relevance of particular norms, values, and beliefs that are constantly shaped by an ever-increasing presence of media, technological advancements, globalization, and hot-button topics (even when such informal institutions do not fundamentally change). As such, the boundaries of both formal and informal institutions are—and hence, the scope of the informal economy is—in a state of flux. That is, these boundaries are both permeable and fluid. To the extent that formal institutional boundaries shift in congruence with informal institutions, societal actors may have less need to undertake informal adjustments to perceived formal institutional imperfections.

In terms of fluidity of formal institutional boundaries, extant research has begun to provide some initial understandings of why boundaries change. For example, Lee and Hung (2014) describe how formal institutions came to recognize the informal shan-zhai mobile phone sector in China. With the intent of forming a pillar industry around cell phones, the Chinese government provided licenses to only a small number of state-owned enterprises. Drawing upon moral legitimacy based on fairness and justice and freed from technological and regulatory constraints, shan-zhai entrepreneurs were able to innovate and grow significantly. Simultaneously, shan-zhai entrepreneurs actively framed their activities as socially acceptable and worked to build cohesive supply chain and inter-industry/political ties. The broader societal acceptance of the informal shan-zhai sector eventually led the government to formally approve all of its activities. Lee and Hung's (2014) results provide a contrasting perspective to the delegitimation of alcohol during the Prohibition Era in the United States that accompanied the temperance movement (Hiatt, Sine, & Tolbert, 2009). Collectively, this research points to the influence of multiple large groups within society possessing different values and beliefs regarding definitions of legitimacy (Webb et al., 2009) and the potential for these large groups to muster collective support in prompting formal institutional change.

Thus far, we have discussed how the boundaries of formal institutions can change in response to the changing relevance of certain norms, values, and beliefs within society. However, it seems that, today, informal institutional boundaries within a particular society are also more dynamic than has been the case historically. A confluence of factors seems to underlie potential changes in informal institutional boundaries. Immigration, for example, introduces new norms, values, and beliefs into societies. The ethnic enclaves that form within a society through immigration can provide pockets of informal institutions that protect local economic activity with potentially conflicting formal institutions (Pessar, 1995; Portes & Jensen, 1989). Not surprisingly, ethnic enclaves have thus been a context for scholars examining informality in developed contexts (e.g., Ahmad, 2008; Stoller, 1996). Beyond immigration, we expect a number of other factors to shape informal institutions and the informal economy within society. Media channels increasingly offer more biased and opinionated discussions of ongoing events in society. Given media's much larger footprint and the ability for media now through technological advancements to be at individuals' fingertips anytime during the day and night, we suspect that the potential exists for differences in informal institutions to be stoked, publicly debated, and eventually shaped in new ways. In our view, entrepreneurial efforts to segment markets in increasingly narrow ways also offer the potential for informal institutions to change. As entrepreneurs *create* new opportunities, they can highlight consumer needs of which the consumers were previously not aware (Alvarez & Barney, 2007), which in turn might shape new norms, values, and beliefs (Giddens, 1984).

Importantly, the development of formal institutions and changes in formal institutional boundaries does not necessarily preclude or displace the use of informal mechanisms. Developing economies are, by definition, undergoing development of formal institutions. In some cases, economic development might consist of more market-friendly policies. In other cases, economic development manifests in formal institutional infrastructures and supporting apparatuses. In our conversations with a local microfinance organization representative in Ghana, the representative discussed their development of a formal savings and loan infrastructure. Despite offering benefits in terms of security and more attractive interest rates relative to the local informal susu collectives, the microfinance organization had difficulty enticing local individuals to convert to their system. It was unclear as to why such difficulties occurred, whether it be due to social pressures to remain in the informal collective, distrust of the competence and goodwill of formal institutional stakeholders, inertia due to existing norms, or other factors. The resistance to change, however, suggests that even in some cases when formal institutional boundaries exist, the informal economy and its expectations and mandates may persist.

Future research. A theory of informal adjustments could benefit from additional research to understand issues such as those suggested by the following questions:

- Why do catalysts trigger formal institutional stakeholders to tangibly versus trivially respond to social movements?

- Why do groups sometimes actively compete for their norms and beliefs to be formalized whereas other times one group simply acquiesces to the other?
- How and why have some formal institutions gained more power and influence in recent history, and how have the formal institutional changes influenced acceleration/deceleration of changes in informal institutional boundaries?

Confluence of Formal and Informal Institutions

A theory of informal adjustments is premised on the notion that informal mechanisms are used to facilitate, govern, and structure economic activities where imperfections exist in formal institutions. We have emphasized changes in informal institutions and the formation of informal supporting apparatuses and infrastructures. More specifically, we seek to shift scholars' efforts from studying formal institutions to incorporate stronger considerations of informal institutions. Importantly, we expect that a more robust and inclusive theoretical framework for understanding informality derives from understanding not only the influence of informal institutions as adjustments but also the confluence of both formal and informal institutions.

London, Esper, Grogan-Kaylor, and Kistruck (2014) provide a useful and informative example of studying the confluence of formal and informal institutions. Using a sample from across numerous base-of-the-pyramid markets in India, the authors show that formal institutional voids moderate the relationship between poverty-based norms and consumers' purchasing decisions. Interestingly, the direct effects of poverty-based norms were predominantly not related to purchasing decisions; only when taking into account variance in the formal institutional environment did the effect of norms become more salient. These findings offer at least some evidence to suggest that the influence of informal institutions becomes stronger in the presence of formal institutional imperfections.

In a second study, Bruton and his co-authors (Bruton, Webb, Yu, & Davis, 2014) use a sample of microentrepreneurs in China to examine the confluence of informal norms and formal institutional voids on the microentrepreneurs' networks and venture performance. They found that formal institutional voids lead to a greater use of network ties. Moreover, gender- and income-based norms moderate this relationship such that female and lower-income microentrepreneurs have smaller networks. In turn, more network ties lead to higher venture performance.

Future research. This research provides a number of important implications to scholars studying informality. First, both studies (Bruton et al., 2014; London et al., 2014) highlight the importance of examining the variance of formal institutional imperfections. Formal institutional voids are not all or nothing, zero or one. Rather, formal institutional voids can vary significantly across regions, and scholars should use or develop measures that fully capture this variance. This implication holds not only for formal institutional voids but all forms of formal institutional imperfections. Second, this research highlights the potential for informal institutional imperfections. The finding by Bruton and his co-authors (2014) that female and lower-income microentrepreneurs have smaller networks suggests that these microentrepreneurs may be marginalized, with less opportunity to access resource-rich networks. Finally, actors can be strategic within contexts of formal institutional imperfections. Upon assessing the challenges in their environments, actors can draw upon informal adjustments in different ways (i.e., strong ties versus weak ties, structural holes, trust and mutuality versus power, etc.) to overcome these challenges. In examining the following research questions, scholars can begin building a foundation for the myriad types of formal institutional imperfections and the various informal adjustments taken to address those imperfections:

- How is the effectiveness of informal institutional adjustments (in terms of entrepreneurial and firm outcomes) influenced by the moderating effects of specific formal institutional imperfections?
- What are the relevant micro-foundations to explain why individuals interpret and respond to their institutional environments differently?

Developed Versus Developing Contexts

As we have discussed the underpinnings of a theory of informal adjustments, we have drawn heavily upon research and examples from developing contexts. This biased lens merely represents our personal inclination for studying relevant phenomena in developing contexts thus far. Nevertheless, significant informal economic activity occurs within developed contexts (Schneider, 2002; Williams & Lansky, 2013; Williams & Nadin, 2014) as well, and the nature of this informality seems to be at least in some cases fundamentally different from what we see in developing contexts. We suspect that at least two reasons may explain differences between informality in developed versus developing contexts. First, developed contexts have a much stronger foundation of formal institutional infrastructures. Informal actors can selectively comply with formal regulations to access certain benefits while at the same time avoiding other requirements that are considered to present undue challenges and costs (Uzo & Mair, 2014). Informal actors can then draw and/or free-ride upon at least some level of formal institutional infrastructure to support growth. Second, developed and developing contexts differ in the nature of their idiosyncratic formal (and informal) institutional imperfections. Formal institutional voids are a highly prevalent form of institutional imperfection within developing economies but rarer in developed economies. Informality in developed economies may be stimulated more by institutional uncertainty, given the potential for environmental trends to outpace formal institutional changes, or ambiguities, given the potential for conflict across policies and regulatory agencies. The types of opportunities available for informal actors and the means through which actors exploit these opportunities within developed contexts would seem likely to differ. As of yet, scholars have a very limited understanding of how informal adjustments differ based on formal institutional imperfections. In particular, we believe this is an important gap in our understanding of the informal economy because we, as a society, may want to encourage actors to exploit through informal adjustments some formal institutional imperfections while seeking to limit other forms of informal adjustments. This logic and expectation suggest the following questions that scholars may wish to pursue:

- What sort of policies should developed economy contexts adopt to promote constructively deviant versus destructively deviant informal adjustments?
- How do developing economy contexts promote shifts of societal actors from relying on informal adjustments to formal institutions?
- In developing economy contexts, how do non-governmental organizations successfully transform informal institutional fields (i.e., their institutional logics, relationships and positions, and governing rules) and incorporate them into more formal, developed fields?

Semi-Formality

Increasingly, scholars have urged a view of informality not as a dichotomy but as a more nuanced and complex, multi-faceted variable (e.g., Godfrey, 2011). How a societal actor seeks to operate in the informal economy is a strategic choice (Siqueira et al., 2014). Actors can selectively comply with certain laws/regulations or draw upon certain formal infrastructures while at the same time avoiding other laws, regulations, or infrastructures (De Castro, Khavul, & Bruton, 2014; Uzo & Mair, 2014) or proactively exploiting other formal institutional imperfections.

The complex nature of informality highlights the complex formal institutional environments in which societal actors operate. Whether in developed or developing contexts, actors operate in polycentric, heterogeneous formal institutional environments. Polycentricity refers to the many different domains (i.e., institutional centers) of policies and regulations and their respective regulatory agencies that govern each domain (Bartjargal et al., 2013). For example, a society can have specific centers in terms of financial, legal, labor, educational, and industry-specific regulatory institutions (i.e., banking, healthcare, defense, etc.), among others. Having multiple centers allows formal institutions to concentrate expertise on specific politico-economic issues and localize efforts on specific markets (Ostrom, 2005). However, multiple centers can serve as a potential source of conflict, either when multiple centers have what are perceived to be overlapping jurisdictions or when gaps exist between the centers' jurisdictions. Such conflict can create uncertainty for societal actors in terms of specific institution-related costs and benefits. In addition, the potential for loopholes exist if the unique institutional centers do not consistently communicate among themselves to resolve issues (Fernandez-Kelly, 2006). Either way, societal actors may be motivated to instead rely on semi-formal adjustments in which they comply with certain formal institutions while avoiding other requirements.

Institutional heterogeneity refers to the varying levels of development within each center (Kistruck et al., 2014). We have referred to formal institutional voids as one type of imperfection. In reality, developing contexts have heterogeneous formal institutional environments, with the level of development of formal institutions varying significantly based upon region (i.e., urban versus rural areas) and centers (i.e., financial versus educational versus labor versus legal, etc.) (Dhanani & Islam, 2002; Granville & Leonard, 2010). Because of this, certain formal institutional centers with minor voids provide more market-related benefits to offset their costs. In comparison, centers characterized by more significant voids present costs that outweigh potential benefits. Actors may choose, then. to operate semi-formally depending on the costs, benefits, and risks associated with selective compliance across formal institutions relative to that of potential informal adjustments.

Future research. In understanding informality, then, scholars may seek to take a finer-grained view of formal and informal institutions, addressing the following questions:

- How can scholars effectively deconstruct formal institutional environments from a single, homogenous category to a complex, multi-faceted phenomena?
- How do formal institutions come to prescribe conflicting definitions or mandates, and what factors influence the relevant formal institutions to resolve such conflict?
- What are the idiosyncratic actor-level and contextual differences that influence the actors' degree of semi-formality?

Methodological Considerations

The typical consideration of informality in terms of illegal yet legitimate economic activities provides methodological challenges to scholars. Especially in developed contexts, where stronger formal institutions have the authority and capacity to enforce laws and regulations, the illegal nature of informal economy activities leads them to be undertaken in clandestine and hidden ways. While hiding primarily from formal institutions which may seek to monitor and enforce these activities, actors also become hidden from scholars who may be interested in studying them. Commonly used approaches to data collection, such as surveys and archival sources, are not likely to produce the quality data that are needed to examine illegal, legitimate economic activities. More creative approaches to data collection are likely required. For example, a more effective approach might be to undertake prison interviews to access a sample of informal entrepreneurs who have likely grown their ventures outside of laws and regulations. Even here, though, the degree to which prisoners would be willing to be honest and totally forthcoming is a potential constraint.

In comparison, activities that are illegal and legitimate in developing economies can often be much less hidden. One reason for a greater openness of informality in developing economies is that these contexts are highly impoverished, and informality has proportionally much higher levels of legitimacy as a means for individuals to meet their subsistence needs in these contexts. To some degree, even formal institutional authorities condone informality as they realize that formal economy opportunities simply do not exist in terms of the breadth and depth needed to support societal needs. Therefore, if scholars can overcome local individuals' tendency to be wary of strangers, survey-based approaches can be used to discern whether actors register their activities (and with whom), what licensure requirements are met, to what extent appropriate social security and taxes are paid, and if relevant regulations are satisfied. Local individuals even seem to respond openly to government-based census surveys measuring informality.

Considering informality as informal adjustments to formal institutional imperfections introduces its own methodological challenges, whether in developed or developing contexts. On the one hand, informal adjustments can occur openly in plain sight. On the other hand, the nature of these phenomena can often take starkly different manifestations than their formal counterparts. Therefore, informal adjustments can be hidden in plain sight, and their underlying mechanisms can be causally ambiguous. Informal finance, for example, is less often found to take place in a physical bank with tellers, safety deposit boxes, savings accounts, a secure safe, and the customary forms of collateral and notarization. Instead, informal bank transactions are handled by a man standing on the street corner with a hefty wad of cash (and likely a hidden security team!) or a network of relationships for collecting savings along with simply a lockbox. Informal enforcement and judicial systems also are likely to be less visible (i.e., no uniforms or badges, police cars, court buildings, etc.). Instead, these informal adjustments may be based on local community norms (e.g., social stigma or ostracization versus jail time), purposefully hidden, or embedded in relationships and informally construed hierarchies.

Future research. Given the nascency of research on informal adjustments, scholarly understanding will benefit from more exploratory and ethnographic approaches, with scholars embedding themselves in the local contexts to truly understand the essence of the norms, values, and beliefs and social structure that defines the informality (Ketchen, Ireland, & Webb, 2014). However, we encourage scholars to also think creatively in terms of how they might inform a theory of informal adjustments using a quantitative approach. In doing so, scholars might consider questions such as the following:

- How can scholars measure institutional boundary change? Given that definitions of legality and legitimacy differ across societies, how can scholars effectively design studies to make cross-country comparisons of institutional boundaries?
- Even if informal adjustments are not visible, are there potentially valid markers or signals of informal adjustments that can be used as proxies?
- Similarly, how can scholars construct a valid measure of semi-formality that captures the variability in which informality occurs but that is also not overly burdensome and complex?
- What are the theoretical implications of measuring the informal economy and informal adjustments in different ways?

CONCLUSION

Unquestionably, the informal economy presents important theoretical and practical implications that organizational scholars can—and need to—inform. Policy efforts to address the informal economy have largely been met with failure. A primary reason for the lack of success in these policy efforts may be the predominant focus on changing formal institutions without regard to informal institutions. Compounding the policy shortcomings are likely the significant diversity of formal institutional imperfections and the variety of informal mechanisms deployed by societal actors as they adjust to these imperfections. Organizational scholars are well positioned to inform the understanding of how institutional environments influence informal rules, organization, and governance. In turn, these insights can translate into more effective policy decisions and decisions regarding infrastructures.

In this chapter, we proposed a theory of informal adjustments as a framework for understanding the informal economy. Our theory is premised on the notion that societal actors assume informal adjustments to facilitate, govern, and structure their activities when imperfections characterize formal institutions. The specific manifestation of an informal adjustment is influenced by the society's specific formal institutional imperfection. We have further sought to identify what theory suggests are key antecedents to societal actors undertaking informal adjustments, variation in the meaning of informality, the influence of dynamic and heterogeneous formal and informal institutional boundaries and environments, a consideration of extant theoretical lenses that can inform our own theory, and the relevance of various methodological approaches. We hope that this foundation will stimulate further efforts to understand the informal economy and informal adjustments that are a part of it.

REFERENCES

Acemoglu, D., & Robinson, J. 2012. *Why nations fail: The origins of power, prosperity, and poverty*. New York: Crown Publishers.

Agnew, R. 1993. Why do they do it? An examination of the intervening mechanisms between "social control" variables and delinquency. *Journal of Research in Crime and Delinquency*, 30: 245–266.

Aharonovitz, G. D., & Nyaga, E. K. 2010. Values, cultural practices, and economic performance: Theory and some evidence from Kenya. *World Development*, 38: 1156–1167.

Ahmad, A. N. 2008. The labour market consequences of human smuggling: 'Illegal' employment in London's migrant economy. *Journal of Ethnic and Migration Studies*, 34: 853–874.

Alvarez, S. A., & Barney, J. B. 2007. Discovery and creation: Alternative theories of entrepreneurial action. *Strategic Entrepreneurship Journal*, 1: 11–26.

Barley, S., & Tolbert, P. 1997. Institutionalization and structuration: Studying the links between action and institution. *Organization Studies*, 18: 93–117.

Bartjargal, B., Hitt, M. A., Tsui, A. S., Arregle, J.-L., Webb, J. W., & Miller, T. 2013. Institutional polycentrism, entrepreneurs' social networks and new venture growth. *Academy of Management Journal*, 56: 1024–1049.

Bird, K., & Shepherd, A. 2003. Livelihoods and chronic poverty in semi-arid Zimbabwe. *World Development*, 31: 591–610.

Bruton, G. D., Pryor, I., Webb, J. W., & Zahra, S. A., 2014. *An examination of the boundary conditions of trust in new ventures: A base-of-the-pyramid perspective*. Working paper, Texas Christian University, Fort Worth, TX.

Bruton, G. D., Webb, J. W., Yu, A., & Davis, B. C. 2014. *Formal institutional voids, marginalization, and network ties: An examination of Chinese microentrepreneurs' performance*. Working Paper, Texas Christian University, Fort Worth, TX.

Carter, M. R., & Maluccio, J. A. 2003. Social capital and coping with economic shocks: An analysis of stunting of South African children. *World Development*, 31: 1147–1163.

Castells, M., & Portes, A. 1989. World underneath: The origins, dynamics, and effects of the informal economy. In A. Portes, M. Castells, & L. A. Benton (Eds.), *The informal economy: Studies in advanced and less developed countries:* 11–37. Baltimore, MD: The Johns Hopkins University Press.

Cleaver, F. 2005. The inequality of social capital and the reproduction of chronic poverty. *World Development*, 33: 893–906.

De Castro, J. O., Khavul, S., & Bruton, G. D. 2014. Shades of grey: How do informal firms navigate between macro and meso institutional environments? *Strategic Entrepreneurship Journal*, 8: 75–94.

De Soto, H. 1989. *The other path*. New York: Harper and Row.

De Soto, H. 2006. Trust, institutions and entrepreneurship. In C. S. Galbraith & C. H. Stiles (Eds.), *Developmental entrepreneurship: Adversity, risk, and isolation* (Volume 5): 3–19. Amsterdam: Emerald.

Dhanani, S., & Islam, I. 2002. Poverty, vulnerability and social protection in a period of crisis: The case of Indonesia. *World Development*, 30: 1211–1231.

Dhanaraj, C., & Khanna, T. 2011. Transforming mental models on emerging markets. *Academy of Management Learning & Education*, 10: 684–701.

Estache, A., & Wren-Lewis, L. 2009. Toward a theory of regulation for developing countries: Following Jean-Jacques Laffont's lead. *Journal of Economic Literature*, 47: 729–770.

Fernandez-Kelly, P. 2006. Introduction. In P. Fernandez-Kelly & J. Shefner (Eds.), *Out of the shadows: Political action and the informal economy in Latin America*: 1–22. University Park, PA: The Pennsylvania State University Press.

Garcia-Rincon, M. F. 2007. Redefining rules: A market for public space in Caracas, Venezuela. In J. Cross, & A. Morales (Eds.), *Street entrepreneurs: People, place and politics in local and global perspective*: 36–57. London: Routledge Taylor and Francis Group.

Giddens, A. 1984. *The constitution of society.* Berkeley, CA: University of California Press.

Godfrey, P. C. 2011. Toward a theory of the informal economy. *Academy of Management Annals*, 5: 231–277.

Goodrick, E., & Salancik, G. R. 1996. Organizational discretion in responding to institutional practices: Hospitals and Cesarean births. *Administrative Science Quarterly*, 41: 1–28.

Granville, B., & Leonard, C. S. 2010. Do informal institutions matter for technological change in Russia? The impact of communist norms and conventions, 1998–2004. *World Development*, 38: 155–169.

Guirkinger, C. 2008. Understanding the coexistence of formal and informal credit markets in Piura, Peru. *World Development*, 36: 1436–1452.

Hart, K. 1973. Informal income opportunities and urban employment in Ghana. *Journal of Modern African Studies*, 11(1): 61–89.

Hiatt, S. R., Sine, W. D., & Tolbert, P. S. 2009. From Pabst to Pepsi: Deinstitutionalization of social practices and the creation of entrepreneurial opportunities. *Administrative Science Quarterly*, 54: 635–667.

Hobbes, T. 1991. *De cive.* Indianapolis, IN: Hackett.

Kaufmann, P. J., & Dant, R. P. 1992. The dimensions of commercial exchange. *Marketing Letters*, 3: 171–185.

Ketchen, D. J., Ireland, R. D., & Webb, J. W. 2014. Toward a research agenda for the informal economy: A survey of the *Strategic Entrepreneurship Journal's* editorial board. *Strategic Entrepreneurship Journal*, 8: 95–100.

Khanna, T., & Palepu, K. 1997. Why focused strategies may be wrong for emerging markets. *Harvard Business Review*, 75(4): 41–51.

Kimura, Y. 2011. Knowledge diffusion and modernization of rural industrial clusters: A paper-manufacturing village in northern Vietnam. *World Development*, 39: 2105–2118.

Kistruck, G. M., Webb, J. W., Sutter, C. J., & Bailey, A. V. G. 2015. The double-edged sword of legitimacy in base-of-the-pyramid markets. *Journal of Business Venturing*, 30(3): 436–451.

Kistruck, G. M., Webb, J. W., Sutter, C. J., & Ireland, R. D. 2011. Microfranchising in base-of- the-pyramid markets: Institutional challenges and adaptations to the franchise model. *Entrepreneurship Theory and Practice*, 35: 503–531.

Lam, L. M., & Paul, S. 2013. Displacement and erosion of informal risk-sharing: Evidence from Nepal. *World Development*, 43: 42–55.

Lee, C.-K. & Hung, S.-C. 2014. Institutional entrepreneurship in the informal economy: China's *shan zhai* mobile phones. *Strategic Entrepreneurship Journal*, 8(1): 16–36.

Levitsky, S., & Murillo, M. V. 2009. Variation in institutional strength. *Annual Review of Political Science*, 12(1): 115–133.

London, T., Esper, H., Grogan-Kaylor, A., & Kistruck, G. M., 2014. Connecting poverty to purchase in informal markets. *Strategic Entrepreneurship Journal*, 8: 37–55.

Mair, J., Martí, I., & Ventresca, M. 2012. Building inclusive markets in rural Bangladesh: How intermediaries work institutional voids. *Academy of Management Journal*, 55: 819–850.

Meirowitz, A., & Tucker, J. A. 2007. Run Boris run: Strategic voting in sequential elections. *Journal of Politics*, 69(1): 88–100.

Nichter, S., & Goldmark, L. 2009. Small firm growth in developing countries. *World Development*, 37: 1453–1464.

North, D. C. 1990. *Institutions, institutional change and economic performance.* New York: Cambridge University Press.

Odegaard, C. V. 2008. Informal trade, contrabando and prosperous socialities in Arequipa, Peru. *Ethnos,* 73: 241–266.

Ostrom, E. 2005. *Understanding institutional diversity.* Princeton, NJ: Princeton University Press.

Palmer, I. 1991. *Gender and population in the adjustment of African economies: Planning for change.* Geneva: International Labour Organization.

Peng M. W., & Heath, P. S. 1996. The growth of the firm in planned economies in transition: Institutions, organizations, and strategic choice. *Academy of Management Review,* 21: 492–528.

Pessar, P. R. 1995. The elusive enclave: Ethnicity, class, and nationality among Latino entrepreneurs in greater Washington, DC. *Human Organization,* 54: 383–392.

Platteau, J.-P., & Abraham, A. 2002. Participatory development in the presence of endogenous community imperfections. *Journal of Development Studies,* 39: 104–136.

Portes, A., & Haller, W. 2005. The informal economy. In N. J. Smelser, & R. Swedberg (Eds.), *The handbook of economic sociology:* 403–425. Princeton, NJ: Princeton University Press.

Portes, A., & Jensen, L. 1989. The enclave and the entrants: Patterns of ethnic enterprise in Miami before and after Mariel. *American Sociological Review,* 54: 929–949.

Portes, A., & Sensenbrenner, J. 1993. Embeddedness and immigration: Notes on the social determinants of economic action. *American Journal of Sociology,* 98: 1320–1350.

Qian, J. U. N., & Strahan, P. E. 2007. How laws and institutions shape financial contracts: The case of bank loans. *Journal of Finance,* 62: 2803–2834.

Rakowski, C. A. 1994. Introduction: What debate? In C. A. Rakowski (Ed.), *Contrapunto: The informal sector debate in Latin America:* 3–10. Albany, NY: State University of New York Press.

Roever, S. 2006. Enforcement and compliance in Lima's street markets: The origins and consequences of policy incoherence towards informal traders. In B. Guha-Khasnobis, R. Kanbur, & E. Ostrom (Eds.), *Linking the formal and informal economy: Concepts and policies:* 246–262. Oxford: Oxford University Press.

Schneider, F. 2002. *Size and measurement of the informal economy in 110 countries around the world.* ANU, Canberra, Australia: Workshop of Australian National Tax Center.

Siqueira, A., Webb, J. W., & Bruton, G. D. Forthcoming. Informal entrepreneurship and industry conditions. *Entrepreneurship Theory and Practice.*

Stoller, P. 1996. Spaces, places, and fields: The politics of West African trading in New York City's informal economy. *American Anthropologist,* 98: 776–788.

Sutter, C. J., Webb, J. W., Kistruck, G. M., & Bailey, A. V. G., 2013. Entrepreneurs' responses to semi-formal illegitimate institutional arrangements. *Journal of Business Venturing,* 28: 743–758.

Uzo, U., & Mair, J. 2014. Source and patterns of organizational defiance of formal institutions: Insights from Nollywood, the Nigerian movie industry. *Strategic Entrepreneurship Journal,* 8: 56–74.

Varley, A. 2007. Gender and property formalization: Conventional and alternative approaches. *World Development,* 35: 1739–1753.

Webb, J. W., Bruton, G. D., Tihanyi, L., & Ireland, R. D. 2013. Research on entrepreneurship in the informal economy: Framing a research agenda. *Journal of Business Venturing,* 28: 598–614.

Webb, J. W., Ireland, R. D., & Ketchen, D. J. 2014. Toward a greater understanding of entrepreneurship and strategy in the informal economy. *Strategic Entrepreneurship Journal*, 8: 1–15.

Webb, J. W., Kistruck, G. M., Ireland, R. D., & Ketchen, D. J. 2010. The entrepreneurial process in bottom of the pyramid markets: The case of multinational corporation/nongovernment organization alliances. *Entrepreneurship Theory and Practice*, 43(3): 555–581.

Webb, J. W., Tihanyi, L., Ireland, R. D., & Sirmon, D. G. 2009. You say illegal, I say legitimate: entrepreneurship in the informal economy. *Academy of Management Review*, 34: 492–510.

Williams, C. C., & Lansky, M. A. 2013. Informal employment in developed and developing economies: Perspectives and policy responses. *International Labour Review*, 152(3–4): 355–380.

Williams, C. C., & Nadin, S. 2014. Evaluating the participation of the unemployed in undeclared work: Evidence from a 27-nation European survey. *European Societies*, 16(1): 68–89.

Williams, C. C., Windebank, J., Baric, M., & Nadin, S. 2013. Public policy innovations: The case of undeclared work. *Management Decision*, 51: 1161–1175.

Williamson, O. E. 2000. The new institutional economics: Taking stock, looking ahead. *Journal of Economic Literature*, 38: 595–613.

Woolcock, M. 1998. Social capital and economic development: Toward a theoretical synthesis and policy framework. *Theory and Society*, 27: 151–208.

Yue, L. Q., Luo, J., & Ingram, P. 2013. The failure of private regulation: Elite control and market crises in the Manhattan banking industry. *Administrative Science Quarterly*, 58: 37–68.

3 Communication, Visibility, and the Informal Economy

A Framework for Future Research

Craig R. Scott and Müge Haseki

Recent scholarship on the informal economy has not only made a persuasive case about the relevance of this sector for management and organizational studies but has also begun to articulate a number of promising research directions in this area (see Bruton, Ireland, & Ketchen, 2012; Godfrey, 2011; McGahan, 2012; Webb, Tihanyi, Ireland, & Sirmon, 2009). Through a focus on economic, sociological, and various managerial perspectives (e.g., organizational behavior, human resource management, stakeholder analysis), these and other authors have highlighted an aspect of the economy toward which management scholars have previously paid limited attention. But as Bruton et al. note, insights beyond the economic, sociological, and managerial would also be useful in our efforts to understand and design a research agenda about these firms and the individuals working in this space. One such perspective comes from the work in communication generally and organizational communication specifically.

While the previously mentioned management scholarship explicitly labels aspects of the informal economy as hidden, shadowy, shady, untracked, and not easily seen, it has rarely interrogated those ideas about how actors in this sector conceal and reveal themselves to others. Other work adds additional terminology for how we talk about this economy: unobserved, invisible, clandestine, underground, concealed, unrecorded, off-the-books, etc. (see Williams, 2006). These terms not only describe an alternative to the more familiar and formal aspects of the economy but also suggest something about the degree of openness and transparency found in this sector. Indeed, the nature of what many firms and workers in the informal economy do may necessitate some degree of reduced visibility and/or some restrictions in their communication with at least certain audiences. Thus, an organizational communication perspective that examines how these organizations and their members communicate their identity can provide new insights into key aspects of this sector.

This chapter seeks to contribute to the conversation by looking at several communication-based tensions surrounding the informal economy and its visibility. Next, a model of hidden organizations based on the communication of identity by firms and their members is introduced to help situate informal economy collectives broadly and to better compare different types to one another. Finally, we use that model to outline several possible research directions as we add an organizational communication perspective to our efforts at understanding the informal economy.

COMMUNICATION AND VISIBILITY TENSIONS IN THE INFORMAL ECONOMY

A variety of issues relevant to communication processes potentially emerge in the informal economy. The actual research examining communication in this economy has focused heavily on information and communication technologies (ICTs). For example, Opiyo and K'Akumu's (2006) study of ICTs in Kenya noted that these tools are utilized by Micro and Small Enterprise (MSE) in ways that encourage growth and improvement of the informal sector—leading them to conclude that ICTs should be more widely available in this market. Molony's (2008) research on mobile phone use by groups of informal construction workers in Tanzania found that this tool was useful in providing contact information when seeking additional work—but, in general, success in finding work is more about word of mouth and the leader's informal network (regardless of mobile phone use). Ilahiane and Sherry (2008) report on a different link with ICTs when those are the tools being marketed in a Moroccan underground economy in which street vendors are essentially unpaid sales representatives. Other work with informal media economies draws attention to media piracy, peer-to-peer file sharing, underground publishing, and other related topics (see Lobato, 2013).

Although that work linking ICTs and media to the informal economy is important, we focus this chapter on a somewhat different role for communication that emerges as we turn our attention more heavily to this other sector. Communication processes typically play a substantial role in both the internal (e.g., coordination, collaboration) and external (e.g., promotion, partnering) operations of organizations. As organizational identity and identification scholars have established, communication also plays a key role in the construction and representation of individual and collective identities both internally and externally (see Ashforth & Mael, 1989). As organizations and organizational members, we often use communication to share our (communicatively constructed) identity with various others. Yet, there is good reason to think this communicative process may operate a bit differently when considering the informal sector. As most definitions suggest, these organizations are operating in at least partially illegal ways— usually because they are not paying taxes, not officially registered, or not complying with certain employment laws—but still producing legal goods/ services (thus, we are not talking about a more criminal or renegade economy). As a result, these firms and those working in this informal space may demand at least some degree of reduced visibility and/or some restrictions in their communication. In some ways, the communication-based measures of success regularly applied to formal economy organizations (e.g., high name recognition) may be nearly opposite of what at least certain informal organizations may need (where such visibility could attract unwanted attention).

Given such differences, we attempt to extend this conversation about organizations and workers in the informal economy by introducing several related dialectical tensions linked specifically to communication as it is (or is not) used to promote (or restrict) visibility in this sector. A number of scholars have drawn on such an approach to help us better understand a variety of organizations, ranging from global software teams (Gibbs, 2009) to negotiation units (Putnam, 2003). A dialectical tension approach "situates tensions as normal, routine features of organizational life and looks for ways in which they can be productive for organizations as they find ways to 'hold together necessary incompatibles'" (Trethewey & Ashcraft, 2004: 84). These tensions may be found within the informal sector or help in describing the formal-informal relationship. Unlike double binds or contradictions from which we cannot readily escape, framing these differences as tensions provides the opportunity for us to more actively engage and manage them. We turn next to a brief mention of several related tensions that can help us think about the informal economy from a perspective emphasizing how one's identity gets communicated to others.

Formal-Informal

We begin with these terms not only because they are how we describe these different sectors of the economy, but also because they are used to talk about communication. Formal communication refers to those interactions that follow the planned structure of the organization and that represent the official, sanctioned organizational messages; informal refers to the many messages not following that planned structure or not officially sanctioned by the organization. While these are often presented as opposing or competing types of communication, they can be used to supplement one another (as when the informal messages reinforce or merely add specifics to the formal interaction). Monge and Contractor (2001) note the continuing interest in differences between formal and informal communication—but also suggest such distinctions have diminished substantially. Furthermore, efforts to shut down or formalize the informal often result in even more informal communication.

This suggests a useful tension between the formal and informal that demands we consider both and the complex relationship between them. Williams and Round (2011) illustrate one aspect of this intertwined relationship in their observations about cash-in-hand payments in Moscow, where employers informally pay their formal workers off the books. Godfrey (2011) has also argued that formal bureaucratic structures can be used by informal entrepreneurs to reduce risks and potential intrusions in what he describes as a semi-formal economy. De Castro, Khavul, and Bruton (2014) showed that formal and informal firms may create a trade system that legitimizes the continuation of the informal system.

Named-Anonymous

Most organizations have a name that they use to refer to themselves and that others associate with them. One's name is perhaps the most common way in which anything is identified (see Marx, 2004, 2006). However, some organizations and/or people associated with them may benefit from being without a name, i.e., anonymous. Anonymity is usefully described in relative terms (or degrees), includes forms of partial anonymity such as pseudonymity (a false name understood to be false), and is a perception of both message senders and receivers (Anonymous, 1998).

Although it has received only minimal attention, Scott and Rains (2005) have argued that we should pay greater attention to anonymity in organizations because of its relevance across a range of communication activities (e.g., whistleblowing and anonymous reporting of wrongdoing, anonymous communication technologies, anonymous feedback systems, anonymous complaints, etc.). Even in the formal economy we may find an organization "doing business as" another company or we find organizations that change names after some crisis to hide a part of their past identity. Tensions between being named or anonymous may surface even more in the informal economy or in the spaces where the formal and informal blur. Here we might find front organizations used as the name and face of an entity that keeps the organization behind it anonymous. We might see pseudonyms used by certain workers in stigmatized industries as an effort to protect themselves from others. If an informal organization does not wish to be identified, we might see the absence of a physical address, limited online presence, and/or missing contact information as providing a sense of organizational anonymity.

Transparent/Recognized-Secretive/Invisible

Several different sets of terms may be used to describe (a) the strategy used by the organization and/or people associated with it when communicating, and (b) the evaluation of the organization and/or people associated with it by others. Transparency refers to "the degree of openness in conveying information" (Ball, 2009: 297). Transparency and recognition can be a goal one has in efforts to communicate in a certain way; moreover, such strategies may produce evaluations suggesting one is relatively transparent and/or generally recognizable. An alternative goal is described by strategies to be secretive or invisible by restricting one's communication with others in various ways; again, such efforts may lead to assessments that an organization or those linked to it is secretive or largely invisible. In our society, we tend to privilege transparency as a goal and an outcome and we generally distrust anything involving secrecy (Bok, 1982). Actors in the formal economy may benefit substantially from the enhanced recognition—but even they must balance that against needs to make certain processes and aspects of organizing largely invisible to others. "Secrets and the safeguarding of secrets are necessary, if not essential, to organizational survival and competitiveness. Secrets are delicate, however, and the controlled and deliberate management of secrets poses serious leadership and organizational challenges" (Dufresne & Offstein, 2008: 102).

This area of tension is perhaps even more pronounced in the informal economy. For example, certain aspects of the complex sex industry operate heavily in the informal economy (e.g., escort services, hotel parties, adult massage, etc.). Some of these organizations and individuals advertise widely but also attempt to keep a relatively low profile to avoid undesired attention from the authorities and the general public. Schlosser's (2004) work about the pornography industry reveals another aspect of this tension between recognition and invisibility in that many facets of the sex trade "are tucked into middle-class and working-class neighborhoods, amid a typical Southern California landscape of palm trees, strip malls, car washes, and fast food joints" (167).

Other scholars have noted that one is able to stay invisible only until they start growing (Webb et al., 2009) or until they make increased profits (DeCastro et al., 2014); yet, for many actors in the informal economy, the entire purpose of their invisibility is to grow and make money. Portes and Haller (2005) argue that the success of informal organizations in highly regulated environments depends heavily on their efforts to conceal themselves and then maintain that secrecy. In Liberia, largely invisible rotating credit associations known as *susu groups* operate in secrecy to avoid market officials and empower women economically (Cruz, 2012). In each case, these informal organizations and the people associated with them must negotiate this tension related to what Gambetta (2009) calls the advertising problem: the need to attract relevant customers and resources when unable to promote goods/services in traditional ways.

Expressive-Silent

Whether talking about the formal or the informal economy, there are a variety of individuals involved with these organizations (as formal employees, off-the-books employees, contractors, customers, suppliers, etc.). They may experience a form of tension in their communication about their own identity as well. As organizational members, we are always balancing our collective and individual identities (Ashforth & Mael, 1989), and this makes us sometimes eager to talk up our organizations but at other times less likely to express any affiliation. The research about organizational identification suggests that when we feel strongly identified we will express ourselves in ways that show affiliation and alignment with the organization; however, a lack of connection or oneness with an organization may lead to negative talk or even a lack of talk.

Clearly, tensions must often be managed in formal employment arrangements as one seeks to communicate both a personal and professional identity or as one attempts to communicatively account for their membership in an organization with a lack of emotional attachment to that collective. These tensions may be experienced in somewhat different ways for more hidden workers in the informal economy, in which loyalty is better demonstrated through silence so as to maintain their hidden positions. Schlosser's (2004) study of the pornography industry created primarily by Reuben Sturman notes that this man would use multiple aliases and a general lack of communication with the media as a way to avoid too much attention from others. Through those somewhat silent strategies, he expressed his commitment to the industry. As a different example of this tension, Williams (2004) talks about voluntary disclosures in which certain government amnesty programs (designed to move informal work to more formal realms) may get people to reveal that they have been operating underground—creating an opportunity in which prior silence may turn to expression.

Public-Private

This tension can reference several issues related to the study of organizations (e.g., whether the organization is privately owned or publicly held or even public in the sense of government-based). In this context, private refers to information that is closely held (e.g., inside the self, internal to the firm) and public reflects a much wider sharing of that information to others (e.g., one's family, the community, or even the general public). Thus, private-public concerns how tightly we control who gets access to key identity information about us. Communicative theories of privacy treat the tension between concealing and revealing private information (which is inaccessible to certain others unless a person or even an organizational actor chooses to disclose it) as a primary principle (Petronio, 2002).

This concealing and revealing tension that characterizes privacy choices implies a concern about different publics or audiences (see McQuail, 1997). Certainly most organizations in any sector of the economy have to think strategically about their relevant publics in deciding not only what to conceal and reveal—but also to whom such disclosures are made. Actors in this sector may try to hide information from legal authorities, certain formal-sector competitors, and other key publics; but they may also make other information publicly available to certain customers, potential members/ employees, and other important stakeholders. Snyder's (2004) study of self-employed workers in New York City's East Village neighborhood provides an account of Sean, an entertainment producer and consultant in his fifties who teaches Tai Chi in the informal sector. When asked how he responds when someone asks him what he does, Sean replied: "Depends who it is. If it's a party with a bunch of Tai Chi people, I would say I teach Tai Chi. I do projects, I tell most people" (223). This distinction between private and public is also seen in the tension between public and private morality as it might apply to the informal sector. We may publicly denounce these informal businesses that try to skirt the law in our communities, but then privately use them to avoid paying extra taxes ourselves (e.g., with a landscaping service). In some ways, this tension is reflected in what Gambetta (2009) calls the communication problem: the need to communicate with known colleagues without unwanted others intercepting or understanding the message.

Other

There are, of course, a variety of other tensions that we can use to talk about various sectors of the economy that may also be especially linked to the informal. There is a need for autonomy to protect oneself from scrutiny but also a desire for interconnectedness to provide resources and security. There are the always present tensions between truth-telling and deception that can be more pronounced when one has to hide certain aspects of who they are from others. There is the need to know about others in the marketplace without being known yourself. Wanting full information on a potential recruit while also wishing to remain blind to his/her legal immigration status represents another tension found in certain parts of the informal economy (Jones, Ram, & Edwards, 2006).

FRAMEWORK ABOUT HIDDEN ORGANIZATIONS APPLIED TO THE INFORMAL ECONOMY

Collectively, these communication-based tensions suggest a value in looking at how organizations and individuals in the informal economy communicate identity in ways that enhance or limit their visibility to certain others. In doing so, it may be useful to consider both informal economy firms as well as underground workers who may be working off-the-books for a formal or informal business or who are more entrepreneurial or self-employed but still best described as part of this alternate economy. To help us in doing this, we draw on a recent framework examining hidden organizations more generally and then use it to talk specifically about various parts of the informal economy.

Scott's (2013) framework attempts to position a variety of more hidden organizations—including terrorist groups, criminal organizations, government intelligence, anonymous support groups, secret societies, and others—in relation to one another and to the more visible organizations in society (see Figure 3.1, adapted from Scott, 2013). The model is based on three

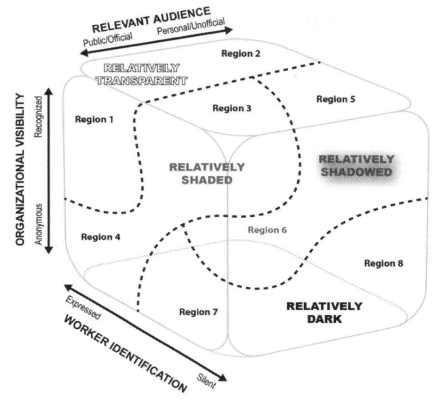

Figure 3.1 Framework for Examining Visibility of Organizations and Workers in the Informal Economy

dimensions that are essentially continua: *organizational visibility, member identification*, and *relevant audience*. The intersections of these continuous dimensions create permeable regions where various organizations operate.

The first primary dimension, degree of organizational visibility, refers to how recognizable or anonymous an organization's identity is (Scott, 2013). In illustrating the differences along this continuum, he suggests that more visibly anonymous organizations tend to conceal information, fly under the radar, or work behind the scenes; moreover, they are less likely to extensively advertise, widely promote themselves or their services, and often lack much resembling marketing or public relations functions. They may use fronts or pseudonyms, use little signage, and have an unfixed or discreet physical existence; they may lack a significant online presence, use communication channels that do not document/record information about the organization, and provide limited data about the organization and its members. They may value their more secretive nature and be typically smaller in size. All of this allows them to be partially or completely unrecognizable.

The second primary dimension in this model examines organizational members and whether they actively express or keep relatively silent about the sense of connection to or affiliation with their organization. For Scott (2013), the hiddenness of an organization depends substantially on the communication of its members—and silence may actually reflect stronger organizational identification if that is part of an effort to help conceal the collective and/or its members. He illustrates the differences along this continuum by noting that relatively silent members usually do not mention who they work for and avoid providing the organization's name—sometimes out of ignorance of the organization with which they are linked. Comments to others about what they do provide relatively little information about the organization and individuals are unlikely to have anything like a business card or detailed email signature. Silent members may be less likely to use "we" statements to talk about the organization and may not be nonverbally linked to it (no display of logo-imprinted clothing or other items). The silence may also be facilitated by a lack of full knowledge about the organization and its identity—making revelation of any secrets by members that much more difficult.

The final dimension in Scott's (2013) model relates to the relevant audience. As he argues, "Questions of visibility, recognizability, and anonymity demand that we ask, 'Visible to whom?' 'Recognizable to what groups?' 'Anonymous to which audiences?' and 'Hidden from whose view?' That degree of organizational visibility may not be the same for all observers" (93). Similarly, our expression of or silence about our affiliation with an organization is also directed toward or away from some audience. In his framework, this dimension is anchored by mass/public and local/limited audiences and it is the least important for influencing organizational hiddenness. To illustrate the differences at the extremes, more local/limited audiences are typically smaller and more immediate. When this is the relevant audience, the organization or its members may not have a public reputation to manage (only a local one). A more local/limited audience focuses attention on local media and greater use of interpersonal/non-mediated communication channels. The activities of these organizations matter most to their local community. When this local audience is most relevant, members come into contact with fewer others and limit expressions of (or are silent about) their organizational attachment to more immediate others. Scott theorizes that these organizations operate in limited places and that local audiences may be more recognizable as distinct audiences. All this stands in contrast to those organizations interacting with a much more mass/public audience.

By combining these three dimensions and looking towards the anchors on each end, Scott (2013) describes eight relatively permeable organizational regions based on how organizations and their members communicate their identity to relevant audiences. He uses those regions to describe different organizations that may operate in those spaces. Adapting the original framework, these regions can be grouped into four broader categories (see Figure 3.1): relatively transparent (visible organizations and expressive members); relatively shaded (public audience and either visible organizations or expressive members but not both); relatively shadowed (local audience and either anonymous organizations or silent members, but not both); and relatively dark (anonymous organizations and silent members).

With that in place, we are nearly ready to discuss how this framework might provide insights into the informal economy and to provide some possible examples. However, two adjustments seem needed here at the outset on two of these dimensions. First, a focus on organizational members exclusively limits the relevance of such a model for understanding underground workers more broadly. Snyder (2004) says underground work is a key part of one's identity for the majority of underground workers—so they may be able to be expressive or be silent about their work even if there is not a formal organizational affiliation. Thus, we talk here about *worker* identification and affiliation with the work. Second, a discussion of the informal economy may necessitate a slight rethinking about the relevant audience in which some of the key issues concern hiding from taxing and certain other authorities. Thus, a more local/limited audience here can be more usefully construed as one's close personal network (with family, friends, and perhaps other workers in that sector). A more public audience would especially include public government officials (including those taxing and police authorities) and the broader communities these officials represent. Thus, we can talk about the audience as personal/unofficial or public/official.

Relatively Transparent Regions

In Scott's (2013) model, the first two regions are where many of the organizations in the formal economy are found. Thus, this is also where we might find an aspect of the informal economy that is largely hidden within otherwise formal organizations. An example would be a legitimate, recognized business with documented employees that decides to also hire some of those workers for additional work that is paid off the books. This type of arrangement conceals the informal aspect by hiding it in plain sight—within a very visible organization with employees who are not generally hiding their affiliation with that organization. Other organizations here could be ones that become so large and successful that they attract the attention that either moves them into the formal economy or causes the organization to be fined/ charged. Webb et al.'s (2009) discussion of Napster reveals the interesting case of an organization whose growth attracted the attention of authorities that eventually would force it into bankruptcy (while other smaller firms doing essentially the same practices were sometimes able to stay in business). In this second region we might also find smaller companies that may advertise locally and have legal employees—but then engage in certain work practices off the books. For example, the tree service or lawn mowing company that does not collect taxes (or offers that option for cash payment) is contributing to the informal economy even though this visible company may promote its services to potential customers in the community and hire workers legally who clearly work for that organization. Perhaps those who run a small catering business out of their home or are regularly running garage sales are also in this region because they express what they do and even advertise it to others—but stay small/local and operate in areas that do not attract too much attention from legal authorities.

Relatively Shaded Regions

Here we might find larger, more visible organizations likely operating in the formal economy but who hire underground labor at a lower cost and with fewer regulations to conduct some of their work. This would seem to include practices found in the New York City (see McGahan, 2012) and Los Angeles (Hsu, 2014) construction industries. These practices avoid paying unemployment insurance and other moneys to local/state officials and also pay the workers at substantially lower rates; yet, those workers will remain silent about the practices because they are either working in those cities illegally or because they can easily be replaced if they raise concerns. It is also possible, but perhaps less likely, that the relatively shaded regions may include front organizations that masquerade as an entity not subject to the tax laws when they really should be contributing. In this case, the paid members and volunteers may have no reason to hide their association with this organization seeking a broad audience—but the actual organization behind those more informal fronts may be concealing its own identity.

Relatively Shadowed Regions

Region 5 in this model could feature certain entrepreneurial efforts in which organizational visibility in a very local community is sought. The visibility is needed for the success of the organization in one's community, but the audience stays quite local so as to avoid attention from public authorities (especially if the business is not registered or paying taxes). In this region of the framework, the entrepreneur or other employees remain relatively silent about their work—perhaps because they are immigrants not legally able to work or perhaps because they lack the required licensing (e.g., unregistered taxi service). Venkatesh's (2006) in-depth analysis of Chicago's South Side ethnic neighborhoods suggests these sorts of informal arrangements. An immigrant woman entrepreneur in the country illegally who starts a hair salon in her neighborhood in the Bronx might be another example. Region 6 may not describe very much of the economy—formal or informal; however, it could include small businesses in a local community "who conceal their identity because either they do not want to attract unnecessary attention to what they actually do or because any expenditure of resources to promote their identity is unnecessary" (Scott, 2013: 176). In this region, we could have an organization or employer not necessarily paying taxes or reporting all income—because, for example, regulations are too complex or costly, they are trying to keep the company solvent, or they are trying to cheat the system. But, the workers themselves are legal and getting paid and have no reason to conceal their involvement in what they may perceive to be a legitimate, law-abiding organization. Especially if one can attract workers and other resources and customers through local network (e.g., a garment manufacturer who mostly employs relatives and close friends and who markets to a limited range of buyers), the organization may be able to operate with anonymity that further conceals them underground.

Relatively Dark Regions

The darkest region in Scott's model can also be applied to certain aspects of the informal economy. Here, an organization stays relatively hidden and its workers remain relatively silent. Certain stigmatized aspects of the informal economy could go here—such as a masseuse who uses a false name when working for a discreet massage parlor that may be operating primarily via the informal economy. Here we might also find a secret sweatshop that employs undocumented workers, all of whom remain hidden from authorities (e.g., the secret sweatshop and 260 workers found under an abandoned market in Russia; see Lawson, 2013); additionally, even market street vendors operate primarily in this space (especially if there is no visible organization or the vendors lack needed permits/licenses). We may also find a few instances of the information economy operating in Region 7, especially when the government that would normally be regulating such work chooses to support it. For example, Alarcón (2009) describes how one government in South America actually assisted informal book publishers in an effort to drive out more formally established publishers who held opposing political views. Government forces may also support informal (as well as more illegal and corrupt) economic practices to complete projects like the venues for the Sochi Olympics (when the formal system was not meeting deadlines; see Economist, 2013). Those construction contractors and book publishers might very well fit into a relatively dark region—remaining largely hidden yet with a level of public support of that concealment.

Having briefly applied the adapted model in Figure 3.1 to the informal economy, it would appear that this framework helps to illustrate some important distinctions between various aspects of this sector. These differences, based on the organization's relative visibility and the worker's relative expressiveness about their work as communicated to either personal/unofficial or more public/official audiences, may help to highlight some communicative aspects of the informal economy that have not previously received adequate attention. Regardless of where we have placed certain organizations or workers in the examples offered here, the broader contribution lies in thinking more about how these issues of communication and visibility allow us to compare and contrast different actors in the informal economy.

POTENTIAL RESEARCH QUESTIONS
SUGGESTED BY FRAMEWORK

We believe this framework as applied to organizations and workers in the informal economy provides a somewhat unique perspective on this sector. It by no means replaces other models and perspectives, but hopefully complements them. By highlighting issues of communication and visibility it points to a variety of future research directions for work on the informal economy. In this final section, we discuss several such possibilities.

Differences in Model Regions

The framework suggests several differences between organizations and workers operating in different regions. Thus, future research of a somewhat comparative nature should examine the extent to which such communicative differences are actually found among various actors in this sector and if those distinctions are ones that really make a difference. Moreover, the model may be helpful in pointing to certain types of informal organizations or informal work that need increased research attention. Combined with Scott's (2013) original work, it can also help more clearly situate the informal economy and its players amid the broader organizational landscape that includes not only formal economy organizations but also a wide range of other hidden collectives—all of whom are concerned to some degree with how they communicate their identity to certain others.

Key Outcomes

In many ways, informal economy scholars are concerned with key outcomes for the organizations and individuals in these sectors; yet, we know very little about how the degree of visibility might constrain and enable such outcomes. Future research should examine how issues of organizational visibility and worker expressiveness might relate to organizational performance, survival, and potential transition to the formal economy. In particular, research can investigate what advantages and disadvantages visibility of an organization provides in times of uncertainty and change. Similarly, research should examine how these aspects of communication relate to individual productivity, satisfaction, and other measures. Perhaps organizations that can avoid more public audiences (at least as we have reframed that idea here) can survive longer in an informal economy—which runs counter to what we might expect in more formal sectors. Similarly, firms with some greater visibility (to the appropriate audiences) may be more productive, and workers who can be more expressive about what they do may often be more satisfied—but these remain largely under-examined relationships in need of further study.

Communication Strategies

When it comes to organizational attempts to be relatively anonymous or worker efforts to remain relatively silent, various concealment strategies must be used. Scott (2013) talks briefly about these for hidden organizations generally, and several of these might apply to the informal economy as well. For example, informal firms could conceal their identity through communication strategies such as maintaining a minimal online presence, using limited or no physical signage or visual identity markers, presenting vague information about their identity, using interpersonal/offline channels, limiting the use or branding of name, or even changing names/locations. Informal workers might remain silent through strategies such as not making pictures or names available to outsiders, not maintaining membership lists, not talking about their work, having limited knowledge/information to share with others, using anonymous channels, not carrying identifying information, or even changing/leaving an employer or type of work. Understanding what specific communication concealment strategies are used by different actors in the informal economy and how those relate to various outcomes represents an additional direction for future research in this area.

Disclosure

A related promising direction in this area is emerging work on organizational self-disclosure. Hatch and Schultz (2010) introduce this concept, arguing, "At an organizational as well as a personal level, allowing yourself to be known is a risk with many rewards" (601). Even though their focus is on brand co-creation, this has interesting implications for actors in the informal economy, in which organizations and their members must communicate their identity to certain audiences while concealing it from unwanted others. Similarly, informal organizations may hesitate to disclose information to their customers even though they want to increase customer loyalty; thus, research can examine how much information is disclosed to customers to maintain customer loyalty without jeopardizing organizational survival. It all points to a need to explore Gambetta's (2009) communication and advertising problems (described earlier) as they apply to the informal sector.

Ethical/Legal Issues

A focus on these visibility issues potentially raises important ethical and legal questions surrounding aspects of the informal economy. Not surprisingly, tensions between being named and being anonymous raise a number of important legal questions (Bronco, 2004). Even in the United States, it is not entirely clear if the right to speak anonymously that is part of an individual's free speech also extends to an organization's rights as a legal entity—and such questions may be very important for several actors in the informal economy. Ethically, we often raise questions when organizations and/or their workers are somehow secretive or hidden. The calls for more transparent communication in the formal sector as a way to promote more ethical behavior may not be as appropriate for much of the informal economy; in fact, for some, greater anonymity and silence may be more socially appropriate. At any rate, ethics surrounding the communication practices of informal actors deserves our attention.

Reputation

It is difficult to talk about how organizations and workers interact with various audiences without talking about their reputation—which is frequently connected to how well a firm communicates with relevant stakeholders (see Fombrun & Rindova, 2000). Yet, the nature of reputation may be less clear for those informal organizations that barely communicate their identity to others. How do we evaluate the reputation of organizations we barely know, but that may still depend on reputation in some ways? How does the less visible nature of some informal organizations hurt their identity and in what ways could that anonymity actually enhance one's reputation with certain audiences? The role of communication in the reputation process for these informal sector organizations clearly needs further exploration.

Other Organizations

The study of the informal economy broadly also has to consider other organizations that arise to support this economy (but may themselves not necessarily be part of that economy). This could be somewhat hidden nonprofits that help provide protections for workers (Martin, 2012) or informal workers unions that have emerged in India and other places (Agarwala, 2008). In some ways, these organizations can act in ways that less visible members of the informal economy cannot. Conversely, we should also consider other organizations that work to uncover some of the less visible aspects of this economy (e.g., undercover operations to identify tax evaders) and who use their communication to reveal what may otherwise be hidden.

CONCLUSION

It should not be surprising that this informal economy—which we regularly describe as hidden, shadowy, shady, untracked, unobserved, invisible, clandestine, underground, concealed, unrecorded, etc.—can be usefully considered in terms of its visibility, or lack thereof, to various others. Without question, the nature of what many actors in the informal economy do often requires at least some degree of reduced visibility and/or some restrictions in their communication with certain others. We see this in communicative tensions that emerge with the informal economy surrounding the formal-informal, named-anonymous, transparent/recognized-secret/invisible, expressive-silent, and public-private. Our goal here has been to provide an organizational communication perspective to explore how these actors in the informal economy conceal and reveal their identity to certain key audiences.

Of course, an effort to examine more anonymous informal organizations and more silent informal workers creates additional challenges for research in this area. These aspects of this economy may be the hardest to access—but that makes this an area where we may be able to contribute substantially to our understanding of the informal economy. We see the informal economy as containing at least some hidden organizations and hidden work that require somewhat unique communication efforts as they navigate a number of tensions. Thus, a communication perspective focused on degrees of visibility can help point to a number of research directions that promise to add to our growing understanding of this vital part of the organizational landscape.

REFERENCES

Agarwala, R. 2008. Reshaping the social contract: Emerging relations between the state and informal labor in India. *Theory and Society*, 37: 375–408.

Alarcón, D. 2009. Life among the pirates. *Granta*, 109: 7. Retrieved from http://www.granta.com/Magazine/Granta-109-Work/Life-Among-the-Pirates/1

Anonymous. 1998. To reveal or not to reveal: A theoretical model of anonymous communication. *Communication Theory*, 8: 381–407.

Ashforth, B. E., & Mael, F. 1989. Social identity theory and the organization. *Academy of Management Review*, 14(1): 20–39.

Ball, C. 2009. What is transparency? *Public Integrity,* 11: 293–308.

Bok, S. 1982. *Secrets: On the ethics of concealment and revelation.* New York: Pantheon Books.

Bronco, a.k.a. Scott, C. R. 2004. Benefits and drawbacks of anonymous online communication: Legal challenges and communicative recommendations. In S. Drucker (Ed.), *Free speech yearbook:* 127–141. Washington, DC: National Communication Association.

Bruton, G., Ireland, D., & Ketchen, D. 2012. Toward a research agenda on the informal economy. *Academy of Management Perspectives*, 26(3): 1–11.

Cruz, J. 2012. *Community through invisibility: Market women's organizing in post-conflict Liberia.* Paper presented at the annual convention of the National Communication Association, Orlando, FL.

De Castro, J. O., Khavul, S., & Bruton, G. D. 2014. Shades of grey: How do informal firms navigate between macro and meso institutional environments? *Strategic Entrepreneurship Journal*, 8(1): 75–94.

Dufresne, R. L., & Offstein, E. H. 2008. On the virtues of secrecy in organizations. *Journal of Management Inquiry*, 17: 102–106.

Economist. 2013. Sochi olympics: Castles in the sand. http://www.economist.com/news/europe/21581764-most-expensive-olympic-games-history-offer-rich-pickings-select-few-castles, July 13.

Fombrun, C. J., & Rindova, V. P. 2000. The road to transparency: Reputation management at Royal Dutch/Shell. In M. Schultz, M. J. Hatch, & M. H. Larsen

(Eds.), *The expressive organization: Linking identity, reputation, and the corporate brand*: 77–96. Oxford: Oxford University Press.

Gambetta, D. 2009. *Codes of the underworld: How criminals communicate*. Princeton, NJ: Princeton University Press.

Godfrey, P. C. 2011. Toward a theory of the informal economy. *Academy of Management Annals*, 5: 231–277.

Gibbs, J. 2009. Dialectics in a global software team: Negotiating tensions across time, space, and culture. *Human Relations*, 62: 905–935.

Hatch, M. J., & Schultz, M. 2010. Toward a theory of brand co-creation with implications for brand governance. *Journal of Brand Management*, 17: 590–604.

Hsu, T. 2014. 1 in 6 California construction workers labors in shadows, study finds. *Los Angeles Times*. http://www.latimes.com/business/la-fi-california-construction-underground-economy-20140829-story.html, August 31.

Ilahiane, H., & Sherry, J. 2008. Joutia: Street vendor entrepreneurship and the informal economy of information and communication technologies in Morocco. *The Journal of North African Studies*, 13: 243–255.

Jones, T., Ram, M., & Edwards, P. 2006. Ethnic minority business and the employment of illegal immigrants. *Entrepreneurship and Regional Development*, 18(2): 133–150.

Lawson, J. 2013. Sweatshop city of 260 migrant workers complete with canteen, cinema and casino found under Moscow street. *Daily Mail*. http://www.dailymail.co.uk/news/article-2336721/Sweatshop-city-260-migrant-workers-complete-canteen-cinema-casino-Moscow-street.html, June 6.

Lobato, R. 2013. Informal economies in international communications: Connecting parallel debates. *SAIS Review*, 33(1): 81–90.

Martin, N. 2012. "There is abuse everywhere": Migrant nonprofit organizations and the problem of precarious work. *Urban Affairs Review*, 48: 389–416.

Marx, G. T. 2004. Internet anonymity as a reflection of broader issues involving technology and society. *Asia-Pacific Review*, 11: 142–166.

Marx, G. T. 2006. Varieties of personal information as influences on attitudes toward surveillance. In K. Haggerty and R. Ericson (Eds.), *The new politics of surveillance and visibility*: 79–110. Toronto: University of Toronto Press.

McGahan, A. M. 2012. Challenges of the informal economy for the field of management. *Academy of Management Perspectives*, 26(3): 12–21.

McQuail, D. 1997. *Audience analysis*. London: Sage.

Molony, T. 2008. The role of mobile phones in Tanzania's informal construction sector: The case of Dar es Salaam. *Urban Forum*, 19: 175–186.

Monge, P. R., & Contractor, N. S. 2001. Emergence of communication networks. In F. M. Jablin & L. L. Putnam (Eds.), *The new handbook of organizational communication: Advances in theory, research and methods*: 440–502. Thousand Oaks, CA: Sage.

Opiyo, R. O., & K'Akumu, O. A. 2006. ICT application in the informal sector: The case of the Kariokor market MSE cluster in Nairobi. *Urban Forum*, 17: 241–261.

Petronio, S. 2002. *The boundaries of privacy: Dialectics of disclosure*. Albany: SUNY Press.

Portes, A., & Haller, W. 2005. The informal economy. In N. Smelser & R. Swedberg (Eds.), *Handbook of economic sociology*: 403–428. Princeton, NJ: Princeton University Press.

Putnam, L. L. 2003. Dialectical tensions and rhetorical tropes in negotiations. *Organizational Studies*, 25: 35–53.

Schlosser, E. 2004. *Reefer madness: Sex, drugs, and cheap labor in the American black market*. Boston: Houghton Mifflin Harcourt.

Scott, C. 2013. *Anonymous agencies, backstreet businesses, and covert collectives: Rethinking organizations in the 21st Century.* Stanford, CA: Stanford University Press.

Scott, C. R., & Rains, S. A. 2005. Anonymous communication in organizations: assessing use and appropriateness. *Management Communication Quarterly,* 19: 157–197.

Snyder, K. A. 2004. Routes to the informal economy in New York's East Village: Crisis, economics, and identity. *Sociological Perspectives,* 47: 215–240.

Trethewey, A., & Ashcraft, K. L. 2004. Practicing disorganization: The development of applied perspectives on living with tension. *Journal of Applied Communication Research,* 32: 81–88.

Venkatesh, S. A. 2006. *Off the books: The underground economy of the urban poor.* Cambridge, MA: Harvard University Press.

Webb, J. W., Tihanyi, L., Ireland, R. D., & Sirmon, D. G. 2009. You say illegal, I say legitimate: Entrepreneurship in the informal economy. *Academy of Management Review,* 34: 492–510.

Williams, C. C. 2004. **Small businesses in the informal economy: The evidence base.** London: Small Business Service. from http://works.bepress.com/colin_williams/4, October 20, 2014.

Williams, C. C. 2006. *The hidden enterprise culture: Entrepreneurship in the underground economy.* Cheltenham, UK: Edward Elgar.

Williams, C. C., & Round, J. 2011. Beyond competing theories of the hidden economy: Some lessons from Moscow. *Journal of Economic Studies,* 38: 171–185.

4 Organization and Contract in the Informal Economy

William S. Schulze and Paul C. Godfrey

Viewed through the lens of formal economic theory, informal economies should not persist, let alone grow. In developing countries, informal economic activity supports survival but not prosperity, does little to enhance individual economic welfare, and has limited ability to manage externalities such as environmental degradation. It has proven stubbornly resistant to reform, as witnessed by generations of well-intentioned investment and intervention by OECD member nations. Yet, across diverse environments, informality has demonstrated that it is robust and capable of supporting life under conditions ranging from war and famine to peace and abundance. Informal organizations also appear to be capable of autonomous governance; actors are able to reach cooperative agreements without the support of the formal institutions in both developed contexts, where support by such institutions is costly and onerous, and in developing economies, where formal institutional support is lacking. And in developed countries, informal economic activity continues to grow in response to the increasing presence of definable social subgroups (Portes & Sensenbrenner, 1993) as well as the burdens imposed by highly complex and bureaucratically unwieldy organizations (Turner, 2004).

In this chapter, we explore how and why the costs of organizing and sustaining productive activity differ so greatly between formal and informal regimes. We use contract as our conceptual vehicle for exploration and juxtapose how contracts emerge in purely informal and purely formal settings. We explore how interested parties establish purpose and identify expectations for processes and outcomes in different social settings. To foreshadow, our analysis underscores the role of the relational contract in traditional, developing, *and* developed economies, and uses these insights to explain how and why relational governance allows informal economies to function without support from the complex and costly web of social institutions that are needed to support and coordinate economic activity in developed economies.

We argue that while traditional and formal contracts may exist as substitute/alternative forms of contracting, relational contracts stand as a complement/supplement to either of these strong forms of contracting. Relational contracting combines the flexibility offered through traditional contracting with elements of formal contract, and allows organizations to respond to episodic upheaval and to experiment with alternative solutions. Elements of formal contract, meanwhile, serve as a backstop that strengthens the traditional elements of contract on which relational contracts are based. Our core insight is that the relational, not formal, contract is the foundational governance mechanism in both developing and developed economies, and that understanding the functional relationship between the two types of contract enriches our understanding of both.

COOPERATION AND CONTRACT

Cooperative action, defined as joint action that is "conscious, deliberate, and purposeful" (Barnard, 1938: 4), can only occur when interested parties establish a common purpose and set expectations for both the processes and outcomes that will leave all parties better off. Contract is the ubiquitous vehicle for creating and clarifying both purpose and expectations; hence, we begin by juxtaposing how those objectives are achieved in informal and formal organizations with two common contractual approaches to cooperative activity and its governance: traditional and formal contracting. Institutional, transactions cost, and other related theories about formal organizations assert that economizing activity leads to the eventual adoption of governance solutions (and contracts) that are tailored and matched to the scale, complexity, and other attributes of the characteristic exchange (Williamson, 1993). In what follows, we consider two broad classes of contracts: formal contracts, which are grounded in explicit, legally enforceable terms and conditions (exemplified by the nexus of contracts view of the cooperative firm classically espoused by Fama and Miller (1972) and recently updated by Bainbridge (2008)); and traditional contracts (which we view as a generalized form of the traditional contract) that feature implicit agreement and rely on social sanction for enforcement (Durkheim, 1933; Granovetter, 1985; Turner, 2004; Weber, 1947).

Archetypal Contracts

Black's Law Dictionary defines a contract as "an agreement between two or more parties creating obligations that are enforceable or otherwise recognizable at law" (Black's Law Dictionary, 1999, c.f. contract). Agreement—which must be voluntary for a contract to be valid at law—represents the foundation of cooperative effort; cooperation without agreement can only be achieved through coercion. The voluntary nature of contracting means that cooperation requires moral as well as physical endeavor since actors are expected to make, and subsequently keep, moral commitments (e.g., honest representation and fidelity) (Barnard, 1938; Locke, 1690/1988). As we note below, the moral component proves an important facet of contract and enhances our understanding of the merits of traditional contracts vis-à-vis formal ones.

Every contract has four elements. *Promises* and *considerations* jointly define the "what" of exchange, in terms of property or services, and the compensation returned (Black's Law Dictionary, 1999). The contract, simply put, clarifies what actors expect to *give* and *get* through cooperation. The third and fourth elements of contract facilitate dispute resolution: *jurisdiction*, or the delineation of which set of laws, rules, norms, or customs will be referred to in order to interpret promises, considerations, events, or contingencies; and *sanctions*, the penalties invoked upon violations of the agreement.

We consider below how each of these four contractual elements— promise, consideration, jurisdiction, and sanction—are treated within the two dominant and archetypal views of contracts in the social science literature: *traditional*, a sociological/anthropological view of contract, and *legal*, an economic/legal perspective. These two archetypes build from different premises regarding the fundamental basis of the contracting parties, the legitimacy invoked to support the contract, the logic of exchange encapsulated in the agreement, and the authority structures that govern the contact.

Traditional and Legal Contracts

Traditional contracting employs family or kinship identity to determine the status of parties (Turner, 2004), calls on the pre-existing and taken-for-granted legitimacy of kinship ties (Weber, 1947), uses altruism as the exchange logic to guide the allocation of resources (Schulze, Lubatkin, & Dino, 2003), and relies on patriarchal authority to implement and govern contractual provisions (Becker, 1981). Legal contracting, in contrast, refers to formally defined or class-based identity in establishing status (Bainbridge, 2008), refers to explicit and consciously negotiated laws, norms, and rules for legitimacy (Newberry & Stiglitz, 1987), uses the logic of balanced reciprocity (quid pro quo) for exchange (Friedman, 1953), and rests on rational, hierarchical authority for implementation and control (Poppo & Zenger, 2002; Williamson, 1985).

Promise. Promises describe what each party will contribute to the cooperative endeavor. Simple contracts, or spot market transactions, make simple promises such as a commitment to pay for and take ownership of a good in trade, and payment and the exchange of goods is usually contemporaneous. Complex contracts are often non-contemporaneous and involve complex promises. Complex promises outline the *what, how, where,* and *when* of the promises made.

A set of generalized expectations about the conduct of each party characterize traditional contracts. Parties expect each other to act diligently in the execution of their responsibilities (e.g., they do "whatever it takes") and comply with norms of good behavior and honest conduct. As a result of these shared expectations, traditional contracts rarely specify the what, how, when, and where of promise, and cooperation proceeds uninhibited by the lack of such precision. Indeed, one of the virtues of the traditional contract is that well-behaved parties can exercise substantial discretion with respect to the what, how, and when of their obligations within a structure that adheres to larger social expectations about performance. Supervision is not required or expected. As a governance mechanism, traditional contracts are unusually flexible and readily adaptable; they enable stable, routine exchange as well as exchange in fluid and uncertain economic and social conditions.

Legal contracts, as an opposite organizing logic, contain detailed and explicit promises by the parties; put simply, they clearly and precisely articulate the what, how, where, and when in terms that can be understood and adjudicated by third parties unfamiliar with the technical details of the transaction. Parties must honor all specified obligations with no expectation of exceeding them. Supervision and monitoring is expected and often required. Legal contracts help avoid the costs of duplicative effort—each party has a clear and delineated task to perform—which allows parties to capture the gains of specialization (Marshall, 1890/2006; Smith, 1776/1965). They are (emphatically) not flexible. Legal contracts require renegotiation to adapt to changed economic and social conditions; indeed, uncertainty around future states helps determine the type of legal contract used to govern transactions (Williamson, 1985).

Consideration. Consideration represents the flip side of promise; the latter specifies what actors give while the former outlines what actors get. In simple contracting, consideration and promise exist symmetrically as one party's promise constitutes the other's consideration. Complex contracts, in contrast, decouple promise and consideration.

Three elements typify consideration in traditional contracting. First, like promise, consideration in traditional contracts is often left open, guided only by expectations of "fair" remuneration specified by the larger institutional setting within which social life takes place (Thornton, Ocasio, & Lounsbury, 2012). Second, traditional contracts, especially those based on family or kinship ties, presume that parties will have an ongoing relationship that supersedes the terms of the contract. This allows partial or full temporal displacement of consideration; e.g., "we'll take care of you next time." Finally, and most critically, traditional consideration includes moral goods such as love, affection, just treatment, or loyalty, in addition to consideration based on physical goods such as money.

The entwinement of moral goods with exchange allows traditionally governed cooperative endeavors to create meaning for participants. *Meaning* derives from inclusion of moral goods in the endeavor, affection flowing from the other parties, and the acceptance of the associated cognitive and normative institutional world views held by the other party (Scott, 2008). Because the meaning-based value of a contract rises with repeated exchange, traditional contracts become *self-enforcing*; repeated exchange further fosters loyalty within the group, enhances productivity and identification, and increases the incentive to interact with individuals within the group as well as those in groups who share similar values (Dixit, 2010; Meyer & Allen, 1997).

Legal contracts, again the archetypal opposite, specify consideration in terms that are as detailed and explicit as the corresponding promises. Exchange also occurs within a closed loop since consideration is rendered when the terms of the contract are fulfilled. Further, discrete decisions about continuation or repetition of the contract are required, they are not silently presumed. Legal contracts also meter consideration, and all consideration is specifically delineated in monetary or barter terms. The standardization of consideration is useful and necessary, since actors must be able to compare opportunities and calibrate their expectations, effort, and willingness to cooperate to the chosen task. Legal contracts, by construction, preclude the exchange of moral goods: One can contract for sexual favors but not for love. Exchange guided solely by legal contract thus lacks the self-enforcing properties of traditional ones; they require explicit incentives (i.e., money) for their creation, perpetuation, and regeneration.

Jurisdiction. Contractual language is never exhaustive, even in the most clearly written legal contract, due to the implausibility and expense of drafting a document that might account for all future contingencies. Consequently, disputes over meaning and intent become inevitable, even among well-intended actors. The jurisdictional element of contracts informs parties which underlying values, norms, rules, or laws will be the point of reference in clarifying promises and considerations. Those values, norms, rules, or laws typically specify how such disputes will be resolved, or at least provide a recipe for the process.

Traditional contracts rely on taken-for-granted, often timeless and unspoken, norms and rules arising from the sedimented customs of family, clan, or ethnic identity and tradition; that is, they rely on the thick morality of everyday life (Walzer, 1994) to interpret ambiguity, resolve disputes, and move cooperative efforts forward. Moral thickness provides actors with a nuanced set of rules—often a historically rich trove of such rules—that allow actors to quickly and clearly resolve disagreements around the typical issues that arise during cooperation.

Legal contracts invoke specific statutes, encoded protocols and standards, or abstract principles such as justice and fairness to clarify situational ambiguity and adjudicate conflicts. Legal contracts rest on authority and are enforced by supporting social institutions, such as the Court (Walzer, 1994). Contracts may be seated in many societal units and sectors; thus, legal contacts must clearly specify which set of statutes and standards provide the interpretive umbrella. For example, many U.S. business contracts specify the laws of Delaware as the jurisdiction for the contact. Disputes will not only be resolved in Delaware's Chancery Courts, they will be resolved according to the unique set of statutes, precedents, and standards of the state of Delaware.

Sanction. Cooperative effort breaks down when parties violate their obligations. Actors may wish to reestablish cooperation or they may seek to recover resources dedicated to the effort; doing so entails specifying a set of mechanisms that assures that contracts will be binding on the parties. As Durkheim (1933: 70) observed, "we must bear in mind that, if a contract has binding force, it is society which confers that force." The question becomes: Which societal organ or institution backs up contracts?

Traditional contracts require collective action and enforcement agreements by leveraging the group's monopoly on inclusion (Durkheim, 1933; Granovetter, 1985; Turner, 2004; Weber, 1947). The threat to one's reputation or standing within a social group constitutes a primordial and powerful enforcement mechanism with ostracism or exclusion from the group serving as the most powerful punishment available. The greater the strength or centrality of shared values, worldviews, and connections that bind the actors into a common social group such as a common religious tradition, ethnic group, or family, the more potent the threat of exclusion: Families disown wayward offspring, tribes banish recalcitrant members, and congregations excommunicate heretical members. Indeed, neuroscientists have confirmed that neural response to the threat of ostracism is identical to that caused by induced physical pain (Eisenberger, Lieberman, & Williams, 2003). The monopoly on inclusion thus operates as a potent sanction that discourages malfeasance on the part of actors[1].

In contrast, legal contract ultimately depends on the State's monopoly on legitimate violence (North, 1981; Weber, 1947) to back up and enforce contracts (Fama & Miller, 1972; Newberry & Stiglitz, 1987; North, 1981). The threat of costly litigation and the potential loss of property encourage compliance by reducing the potential gains of deviant behavior. The actual loss of property or freedom stemming from contract violation clearly disadvantages the affected party; the sanction also creates a chilling effect on others that help reduce current and future defections from expected action and performance. The costs of litigation, however, reduce the likelihood of enforcement such that economic gains from deviant behavior not only remain available but can become a strategic objective. Thus, while the advantage of the State's monopoly on violence rests in both its finality of sanction—with the ultimate sanction for certain violations being the loss of life—and in its ability to encroach on the lives of individual miscreants, it is a coarse and clumsy tool, especially when compared to the precision and nuance with which social sanctions can be calibrated and imposed.

Having defined and elaborated the elements of the traditional and legal contract, we now turn to the task of delineating their effects on the costs and rewards of cooperation in the informal and formal economies.

Cooperation in Informal and Formal Settings

We consider first the archetypal traditional contracting arrangement, the Oikos or household economy. For Weber (1947) and Booth (1993), the Oikos represents the archetypal cooperative endeavor, efficiently and effectively structured by traditional contracting. Booth (1993: 6) considers the

Oikos as a "natural" economy, contrasted with an artificial or market economy, in which family members in the household (nuclear or extended) enjoyed membership status and standing while others working for the household were either in servitude or slavery and thus enjoyed neither status nor standing within the household.

The objective of the Oikos differed from the market in that surplus had no intrinsic value (Weber, 1958). Rather, families strove for autarchy and satisfied their needs through the efforts of the household and command over its own resources (Booth, 1993). Family (and, more broadly, clan) membership defines standing within the Oikos; legitimacy comes from the timeless authority of the family. Altruism and patriarchal authority determine the pattern and governance of cooperative activity. Roles are multi-faceted, and members do "what needs to be done" in return for being "taken care of" in terms of both physical and moral goods. Family-based norms and thick customs provide guidance for dealing with ambiguity and uncertainty, and the ultimate sanction for non-compliance would be banishment. The Oikos represents not only the ancient Greek household but also household-based economic activity today in many places around the world, from Prahalad's (2005) Bottom of the Pyramid to emerging economies characterized by reliance on traditional institutions and norms (Peng, 2003). Fukuyama (1995) outlines Oikos-like corporate structures in China (Ja enterprises) and Korea (the Chaebol).

When will actors choose to replace or supplement traditional contract with elements of legal contracts? The strengths of traditional contracting provide the answer; the effectiveness of traditional contract relies on homogeneity in values and expectations across parties. Diversity in values—that is, diversity in expectations about what constitutes diligent conduct and moral integrity—limits actors ability to effectively contract with those not in the family/clan/tribe. While growing demand may motivate members of the Oikos to establish relationships with outsiders, those outsiders should be leery of dealing with members of the Oikos on their own terms.[2] While personal knowledge of the parties may exist, and solutions to distribution problems may be within contractual reach, dispute resolution becomes problematic due to expectations that outsiders would have about the efficacy of resolving disputes with the Oikos as well as the standards used to determine the fairness of any proposed solution.

Jurisdiction and sanction create their own set of problems. Outsiders do not possess the same thick morality, customs, and norms of members of the Oikos: They operate according to their own set of thick morals and customs. Since implicit reliance on the Oikos would cause each party to invoke different jurisdictional standards for dispute resolution, parties will either create an explicit agreement to negotiate interpretation (a proto-legal version of case law) or they may invoke formal jurisdictional elements from local, regional, or national institutions. Sanctions evolve similarly, since socio-economic barriers reduce the effectiveness of exclusion and other traditional forms of enforcement. The parties may adopt some form of market-based sanction like reputational loss or private sanction (Newberry & Stiglitz, 1988), or they may adjudicate their disputes in local courts according to local laws. Moral and cultural diversity thus requires the development of formal or semi-formal mechanisms of resolution to provide reasonable expectations that any disputes or ambiguities will be effectively resolved.

Can actors find an interim solution, a contract that combines the flexibility and meaning of the Oikos with the scalability and security of the law? We answer affirmatively and argue that the relational contract not only provides an intermediate solution but also provides advantages such that they are the dominant *de facto* contractual form and are used to govern most transactions in developing and developed economies alike.

Relational Contracts

The relational contract represents an extension of the traditional contract, but is differentiated because it draws on elements of legal contracting to "backstop," or reinforce traditional modes of governance. Relational contracts arise at the boundary where tradition, custom, norms, and shared values can no longer be relied upon to shape and enforce each element of contract; legal contracting therefore emerges when traditional contracts fail to provide adequate governance. Relational contracts combine elements of traditional and legal contracts, and use each to selectively redress specific transactional features. Use of the relational contract allows actors to preserve the dimensions of traditional contract that generate meaning and the moral value that attends exchange. Relational contracts incorporate dimensions of formal or legal contracting that complement traditional contractual elements and strengthen the overall exchange relationship. We view the traditional contract as foundational, with elements of formal contract arising, when needed, as its complement, with the ensuing whole constituting a relational contract. The decision to remain informal, or at least to resist outright formalization, is in this sense both rational and value-enriching. Table 4.1 outlines essential differences between traditional, relational, and legal contracts.

Barnard (1938: 172) describes the evolution of relational contracts:

> Laws don't create Teamplay. It is not called into play by law. For every written rule there are a thousand unwritten rules by which the course of business is guided, which govern the millions of daily transactions of which business consists. The rules are not applied from the top down, by arbitrary authority. They grow out of actual practice—from the desire to achieve common ends and further the common good. They are observed *voluntarily*, because they have the backing of experience and common sense. (Emphasis and capitalization are original.)

Table 4.1 Archetypes of Contract

Element	Traditional	Relational	Legal
Basis	Family/ kinship identity	Personal identity	Formal/class identity
Legitimacy	Taken for granted	Explicit, negotiated	Explicit, negotiated
Logic	Altruism	Generalized reciprocity	Balanced reciprocity
Governance	Patriarchal authority	Negotiated atructures	Rational/legal authority
Contracting Elements			
Promise	Vague	Incomplete	Explicit
Consideration	Moral goods	Moral and physical goods	Physical goods
Jurisdiction	Custom, thick morality	Case, negotiated morality	Statute, thin morality
Sanction	Monopoly on social Inclusion	Social inclusion and violence	Monopoly on violence
Archetypal Organization	Oikos— household	Business corporation	Administrative state agency

Along with Barnard, we submit that those wanting to create purposive joint action will strive to balance tradition and law because actors desire the advantages of both forms of governance. The flexibility, meaning, speed, and efficiency of traditional arrangements create real value in production and exchange; they allow actors to respond to changing conditions or operate in stable conditions with lower costs. Moral goods, which are the concomitant product of exchange, also incentivize and self-enforce cooperation at little or no direct monetary cost. The specialization, standardization, scalability, and security that legal contracts engender reduce risk and provide a concomitant set of advantages, albeit at greater financial cost. While the archetypes of traditional and legal contracts entice scholars with their elegance and simplicity, the demands of actually getting work done in complex environments and the non-mutually exclusive basis of the two archetypes should lead actors to facilitate cooperation, most of the time, through relational contracts (Saxenian, 2000)[3].

The basis of relational contract depends neither on the family/kinship status of an individual nor on his or her membership in identified social classes or groups but rather on the identity of the individual and strength of their identification with other individuals in exchange-relevant groups. Relational contracts become legitimate through a mix of explicit, private negotiation, and unconscious mutual adjustment between the parties. Generalized reciprocity, a middle position between altruism and balanced reciprocity, operates as the exchange and transactional logic: Parties contribute with an expectation of commensurate reciprocity although the timing and nature of that reciprocity may be unspecified. Authority or governance comes by mutual adjustment and agreement, and status differences, if any, are implicitly understood, accepted, and viewed as legitimate. Non-family employees, for example, understand that the family members who are employed by the family firm may enjoy privileges that are not available to other employees. Parties are expected to adhere to social norms that govern exchange, and violation leads to social sanction varying from a loss of reputation as a moral actor to ostracism.

Relational contracts exist because parties are able to simultaneously lever the advantages both traditional and legal contract. Some elements of promise may be detailed and explicit (e.g., compliance with a delivery date), while others may be implicit to the agreement (e.g., ability to exercise discretion about the exact processes used or the source of materials). Consideration necessarily includes both moral and physical goods; indeed, Barnard (1938) argues that in any business relationship in which personal identity matters, some form of moral goods (loyalty, fealty, friendship, respect) will be exchanged. Parts of contracts may be interpreted by reference to State or statute (e.g., financial penalties) while other parts may be covered by the umbrella of established traditions, for example, a loss of reputation or social standing (Berger and Luckmann [1967]). In the main, interpretation of relational contracts will follow common law practice in that both statute and custom have bearing on the interpretation of the agreement and the consequences of violation.

Importantly, the sanctioning mechanisms of the State's monopoly on violence and the Group's monopoly on inclusion are not mutually exclusive; both can be present in the same *set* of governance arrangements at the same *time*. Metaphorically, the monopoly on violence threatens the body and mind while the monopoly on inclusion holds the heart and soul; since humans are complex mixes of physical, emotional, and spiritual elements, the sanctions may co-exist and may work either separately (e.g., excommunication but not execution or execution without excommunication) or together (execution and excommunication).

In either case, for both jurisdiction and sanction, proto-legal or legal elements supplement traditional elements of the relational contract, and actors now have alternative means to create and enforce agreements. Movement outside the Oikos entails two additional changes that characterize relational contracting. First, personal identity supplants family identity as the basis of cooperation. Second, generalized reciprocity displaces altruism as the guiding exchange logic. Because the parties no longer belong to the same family and are bound by the same patriarchal authority, they trade based on personal trust and the hope that their vague and implicit allocations of effort and resources will be repaid by the other party. That trust and hope, however, has some final fallback position and protection through either market-based or legal sanction.

The Benefits of Relational Contracting

The value of the relational contract lies in its ability to selectively tailor its features to the social *and* economic context in which exchange occurs. Doing so provides actors with the ability to leverage the efficiencies of traditional contracting while only incurring legal governance costs where needed. For example, as noted earlier by Barnard, cooperation proceeds not as the product of formal contract but rather from a grounded set of expectations, behaviors, and practices that rise through repeated exchange between parties. Party identity matters because the moral product of exchange cannot be generated by exchange between anonymous parties transacting in monetized units but rather among individuals and between groups who share common ties and similar values. Individual identity, and the strength of the individual's identity with their referent group, shapes the extent to which they derive benefits from exchange as well as the extent to which ongoing exchange and the manner of its conduct becomes self-enforcing. While the "thousand unwritten rules" of business are the product of experience and common sense, they persist because exchange generates its own incentives in the form of moral and affective goods that participants derive from the process. One does not expect unwritten rules to be efficient in the strictest sense of the word, but it is likely they are highly effective inasmuch as they incentivize repeated high-quality exchange without the added encumbrance of oversight or a need to enforce compliance.

The benefits of relational governance, and its ubiquity in both developed and developing economies, can be attributed to this effectiveness. Where legal contract requires the presence of bureaucratic institutions and elaborate monitoring mechanisms to assure performance and compliance, relational contracts are negotiated among exchange partners and become self-enforcing with time. While the rewards of relational contracting make their use ubiquitous within groups, whether they will be used across groups or between organizations depends on the strength of the relational ties between groups. For example, exchange agreements among parties who are known to each other from past experience or reputation, or whose identity with a group or organization is viewed as strong and legitimate, are negotiated informally.

The fact that parties "shake hands," on a deal, or reach verbal agreement, is often viewed as binding, regardless of the fact that courts uniformly require written agreements. In fact, requiring legal contracts in these "high trust" circumstances is viewed as soiling the transaction, leading to mere monetization of it and the concomitant loss of personal value and worth.[4]

Parties also resist legalistic metering, since efforts to confirm that parties are fulfilling their moral obligation to each other can itself be viewed as a sign of distrust. The adage "trust but verify" describes how elements of formal contract are used to backstop relational contracts. In contrast, exchange among anonymous parties usually requires negotiation, specification of the four elements of contract, ongoing oversight, and, on occasion, requires intermediaries to post performance bonds.[5]

Scale and complexity also limit the extent to which relational contract can govern exchange. Multi-party and other complex exchanges, such as those conducted over long distances or over time, must explicitly address jurisdiction and sanction issues, since dispute resolution constitutes the primary "backstop" when dealing with strangers. Promise and consideration elements of the same agreement, on the other hand, may be reached informally. Informal agreements, as facilitated by relational contract, allow parties to adapt to circumstance and adjust to uncertain internal and external environments. Communication between parties often flows through informal communication networks, and decisions are made by parties directly involved in the activity, as opposed to those in supervisory or other positions of authority.

Interestingly, in cases in which greater authority and arbitration become necessary in relational contracting, the identity of the arbitrator matters because personal knowledge about the transactions and the personalities of the individuals involved must be taken into account. Failure to do so means that value-preserving decisions (i.e., decisions preserve the dignity of the actors involved) will not be reached, and the meaning element of relational contacts will cease to function. Anonymous authorities, or decisions made in accordance with formal contract, lead to less optimal outcomes since the self-enforcing character of exchange evaporates when meaning disappears.

We argue that relational governance works within organizations and exchanges in which stable membership, repeated exchange, and strong identification within and between groups allow it to generate meaningful exchange. We suspect that relational contracting, with its blend of formality and informality, exists as the predominate form of contract. Its use will, however, decline as scale, scope, and complexity challenge the bounds of its effectiveness in the governance of between-group and multi-organizational exchange. Very large scale and complexity, both within and across organizations, are characterized by formal contract and bureaucracy.

IMPLICATIONS AND DISCUSSION

Relational governance sits squarely at the boundary of informal and formal economic activity; Godfrey and Dyer (2015) would classify relational governance as semi-formal exchange. We see the viability and optimality of relational governance in exchange as driven both by its formal/legalistic efficiency and the rewards of traditional/relational exchange. Traditional contracts provide the parties with a flexible and meaning-rich mode of exchange; however, parties forego certain risk mitigation advantages and the ability to scale exchange to deal effectively with actors from outside the thick social setting. Formal governance, in contrast, offers both risk mitigation and scale through explicit promise/consideration and clear jurisdiction and sanctioning mechanisms. Formality requires the monetization and depersonalization of exchange as well as the metering of utility; individual meaning and notions of belonging and worth are lost with formalization. The decision to formalize, then, requires a calculus that incorporates the full person—both his/her social and economic aspects. Actors must weigh not only the gains in economic wealth available but also the corresponding losses in social wealth associated with its adoption. We argue that the notion that actors balance meaning against gain merits consideration as it explains the persistence of informal contracting in both the developed and developing world.

When would rational actors in a developing country choose formality? Extant Western perspectives suggest that rational actors have few reasons to eschew the protections and benefits that attend formalization; therefore, informal economic activity should exist at best as a transitional form until formalization can fully occur (Hart, 1973). However, informality persists despite decades of effort by OECD countries to formalize developing economies (see Godfrey, 2013 for a review). Resistance, we assert, comes from the duality of human motivations. Formality makes sense when the economic advantages it proffers offset the social costs it imposes. To the extent that the desire for identity, meaning, belonging, and other moral goods available through traditional contracting are universal desires among people, formalization faces substantial hurdles and a high bar for adoption. Relational contracting, even when supported by weak institutional structures, often offers an acceptable trade-off between meaning and legal protection.

When we consider the case of actors in developed contexts, we find the same answer. We believe, and our anecdotal experiences corroborate, that the desire for identity, meaning, and belonging exist among all humans: Rational actors in developed economies may, like their developing country counterparts, eschew strict formalization in favor of greater reliance on relational contracting. Relational contracting provides a triple advantage for those working in highly developed settings: 1) a legal "backstop" or platform that provides some level of risk mitigation; 2) the flexibility that comes from the informal nature of traditional contracting (e.g., "do what it takes," "reward fairly"); and 3) an ongoing source of internal identity support and maintenance (through the vehicle of personal reputation) and belonging and status within a group of exchange partners.

One implication of our work concerns the development of human capital and the incentives for economic specialization. Specialization usually requires actors to acquire new and unique skills, skills that are risky to acquire under conditions of underspecified or unenforceable property rights. Absent such assurances, investments in specialized skills place the actor at risk of exploitation. One can easily tease out the implication for the archetypal Oikos: Tradition makes a poor substitute for articulated property rights, and so we would expect little specialization. This conventional Western belief stands at odds with evidence about the productivity, and nature of production, in family-controlled enterprises in developed economies (Carney & Gedajlovic, 2002). Tradition-based property rights, while clearly not grounded in law, go beyond the ownership of physical property to include assurances of continued employment or job mobility and flexibility in labor contract.

Family enterprise stands as a predominant form of economic organization in the developed world (based on the number of enterprises), and family/kinship economic organization can be found throughout the developing world's informal economies. Interestingly, family identity also provides employees with the assurances of continued employment and confidence that their specialized skills will not be withdrawn from use or expropriated; such assurances prove sufficient to motivate employees to develop specialized, transaction- or asset-specific skills. Family-controlled firms are therefore able to produce high-value goods in informal and developing economies despite the absence of formal institutional support.

As in traditional societies, however, family ownership of assets only motivates specialization if the family sends credible signals of a commitment to ongoing and unaltered use of those assets by their owners. In the Oikos, ownership conveys the right to use and control access to assets but not to destroy it or alter its use, since doing so would undermine the legitimacy of the family's socio-cultural claims to altruism and loyalty. Put simply, the patron of the community remains the patron as long as s/he continues to fulfill his/her obligations to it. Failure to do so by withdrawing assets like land from communal or traditional use or exploiting human capital, once developed, represents opportunistic exploitation of the situation and undermines the legitimacy of the patron's claim on those assets.

Another implication of the analysis is that formalization is costly not only in terms of the cost of achieving the levels of social and economic accomplishment required to create and sustain legitimate legal and regulatory institutions but also in terms of the loss of socio-economic value that attend formalization. The notion that formalization impoverishes exchange, and thereby reduces the bonds and ties that support the generation of meaning and moral value, brings into relief why legal and regulatory institutions are necessary in formal economies as well as why formal economies find it necessary to sanction violence against its members in an endeavor to support and sustain itself. The decision to organize informally, and to rely on tradition, custom, and social norms to support and enforce trade, thus seems to be rational not only in terms of costs of operation but also in terms of mere civility. Notions that formal organizations are normatively or ethically superior should be reconsidered.

In this chapter, we have explored the use of three forms of contract—traditional, legal, and relational—in both the formal and informal economy. Breaking contract into its four foundational elements supports our assertion that there is no bright line dividing formal and informal economic activity. Rather, our analysis suggests that the two are linked, and that traditional and legal contracting exist as complements, rather than alternative choices, for exchange governance. The decision to operate using informal economic arrangements, even within ostensibly formal economies, is rational when one considers a model of humanity that contains both social and economic elements. In our view, the serious study of informality holds rich promise for organizational scholars hoping to capture the deep and multi-faceted nature of social and economic life.

NOTES

1. Several scholars note the potential for reputation loss as an enforcement mechanism in economic cooperation and exchange. Reputation loss represents a weaker form of social inclusion; although a powerful sanction its focus on the instrumental value of being a trading partner lacks the power and punch of losing one's friends or status and standing within a valued group.
2. Such a need may arise endogenously, if the Oikos changed its internal goals from autarky to external trade, or exogenously if key resources could only be acquired through cooperation with others.
3. The simplicity of the bifurcation of legal and traditional forms of organizations can be found in most of the economics literature we cite here as well as development economics (Ray, 1998). Weber and Durkheim both found the ease of comparing traditional to rational societies an appealing frame for their work in the early 19th century. Management scholars also find the dichotomy a seductively simple way to formulate research questions. See Xia, Boals, and Delios (2009) for an example in the entry modes decision in new country contexts.
4. Prenuptial agreements are viewed as risky and often eschewed despite their economic merits.
5. ebay both gathers and publishes data on seller and buyer performance, but also provides financial guarantees scaled to the size of the transaction.

REFERENCES

Bainbridge, S. M. 2008. *The new corporate governance in theory and practice*. New York, NY: Oxford University press.

Barnard, C. I. 1938. *The functions of the executive*. Cambridge, MA: Harvard University Press.

Becker, G. S. (1981). *A treatise on the family*. Cambridge, MA: Harvard University Press.

Berger, P. L., & Luckmann, T. 1967. *The social construction of reality : a treatise in the sociology of knowledge*. New York [etc.]: Anchor Books.

Black's Law Dictionary. 1999. 7th ed. St. Paul, MN: West Group.

Booth, W. J. 1993. *Households : on the moral architecture of the economy*. Ithaca, NY: Cornell University Press.

Carney, M., & Gedajlovic, E. 2002. The co-evolution of institutional environments and organizational strategies: The rise of family business groups in the ASEAN region. *Organization Studies*, 23(1): 1–29.

Dixit, A. 2010. *Relation-based governance and competition.* Working paper, Princeton, NJ: Princeton University Press.

Durkheim, E. 1933/1984. *The division of labor in society* (W. D. Halls, Trans.). New York, NY: The Free Press.

Eisenberger, N. I., Lieberman, M. D., & Williams, K. D. 2003. Does rejection hurt? An FMRI study of social exclusion. *Science*, 10: 290–292.

Fama, E. F., & Miller, M. H. 1972. *The theory of finance.* Hinsdale, IL: Dryden Press.

Friedman, M. 1953. *Essays in positive economics.* Chicago: University of Chicago Press.

Fukuyama, F. 1995. *Trust: The social virtues and the creation of prosperity.* New York, NY: The Free Press.

Godfrey, P. 2013. *More than money: Five forms of capital to create wealth and eliminate poverty.* Stanford, CA: Stanford University Press.

Godfrey, P., & Dyer, G. (2015). Subsistence entrepreneurs and formal institutions: Semi-formal governance among Ghanaian entrepreneurs. In P. C. Godfrey (Ed.), *Management, society and the informal economy*: 142–161 New York: Routledge.

Granovetter, M. 1985. Economic action and social structure: The problem of embeddedness. *American Journal of Sociology*, 91(3): 481–510.

Hart, K. 1973. Informal income opportunities and urban employment in Ghana. *The Journal of Modern African Studies*, 11(1): 61–89.

Locke, J. 1690/1988. *Two treatises of government.* Cambridge: Cambridge University Press.

Marshall, A. 1890/2006. *Principles of economics, abridged edition.* New York, NY: Cosimo Classics.

Meyer, J. P., & Allen, N. J. 1997. *Commitment in the workplace: Theory, research, and application.* Thousand Oaks, CA: Sage Publications.

Newbery, D. M., & Stiglitz, J. 1987. Wage rigidity, implicit contracts, unemployment and economic efficiency. *The Economic Journal*, 97(June): 416–430.

North, D. C. 1981. *Structure and change in economic history.* New York: W. W. Norton.

Peng, M. W. 2003. Institutional transitions and strategic choices. *Academy of Management Review*, 28(2): 275–296.

Poppo, L., & Zenger, T. 2002. Do formal contracts and relational governance function as substitutes or complements? *Strategic Management Journal*, 23(8): 707–725.

Portes, A., & Sensenbrenner, J. 1993. Embeddedness and immigration: Notes on the social determinants of economic action. *The American Journal of Sociology*, 98(6): 1320–1350.

Prahalad, C. K. 2005. *The fortune at the bottom of the Pyramid.* Pennsylvania: Wharton School Publishing.

Ray, D. 1998. *Development economics.* Princeton, NJ: Princeton University Press.

Saxenian, A. 2000. The origins and dymanics of production networks in Silicon Valley. In M. Kenney (Ed.), *Understanding Silicon Valley*: 141–164. Stanford, CA: Stanford University Press.

Schulze, W. S., Lubatkin, M. H., & Dino, R. N. 2003. Toward a theory of agency and altruism in family firms. *Journal of Business Venturing*, 18(4): 473–490.

Scott, W. R. 2008. *Institutions and organizations* (3rd ed.). Thousand Oaks, CA: Sage.

Smith, A. 1759/1984. *The theory of moral sentiments.* Indianapolis, IN: Liberty Fund.

Newbery, D. M., & Stiglitz, J. E. 1987. Wage Rigidity, Implicit Contracts, Unemployment and Economic Efficiency. *The Economic Journal*, 97(386): 416–430.

Thornton, P. H., Ocasio, W., & Lounsbury, M. 2012. *The institutional logics perspective: A new approach to culture, structure and process.* Oxford: Oxford University Press.

Turner, J. H. 2004. *Human institutions: A theory of societal evolution.* Lanham, MD: Rowman and Littlefield.

Walzer, M. 1994. *Thick and thin: Moral argument at home and abroad.* Notre Dame, IN: University of Notre Dame Press.

Weber, M. 1947. *The theory of social and economic organization* (A. M. Henderson & T. Parsons, Trans.). New York: Macmillan Publishing Co, Inc.

Weber, M. 1958. *The protestant ethic and the spirit of capitalism* (T. Parsons, Trans.). New York: Charles Scribner's Sons.

Williamson, O. E. 1985. *The economic institutions of capitalism.* New York: Free Press.

Williamson, O. E. 1993. Calculativeness, trust and economic organization. *Journal of Law and Economics*, 36(1): 453–486.

Xia, J., Boal, K., & Delios, A. 2009. When experience meets national institutional environmental change: Foreign entry attempts of US firms in the central and eastern European region. *Strategic Management Journal*, 30:1286–1309.

5 Comparative Economic Organization Revisited

Hybrid Governance in the Informal Economy

Paul C. Godfrey and Robert J. Jensen

Hybrid organizational forms such as micro-franchising represent a form of social entrepreneurship gaining traction in Base of the Pyramid (BoP) countries. A recent survey by Jensen, Sutter, and Mealey (2011) counts over 92 identifiable hybrid organizations in BoP markets in 2011, up from a mere handful five years earlier. If emerging economies can be classified as low-income, high-growth countries, then BoP markets might be thought of as low-income, low-growth environments (Khanna & Palepu, 2010) and may constitute "pre-emergent" economies. A robust theory of micro-franchising[1] and other new hybrid organizational forms would facilitate deeper conceptual work and a clearer empirical agenda that should improve our understanding of organizational forms in the informal economy, a feature of many BoP environments (Schneider, Buehn, & Montenegro, 2010).

Micro-franchising represents a "business in a box" concept that creates a joint ownership structure between franchisor and franchisee in which each owns a set of assets and the parties share ownership of others; thus, micro-franchising falls under the rubric of hybrid governance structures (Mennard, 2006; Williamson, 1991). The "micro" in micro-franchising comes from the low levels of investment required for entry and the small scale of business operations. Categorizing micro-franchises as hybrid governance structures suggests that the logic of Transaction Cost Economics (TCE), a core theoretical paradigm in strategic management (Jones & Hill, 1988; Poppo & Zenger, 2004), and Contract Theory should prove useful conceptual tools to examine and establish the conditions under which micro-franchising will be a preferred business structure in the BoP's informal economy.

In this chapter, we hope to link the study of the informal economy to the mainstream literatures and theoretical paradigms in strategic management. The BoP's informal marketplaces provide a new and different context within which to "stress test" TCE and Contract Theory, paradigms grounded and elaborated within the institutional framework of the developed world (Bolton & Dewatripont, 2005). As we elaborate below, BoP markets feature an institutional environment traditionally viewed as "weaker" than those found in the developed world (Seelos & Mair, 2007; North, 1990), and informal activity constitutes something on the order of half of economic output (see Schneider et al., 2010 for a country-by-country list). BoP markets typically consist of a preponderance of small scale, technologically unsophisticated enterprises with few specialized assets and low levels of capital investment, either financial or human (LaPorta & Shliefer, 2008). These factors result in the predominance of informal or relationship-based contracts as the mode of transactional governance (Godfrey, 2011; Meagher, 1990).

We aim at two contributions to the larger strategy and entrepreneurship literatures. First, we identify the contribution of Transaction Cost Economics and its intellectual parent, Contract Theory, as we use this set of constructs and logic to show why and when hybrid governance will represent an efficient, optimal governance/contract structure in informal economy contexts. Second, we contribute to Contract Theory by examining how optimal governance structures differ in informal versus formal, developed-world markets. As our title suggests, we are paying homage to the seminal work of Williamson (1991) on hybrid governance structures, and we hope to perform a comparative economic analysis across contexts to understand the viability of market (or classical contracting), hybrid forms (relational contracting), or hierarchy (typified by the employment contract) as optimal governance forms. Contrary to current work in TCE, which predicts few hybrid arrangements in highly uncertain contexts (characteristic of both BoP and other newly emerging markets), we conclude that hybrid governance structures possess clear efficiency advantages within the context of BoP markets.

Our argument proceeds as follows. We begin by outlining key differences between BoP, emerging, and developed markets, both in terms of institutions and organizations. Next, we review the core logic of Contract Theory, of which Transaction Cost Economics (TCE) can be considered a subset. We then consider the implications of the differences between informal and formal economies on the effective range of market, hybrid, and hierarchy as governance structures. Our paper concludes with a discussion of the implications of our modeling for theory and research within strategic entrepreneurship and management as well as implications for public policy makers and others interested in alleviating poverty.

BOP MARKETPLACES

BoP markets, as we describe below, can be considered pre-emergent, or at the lower boundary of emerging economies, and can be characterized by limited or stagnant economic growth and severe resource constraints (Collier, 2007) as well as governments pursuing multiple agendas, which may or may not include a serious commitment to economic growth and development (Easterly, 2001, 2006). Characterizing BoP marketplaces—once one moves beyond the income of its participants—proves difficult. As a conceptual benchmark, however, the bottom quintile of countries on the World Bank's Development Indicators[2] stands as a useful guide for inclusion in the BoP. We focus our discussion on two important features of BoP markets: a prevalence of informal economic activity and small scale, low technology operations.

Seelos and Mair (2007: 52) use the term "weak institutional arrangements" to describe BoP markets; however, our personal experience as well as decades of economic development practice indicate that the institutional environments of BoP marketplaces prove remarkably robust and resistant to change (see Farella (1984) for a characterization of Navajo institutions, for example, and Easterly (2001, 2006) for a similar description in Sub-Saharan Africa and Eastern Europe). Three common elements of many developing countries constitute BoP institutional environments: incomplete, impotent, and immoral institutions. Incomplete institutions can be characterized by uneven distribution of laws, policies, enforcement agencies, or customs. Institutions such as education systems, health and environmental regulatory agencies, consumer or investor protection, and even police and basic social services may be poorly developed or diffused. Roads, bridges, airports, ports, electrical grids, and other infrastructural elements may be obsolete, missing, or provide services in major cities (or portions of major cities) but not rural areas. Finally, the normative and cognitive mental maps, norms, and informal rules that facilitate a market economy may be missing or given different interpretations at the BoP (Di Tella, Galiana, & Shagrodsky, 2004; Payne, 2005).

Some institutions exist in a BoP environment, but they prove unable to implement and execute their mission and core objectives; we term these impotent institutions. Although property rights protections may exist *de jure*, the *de facto* conditions in these environments result in highly tenuous application of those rights. Intellectual property protections may be poorly enforced, and violations of copyright laws, patents, or other intellectual property protections may even be encouraged. Getting work done in impotent institutions may rely on personal relationships or friendships or other informal mechanisms (Spicer, McDermott, & Kogut, 2000).

Finally, immoral institutions feature implementation based on arbitrary, capricious, or clearly self-serving criteria. Immoral courts stand opposed to the unbiased umpires of contract language posited in Contract Theory (Bolton & Dewatripont, 2005); graft, corruption, self-dealing, and other forms of wealth extraction and personal expropriation characterize immoral institutions (Johnson, Kaufman, & Zoido-Lobotan, 1998).

Informal Activity

LaPorta and Shliefer (2008: 1) define the informal economy as "economic activity that [is] conducted by unregistered firms or by registered firms but hidden from taxation." Castells and Portes, (1989: 12) state: "the informal economy is . . . characterized by one central feature: it is unregulated by the institutions of society, in a legal and social environment in which similar activities are regulated." Informal economic activity creates vulnerability among its participants as they operate outside the canopy of laws and regulations designed to forestall many forms of exploitation. Hart (1973), Bosoit and Child (1996), and Godfrey (2011) all identify another key feature of informal activity: the reliance on custom, social capital, and other relational mechanisms to govern transactions. As North (1990) notes, this focus allows for highly efficient activity as social norms and sanctions prove remarkably effective in controlling behavior Bernstein (2001) documents this power in the cotton industry within a formal economy. That effectiveness comes at a cost, however, as the breadth of common relationships or shared customs limits the reach of these enforcement mechanisms. What informal participants save in transaction costs they often lose in scale and scope (Furubotn & Richter, 2005).

Informal economic activity leverages the referent group's monopoly on inclusion to enforce agreements (Durkheim, 1933; Granovetter, 1985; Turner, 2004; Weber, 1947). The threat to one's standing within a social group constitutes a primordial and powerful enforcement mechanism, with ostracism or exclusion from the group serving as the most effective punishment available. The greater the strength or centrality of shared values, worldviews, and connections that bind the actors into a common social group, such as a common religious tradition, ethnic group, or family, the more potent the threat of exclusion. The monopoly on inclusion thus operates as a potent sanction that discourages malfeasance on the part of actors.

Small Scale, Low Technology

Entrepreneurs at the BoP operate at smaller scale with lower absolute levels of managerial talent and skill than their developed world counterparts (LaPorta & Shliefer, 2008). Because BoP entrepreneurs most often have limited (to no) start-up capital, their businesses tend to feature low levels of investment in infrastructure, inventory, operating capital, and technology (Brau, Hiatt, & Woodworth, 2009). De Soto (2000) observes that BoP entrepreneurs often lack legal title to their land, which precludes obtaining financing to capitalize their businesses; they also often operate at intentionally small scale in order to avoid detection and extortion from larger entities, public or private. Lower levels of technological prowess and few, if any, economies of scale mean that BoP entrepreneurs, both formal and informal, operate at higher costs compared to larger multi-national corporations producing and selling similar goods. They become price competitive by reducing their own profit or other labor costs, and they become subsistence rather than growth entrepreneurs (Webb, Tihani, Ireland, & Sirmon, 2009).

Small scale and lower levels of technology have two implications for our purposes. First, these businesses entail lower levels of asset specificity as compared to firms in developed markets. Physical assets such as hand tools, weaving stools, tables, and even shop enclosures tend to be generic and fungible between uses and individuals; few assets in the informal economy have any firm-specific characteristics.[3] Human capital also exhibit low levels of specificity; common work includes construction or field labor, basic services such as hair/beauty care or bookkeeping, selling, or arts and crafts production. While some may enjoy more specialization than others (e.g., weaving versus concrete mixing), little human capital is tied to any particular employment arrangement or specific transaction. Micro-franchisors do not generate significant amounts of asset risk in their operations; the capital assets deployed can often be redeployed in new locations without loss of value.

Second, because these firms feature lower levels of technology, often a generation or more behind that found in developed markets, these entrepreneurs face a greater threat of obsolescence, and business models may be more transitory than in developed markets. While the technological development path might be known with certainty, the timing of generational obsolescence may preclude investments to sustain current technologies or expand their reach in current markets. The Grameen "phone ladies" represented a classic example of micro-franchising (Fairbourne, Gibson, & Dyer, 2007); however, advances in telephony technology have made that model obsolete, and Grameen Phone now sells handsets and voice/data plans.[4]

These two forces combine to make business operations in informal economic markets simpler, more flexible, governed by interpersonal relations, and more subject to obsolescence than similar businesses in the developed world. With an overview of informal BoP marketplaces now in place, we turn our attention to describing Transaction Cost Economics (TCE) and Contract Theory before we move to the core contribution of our paper: examining the impact the unique characteristics of BoP markets have on the optimal type of governance structures in these environments.

OPTIMAL GOVERNANCE: TCE AND CONTRACT THEORY

We model contracts, following Bolton and Dewatripont (2005), as a value creating instrument where V (value) = $f(\zeta^c, \zeta^r, \zeta^e)$. ζ^c captures the market, or classical elements, of the contract, including third-party enforcement; ζ^r represents relational features, including self-enforcement (Baker, Gibbons, & Murphy, 2002); and ζ^e describes a particular type of self-enforcing contract, the employment contract that relies on a formal grant of authority or fiat from one party to another to enforce and resolve contract disputes (Simon, 1951; Smith & King, 2009). Table 5.1 outlines key features of these three archetypal governance contracts as modeled in the extant literature.

Table 5.1 Generalized Governance Forms, Extant Models (see Williamson, 1991)

Element	Market (ζ^c)	Hybrid (ζ^r)	Hierarchy (ζ^e)
Asset ownership	Independent	Joint	Single
Contractual Archetypes	Classical	Relational	Employment
Contractual form[5]	$\zeta^c > 0, \zeta^r = 0$	$\zeta^c \geq 0, \zeta^r > 0$	$\zeta^c \geq 0, \zeta^r \geq 0,$ $\zeta^e > 0$
Foresight (F)	Perfect	Imperfect	Imperfect
Verifiability (V)	Yes	No	No
Asset specificity (A)	Low	Moderate	High
Impact w.r.t (F, V, A)	$\zeta^{c'} > 0, \zeta^{c''} > 0$	$\zeta^{r'} > 0, \zeta^{r''} > 0$	$\zeta^{e'} > 0, \zeta^{e''} > 0$
Dispute resolution	Arbitration/ Courts	Negotiation	Fiat
Features to control:			
Adverse selection	Price/Auctions	Screens/Bonds	Non-price signals
Moral hazard	Stipulations	Hostages	Ownership
BoP examples	Micro-credit	Micro-franchising	Aid workers

Contract Theory

TCE represents a sub-field nested within the larger field of Contract Theory (Furubotn & Richter, 2005). In the standard TCE framework, opportunism (O), which Williamson (1985: 47) defines as "self-interest seeking with guile," creates a fundamental desire and potential for hold-up (H); asset specificity (ASP) defines the magnitude of potential losses, and uncertainty (U) increases the probability, or likelihood, of contractual expropriation or hold-up. We define these relationships more formally: $\partial H / \partial O > 0$ captures the individual-level propensity for hold-up, $\partial H / \partial U > 0$, the market risk, and $\partial H / \partial ASP > 0$ the potential loss. Why expand TCE into a Contract Theory framework? Because Contract Theory provides a more detailed and nuanced set of constructs to understand opportunism and uncertainty that allows us to investigate the impacts of informal arrangements on the type and form of optimal contracts. We now discuss how contract theory treats some familiar and important TCE constructs: asset specificity, uncertainty (imperfect foresight), and opportunism (cast as responses to unobservability).

Asset Specificity. Contract theorists model asset specificity in, generally, the same vein as TCE. Specificity exists to the extent that an asset's value (or quasi-rent) in its next-best use lies significantly below its value in the current transactional regime (Klein, Crawford, & Alchian, 1972). Grossman and Hart (1986), for example, accept the generalized notion of specialized assets but note that the importance of the asset to the endeavor, not its degree of specialization, can become the deciding factor in governance form. Contract theory broadens the conceptual space in which assets may be considered specialized, although the fundamental relationship between asset specificity and hold-up remains $\frac{\partial H}{\partial ASP} > 0$.

Imperfect Foresight. In Contract Theory, uncertainty arises from two sources: imperfect foresight by actors regarding the world, and the inherent unobservability of key contract-related information or behaviors. In an ideal world, economic actors have perfect foresight. Perfect foresight does not mean that actors know the future; it means they can anticipate potential futures that may arise and a set of economic values for each potential state. A world of perfect foresight can be modeled as a complete set of Arrow-Debreu securities (Bolton & Dewatripont, 2005). An Arrow-Debreu security is one in which the value v = 1 if some state of nature comes to fruition, 0 otherwise. The complete set can be modeled as $V = \sum_{i=1}^{n} p_i v_i$, where V represents the total future value, and p_i the probability of each potential state, where $\sum_{i=1}^{n} p_i = 1$.

Imperfect foresight (IF) can be defined as a set of Arrow-Debreu securities, such that $\sum_{i=1}^{n} p_i < 1$ actors do not know all potential future states. Imperfect foresight gives rise to incomplete contracts, i.e., contracts which fully specify promises and considerations for known potential futures but cannot specify clauses for unknown futures. Incomplete contracts are contracts with holes, holes where third party enforcement mechanisms such as courts provide no relief because they cannot interpret missing contractual clauses (Furubotn & Richter, 2005). Incomplete contracts use relational contractual mechanisms to fill the holes such that the value of both $\zeta^c > 0$ and $\zeta^r > 0$. The most common self-enforcing mechanism may be the promise to renegotiate the contract in "good faith" when unanticipated states of nature appear. As implied in TCE theory, the relationship between imperfect foresight and hold-up can be expressed as $\frac{\partial H}{\partial IF} > 0$.

Unobservability. Inputs, throughputs, or outputs involved in a contractual arrangement may be unobservable to either of the parties involved and/or to a third-party adjudicator. Contract theorists traditionally model input unobservability as the problem of hidden information about inputs, typified by Adverse Selection (ASE), and unobservability in throughputs as the problem of hidden action, or the problem of Moral Hazard (MH). Actors employ a variety of contractual features to resolve problems of hidden information and hidden action.

Hidden information can be illustrated by two examples: An employer doesn't know the ability of potential employees before they are hired (as in Spence, 1973, 1976), or buyers often don't know the quality of merchandise offered at sale (as in Ackerlof, 1970). In the former case, employers will employ screens such as examining the caliber of education as a signal of a worker's potential quality, while in the latter case the seller may bond him or herself through a warranty in order to signal the quality of the product. We foreshadow our argument around hybrids by noting that contractual features such as franchise fees serve both purposes; they act as screens for the franchisor to self-select those most interested and able to make the endeavor a success and simultaneously represent a bond on the part of the franchisee to signal his or her ability and earnestness. Problems of Adverse Selection exacerbate hold-up, shown as $\frac{\partial H}{\partial ASE} > 0$.

Alchian and Demsetz (1972), Jensen and Meckling (1976), and Fama (1980) all consider variations of the problem of hidden action or moral hazard as typified in the principal agent relationship. After the contract is signed, the agent may have little incentive to fulfill the contract and pursue his/her own ends (for example, shirking effort instead of working hard) if the principal cannot observe the actions of the agent or link that action to outcomes (was inferior production the result of bad inputs or shirking?). Alchian and Demsetz (1972) classify this as the problem of team production and argue that contractual features that align the two parties' incentives should remedy the threat of moral hazard. As Bolton and Dewatripont (2005) note, the optimal tactical features in an incentive aligning contract may be difficult to specify; however, the principle of incentive alignment is quite straightforward. The threat of hold-up increases with Moral Hazard and $\frac{\partial H}{\partial MH} > 0$.

Inputs or throughputs may be observable to the parties, but unobservable, and hence unverifiable, to a third-party arbitrator. Contractual provisions such as "time is of the essence" and working in "good faith" to resolve disputes may prove difficult for courts or others to verify. Situational complexity, causal ambiguity, and plausible deniability make it difficult for courts, featuring non-content-expert judges, to determine whether a party violated "time is of the essence" or truly failed to negotiate in "good faith." Bernstein (2001) describes how the cotton industry established its own commercial legal system and supporting social structures to enforce agreements with provisions not verifiable in traditional courts. The implicit employment contract described by Newberry and Stiglitz (1987), in which employers make informal and implicit promises about layoffs and employment security, provides another example of a third-party unverifiable (3PU) contract. Hold-up becomes a greater problem when third parties cannot adjudicate contract disputes, or $\frac{\partial H}{\partial 3PU} > 0$.

OPTIMAL CONTRACTING AT THE BOP

In this section we overlay the unique features of informal marketplaces on the constructs and architecture of Contract Theory. We perform a comparative economic analysis of informal versus formal markets, given that both TCE and Contract Theory have been developed and deployed within a developed world framework. We begin with a discussion of asset specificity in its own right, as we believe that the nature of informal markets changes the fundamental character of asset specificity. We then consider the impacts of imperfect foresight, third-party unobservability, adverse selection, and moral hazard on the relative contracting costs of classical (market), employment (hierarchical), and relational (hybrid) regimes.

Market Contracting in the Informal, BoP Economy

Asset specificity. In informal markets, the nature of asset specificity changes, moving from the unilateral asset dependency modeled in formal, developed economies (Klein, Crawford, & Alchian, 1972; Williamson, 1985) toward a condition of bilateral asset interdependence (see Grossman & Hart, 1986). Because of the low levels of technology and low costs of physical assets held by the principal (franchisor), the degree of asset specificity the franchisor brings to the contract is typically limited; conversely, the franchisee, a small micro-entrepreneur, typically brings little of specialized value in terms of physical, financial, or human resources. The franchisor does transfer some specialized knowledge and skill to the franchisee, but much of this knowledge concerns generic issues such as operations management, accounting, and financial management, which have value in any business endeavor. In the strictest sense of asset specificity (assets with a marked drop in value from the current use to the next-best use), most assets in informal economic agreements could best be classified as generic (Fairbourne et al., 2007).

The franchise brand represents one potential specialized asset that the actions of the franchisor (e.g., advertising, training, etc.) as well as the franchisee (e.g., execution, action that reinforces brand value, etc.) affect. In addition, the franchisee brings a set of important assets to the relationship, namely, a deep knowledge of the market, the types of people likely to purchase items, and a personal reputation and credibility that may represent an important brand signal in the market. Put simply, the franchisee brings valuable social capital to the relationship (Coleman, 1988; Francois, 2002; Putnam, 2000). Given the lack of commensurate formal institutions, the foreignness of most franchisors to the market,[6] and the embedded nature of informal economic activity, these relational assets and knowledge constitute valuable and important assets for the business (Grossman & Hart, 1986). The franchisee can transfer these base assets of embedded knowledge to other opportunities just as the franchisor can transfer its assets to different franchisees; however, as the franchisee and franchisor work together they co-create value as the franchisee lends the franchisor his/her credibility, and over time the brand and the micro-franchisor's assets enhance the reputation, credibility, and stature of the franchisee among his or her market and social groups.

The assets each party brings to the transaction become more valuable over time in the presence of each other, and the venture creates what we term bilateral asset interdependence. Unlike traditional asset specificity in which one partner becomes more dependent on the other over time, this bilateral mutual dependence, or interdependence, diminishes the potential losses of hold-up behaviors. Counter to the logic of asset specificity, where $\frac{\partial H}{\partial ASP} > 0$, increases in the level of bilateral asset interdependence (BAI) reduce the threat of hold-up, $\frac{\partial H}{\partial BAI} < 0$, as each party sustains substantial self-losses if they attempt to expropriate wealth from the other party.

Imperfect Foresight. The incomplete nature of BoP institutional environments creates several challenges to market contracting. First, the lack of market institutions raises the ex-ante costs of contracting as parties must invest more time and energy in understanding valuations, prices, and trends. The lack of reporting or rating agencies obscures relevant information (i.e., little to no transparency) that makes complete specification of current and future states problematic. Underdeveloped infrastructure (particularly electricity supplies, public services, and law enforcement) combine to complexify and problematize the specification of possible future states.

Impotent institutions further increase uncertainty and obviate planning as the unreliable and stochastic nature of service provision and enforcement reduce the probability that anticipated future states will occur as predicted. The lack of a capitalist mindset tends to make the economic behavior of individuals more variable and less predictable; BoP actors may be less likely to display the type of economic rationality possessed by their developed world counterparts (Payne, 2005).

The net effect of increases in imperfect foresight is to make classical contracting more problematic. By their nature, classical contracts at the BoP will be more incomplete and have additional ex-ante holes than comparable contracts in the developed world. Increases in ex-ante contracting problems translate to increased costs ex post as aggrieved parties must spend more to adjudicate contractual holes with lower probably of success due to the stochastic nature of institutional responses.

Third-Party Unobservability. When insecure institutions characterize a BoP market, third-party enforcement (even when contractual terms are observable) becomes more difficult. Legal recourse may be unavailable due to resource constraints, backlogs, poor evidentiary procedures, or time lags between contract violations and adjudication. Courts may be unreliable, even when available, due to the stochastic, arbitrary, and/or capricious rules used in deciding the merits of claims. Third-party judicial relief may prove untenable due to systematic bias—such as laws that favor domestic versus foreign entities—or the presence of corruption, side payments, or bribes. Lack of deep knowledge of embedded markets may lead to stipulations enforced against the contractor rather than for him/her (see Klein, 1996). BoP markets lack the "umpire-like" court systems stipulated in classical contracting models: Judges may in fact interpret and redefine contractual provisions rather than merely adhere to and enforce them. Sporadic rule of law and immoral administration of those laws raises the costs of adjudication and lowers the likelihood of effective third-party relief, all of which work to raise the overall cost (particularly relative to payoff) of classical contracts. This logic implies that market (classical) contracting will be less efficient in informal markets when compared to market contracting in formal economies.

Hierarchical Contracting in Informal BoP Markets

To the extent that BoP states build on the insecure institutions outlined above, the effect is to raise the cost of subsuming transactions within a hierarchy. Consider first imperfect foresight. The lack of market institutions requires that firms, if they desire accurate market information, perform this activity in house, raising the absolute cost of hierarchy. Embedded informal economic markets and similar social norms make the cultural rules of the market less apparent and harder to understand. Obtaining pragmatic legitimacy and acting accordingly in socially appropriate ways may be more difficult for outsiders and result in costly mistakes.

In terms of third-party unverifiability, LaPorta and Shliefer (2008) find that corruption and bribery costs were higher for formal firms than informal ones, most likely because firms in the formal economy have (perceived or actual) deeper pockets and more touch points with state agencies. Godfrey and Dyer (2011) explain that Ghana's socialist legacy creates a moderately anti-corporate legal orientation; strong laws exist around labor organization and worker protection, meaning that it becomes more difficult to fire employees. On the other hand, property rights law, and the body of precedent supporting such laws, exhibit lower levels of development; many squatter entrepreneurs who would like to purchase their land can't because neither they nor the state know who holds title to the property. Di Tella, Galiana, and Shagrodsky (2004) describe a similar situation in Argentina, and De Soto (2000) has performed similar analysis in several BoP countries.

Lower levels of technology mean that ownership of assets becomes more risky as technological leaps may leave the organization with obsolete technologies or business models, further raising the costs for hierarchies. For example, Grameen Phone became famous because of its "phone ladies," micro-entrepreneurs who owned a phone through a Grameen plan and sold individual minutes to customers by the call (Fairbourne et al., 2007). Advancements in cell-phone technology have displaced this business model, and now Grameen sells hardware directly. Had Grameen operated as a firm rather than a hybrid, they would have borne all the costs alone.

BoP markets also feature low levels of education beyond secondary schools;[7] the lack of more advanced educational attainment removes one set of signals to control for problems of adverse selection. Poor physical infrastructure in BoP markets raises communication and monitoring costs. Finally, the lack of a mindset of capitalism among many BoP participants leads to greater potential for moral hazard in the face of the firm's low-powered incentives. Coupled with labor friendly legal philosophies, it may be easier for firms at the BoP to hire lower ability employees but harder to get rid of them.

The nature of BoP markets raises, not lowers, the cost of hierarchical organization. Founders must invest more in human resources to collect and process information, they may work in legal environments with a predisposition (either *de jure* or *de facto*) towards deciding in favor of labor or local parties, and their technology and other assets may have a greater risk of obsolescence and fewer property rights protections. Put simply, hierarchy becomes an expensive solution to problems of potential hold-up, and we assert that hierarchy will be less prevalent and predominant in informal markets than in formal ones.

Hybrid Contracting in Informal BoP Markets

The impact of BoP market structures and institutions has the opposite effect on hybrid forms than on market or hierarchical contracting: the structures drive down, rather than up, the cost of establishing and operating hybrid contracts such as micro-franchises. North (1990) notes that BoP markets engage in trade within kinship/friendship networks to avoid the problems of differing expectations and difficult enforcement found with strangers. Social norms and family/clan/tribal cognitive and regulatory institutions have evolved to fill the holes created by the lack of formal or legal systems (Venkatesh, 2006).

Centuries-old and well-developed social networks (Coleman, 1988) provide both the bridging capital (Portes and Sensenbrenner, 1993; Putnam, 2000) that mitigates problems of adverse selection and the bonding capital that mitigates the lack of formal third-party enforcement (North, 1990; Polyani, 1957). Informal structures tend to reduce costs and speed the time to resolution for most disputes (Bernstein, 2001). The deeply embedded nature of transacting in BoP settings allows social structures, such as families, tribes and clans, to provide the regulatory institutions to establish a shared cognitive (world views) framework and enforce normative rules and morals. This embedded institutional make-up greatly facilitates trade within the limited group and even enables highly sophisticated transactions and exchanges (see Meagher, 1990 for an example of foreign currency exchange networks in Uganda). Enforcement in these networks relies on concerns of personal standing, making them truly self-enforcing, and are often supplemented with non-economic ties such as friendship or kinship.

In short, the existence of robust informal economic and social structures offer participants, whether they are BoP subsistence entrepreneurs, micro-franchisors, or other social entrepreneurs, the opportunity to leverage a well-articulated and effective institutional infrastructure to create relational contracts that have both strong self-enforcement mechanisms (see Barney and Hansen, 1994; Meagher, 1990) and effective substitutes for state-supported institutions (Bernstein, 2001; De Soto, 2000).

The logic of our argument can be summarized by Figure 5.1, which shows BoP impacts on the three contractual archetypes. The dotted lines (M, R, E) represent the optimal contracting modalities in a developed-world

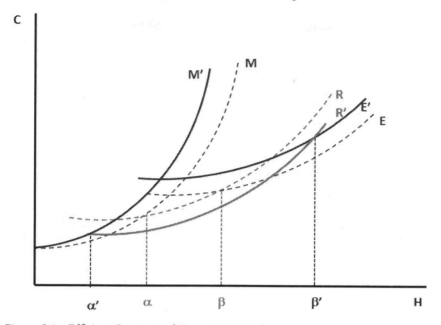

Figure 5.1 Efficient Contractual Form, BoP Markets

Source: M' denotes Market Contracting, R' denotes relational or hybrid contractual forms, and E' represents the hierarchical (employment) contract

context (Williamson, 1991); the solid curves (M', R', E') illustrate how these modalities change in BoP contexts. We choose a conservative shift for the market curve; we assume that at very low threats of hold-up the contracting costs will not differ between a BoP and developed market. The BoP market cost curve pivots to the left and becomes progressively steeper, reflecting the increased comparative costs of contracting in a BoP environment. This shift forces the crossover point between market and relational contracting, α, to the left. BoP markets favor relational contracting. The employment contract curve shifts up from its position in the developed world, showing that hierarchical contracting becomes more expensive at each point. This shifts the relational contracting vs. hierarchy crossover, β, to the right and makes hybrid structures more attractive. The relational contract curve shifts down at every point, reflecting the lower costs of establishing and maintaining self-enforcing hybrid contracts in BoP environments. As the figure shows, and our analysis indicates, hybrid governance structures enjoy economic efficiency properties (i.e., lower transaction costs) over a broader range of transactions in BoP environments compared to developed ones. Depending on the level of institutional insecurity hybrids, may present either a pervasive or predominant form of organizing in BoP markets.

As uncertainty increases, measured by imperfect foresight and unobservability (third-party unverifiability, threats of adverse selection, and moral hazard), hybrid contracts become more, not less, advantageous. First, the institutional infrastructure underpinning both market and hierarchical contracting becomes more tenuous, reducing the viability of these forms of contracting. Second, the advantages of joint ownership and control of assets, higher powered incentives for behavior, and the development of increasing levels of bilateral asset interdependence gives hybrid governance flexibility, risk reduction, and incentive alignment in highly uncertain environments. Our model implies that markets and hierarchies may be the endangered species in BoP environments. Post-conflict and war-torn countries such as Somalia or Cote d'Ivoire may feature economies with few true market transactions, a handful of formal hierarchies, and a vast majority of transactions concluded within hybrid forms (Collier, 2007).

DISCUSSION

Our investigation highlights the importance of contextual settings and assumptions for different theoretical paradigms; specifically, the unique features of BoP marketplaces lead to a different set of explanations and predictions from the TCE model. Hybrid forms become more appealing, and enjoy a greater range of optimal efficiency, when compared with their role in the developed world (compare figures 1, 2, and 3). We suggest that other theories of strategy and entrepreneurship, such as the resource-based view, models of successful entrepreneurs (Ricketts, 2006; Shane & Venkatraman, 2000), or business model development (Alvarez & Barney, 2007), should be subjected to a similar comparative analysis. We don't speculate about the results of such inquiry; however, given the conclusions in this chapter, we believe that the results will yield more robust theories of both strategy and entrepreneurship. By "stress testing" extant theories of strategy and entrepreneurship in BoP contexts we believe that constructs will become sharper, limiting constraints clearer, and the overall explanatory power of our models more complete.

What remains, however, is to systematically identify the types of informal activities that utilize hybrid governance mechanisms and a more robust census of these types of organizations around the world. A sharper definition of the institutional supports, political structures, and social norms that sustain informal activity can guide business and public policy makers to identify those elements of BoP markets for which change can yield meaningful development.

CONCLUSION

Micro-franchising represents a potentially powerful business model to help alleviate poverty at the BoP. Our argument finds that hybrid organizational forms, such as micro-franchises, provide an efficient governance structure for economic activity at the BoP. We find that the types of uncertainty found in BoP environments (imperfect foresight, third-party unobservability, moral hazard, and adverse selection), contrary to current TCE predictions, favor hybrid forms over both many market transactions and hierarchical organizational forms.

NOTES

1. Our paper considers micro-franchising as a concrete example of the more abstract construct of hybrid organizational forms. We will move between the terms micro-franchising and hybrid organizations throughout the chapter.
2. Data on the World Development Indicators can be found at http://data.worldbank.org/data-catalog/world-development-indicators.
3. Authors' observations based on visits to BoP markets in Africa, Latin America, and Native American environments.
4. See http://www.grameenphone.com/ for a complete description.
5. This presentation does not imply that Markets, Hybrids, and Hierarchies exist in a Gutman-type relationship. Rather, the notation incorporates contracting within the shadow of the state. Relational contracts may, or may not, choose to cover certain contingencies by reference to law and court adjudication (Bolton and Dewatripont, 2005). Similarly, employment contracts may rely on non-authority based mechanisms (i.e., friendship, norms of reciprocity) to both enforce compliance and provide rewards.
6. Even if the franchisor is from the same country, they typically are firms that have sold primarily to the upper classes. While they may, in general, be familiar with the country and its institutions, the instantiation of those institutions in the BoP marketplace may be different enough to render the franchisor "foreign."
7. In some BoP countries, education beyond primary school may be lacking for most of the population.

REFERENCES

Ackerlof, G. A. 1970. The market for 'Lemons": Quality uncertainty and the market mechanism. *Quarterly Journal of Economics*, 84: 488–500.
Alchain, A. A., & Demsetz, H. 1972. Production, information costs, and economic organization. *American Economic Review*, 62: 777–795.
Alvarez, S. A., & Barney, J. B. 2007. Discovery and creation: Alternative theories of entrepreneurial action. *Strategic Entrepreneurship Journal*, 1(1–2): 11–26.
Baker, G., Gibbons, R., & Murphy, K. J. 2002. Relational contracts and the theory of the firm. *Quarterly Journal of Economics*, 39–84.
Barney, J. B., & Hansen, M. H. 1994. Trustworthiness as a source of competitive advantage. *Strategic Management Journal*, 15(special issue): 175–190.
Bernstein, L. 2001. Private commercial law in the cotton industry: Creating cooperation through rules, norms, and institutions. *Michigan Law Review*, 99: 1724–1790.
Bolton, P., & Dewatripont, M. 2005. *Contract theory*. Boston: MIT Press.
Bosoit, M., & Child, J. 1996. From fiefs to clans and network capitalism: Explaining China's emerging economic order. *Administrative Science Quarterly*, 41(4): 600–628.

Brau, J. C., Hiatt, S., & Woodworth, W. 2009. Evaluating impacts of microfinance institutions using Guatemalan data. *Managerial Finance*, 35(12): 953–974.

Castells, M., & Portes, A. 1989. World underneath: The origins, dynamics, and effects of the informal economy. In A. Portes, M. Castells, & L. A. Benton (Eds.), *The informal economy: Studies in advanced and less developed countries*: 11–37. Baltimore: Johns Hopkins University Press.

Coleman, J. T. 1988. Social capital in the creation of human capital. *The American Journal of Sociology*, 94(supplement: organizations and institutions: Sociological and economic approaches to the analysis of socia structure): 95–120.

Collier, P. 2007. *The bottom billion*. Oxford: Oxford University Press.

De Soto, H. 2000. *The mystery of capital*. New York: Basic Books.

DiTella, R., Galiana, S., & Schargrodsky, E. 2004. Property rights and beliefs: Evidence from the allocation of land titles to squatters. Ronald Coase Institute Working Paper Series.

Durkheim, E. 1933/1984. *The division of labor in society*. New York, NY: The Free Press.

Easterly, W. R. 2001. *The elusive quest for growth: Economists' adventures and misadventures in the tropics*. Cambridge, MA: MIT Press.

Easterly, W. R. 2006. *The white man's burden: Why the West's efforts to aid the Rest have done so much ill and so little good*. New York: Penguin Books.

Eisenberger, N. I., Lieberman, M. D., & Williams, K. D. 2003. Does rejection hurt? An FMRI study of social exclusion. *Science*, 10: 290–292.

Fairbourne, J. S., Gibson, S. W., & Dyer, W. G. 2007. *Microfranchising: Creating wealth at the bottom of the pyramid*. Northampton, MA: Edward Elgard.

Fama, E. 1980. Agency problems and the theory of the firm. *Journal of Political Economy*, 88: 288–307.

Farella, J. R. 1984. *The main stalk: A synthesis of Navajo philosophy*. Tucson: University of Arizona Press.

Francois, P. 2002. *Social capital and economic development*. London: Routledge.

Furubotn, E., & Richter, R. 2005. *Institutions and economic theory*. Ann Arbor, MI: University of Michigan Press.

Godfrey, P. C. 2011. Toward a theory of the informal economy. *Academy of Management Annals*, 5: 1–47.

Godfrey, P. C., & Dyer, W. G. 2011. *Subsistence entrepreneurs and formal institutions: Semi-formal governance among Ghanaian entrepreneurs*: 25. Ballard Center Working Paper Series. Provo, UT: Melvin J. Ballard Center for Economic Self-Reliance.

Granovetter, M. 1985. Economic action and social structure: The problem of embeddedness. *American Journal of Sociology*, 91(3): 481–510.

Grossman, S. J., & Hart, O. D. 1986. The costs and benefits of ownership: A theory of vertical and lateral integration. *The Journal of Political Economy*, 94(4): 691–719.

Hart, K. 1973. Informal income opportunities in urban employment in Ghana. *Journal of Modern African Studies*, 11(1): 61–89.

Jensen, M. C., & Meckling, W. H. 1976. Theory of the firm: Managerial behavior, agency costs, and ownership structure. *Journal of Financial Economics*, 3(4): 305–360.

Jensen, R. J., Sutter, C. J., & Mealey, C. 2011. *Hybrid governance forms at the BoP*. Paper presented at the Strategic Management Society Conference—CK Prahalad, San Diego, CA.

Johnson, S., Kaufmann, D., & Zoido-Lobaton, P. 1998. Regulatory discretion and the unofficial economy. *The American Economic Review*, 88(2): 387–392.

Jones, G. R., & Hill, C. W. L. 1988. Transaction cost analysis of strategy-structure choice. *Strategic Management Journal*, 9(2): 159–172.

Khanna, T., & Palepu, K. 2000. Is group affiliation profitable in emerging markets? An analysis of diversified Indian business groups. *The Journal of Finance*, 55(2): 867–891.

Klein, B. 1996. Why hold-ups occur: The self-enforcing range of contractual relationships. *Economic Inquiry*, 34(3): 444.

Klein, B., Crawford, R. G., & Alchian, A. A. 1972. Vertical integration, appropriable rents, and the competitive contracting process. *Journal of Law and Economics*, 21(2): 297–326.

LaPorta, R., & Shleifer, A. 2008. *The unofficial economy and economic development*: 1–75. Working Paper Series. Washington, DC: National Bureau of Economic Research.

Meagher, K. 1990. The hidden economy: Informal and parallel trade in Northwestern Uganda. *Review of African Political Economy*, 47(Spring): 64–83.

Mennard, C. 2006. Hybrid organization of production and distribution. *Revista de Analisis Economico*, 21(2): 25–41.

Newbery, D. M., & Stiglitz, J. 1987. Wage rigidity, implicit contracts, unemployment and economic efficiency. *The Economic Journal*, 97(June): 416–430.

North, D. C. 1990. *Institutions, institutional change and economic performance*. New York: Cambridge University Press.

Payne, R. K. 2005. *A framework for understanding poverty*. Highlands, TX: Aha process, Inc.

Polanyi, K. 1957. *Trade and market in the early empires; economies in history and theory*. Glencoe, IL: Free Press.

Poppo, L., & Zenger, T. 2004. Testing alternative theories of the firm: Transaction cost, knowledge-based, and measurement explanations for make-or-buy decisions in information services. *Strategic Management Journal*, 19: 853–877.

Portes, A., & Sensenbrenner, J. 1993. Embeddedness and immigration: Notes on the social determinants of economic action. *American Journal of Sociology*, 98(6): 1320–1350.

Putnam, R. D. 2000. *Bowling alone: The collapse and revival of American community*. New York: Simon &Schuster.

Ricketts, M. 2006. Theories of entrepreneurship: Historical development and critical assessment In M. Casson, B. Yeung, A. Basu, & N. Wadeson (Eds.), *The Oxford Handbook of Entrepreneurship*: 33–58. Oxford: Oxford University Press.

Schneider, F., Buehn, A., & Montenegro, C. E. 2010. New estimates for the shadow economies all over the world. *International Economic Journal*, 24(4): 443–461.

Seelos, C., & Mair, J. 2007. Profitable business models and market creation in the context of deep poverty: A strategic view. *Academy of Management Perspectives*, 21(4): 49–63.

Shane, S., & Venkataraman, S. 2000. The promise of entrepreneurship as a field of research *Academy of Management Review*, 25(1): 217–226.

Simon, H. A. 1951. A formal theory of the employment relationship. *Econometrica*, 19(3): 293–305.

Smith, D. G., & King, B. G. 2009. Contracts as organizations. *Arizona Law Review*, 51(1): 1–45.

Spence, M. 1973. Job market signaling. *The Quarterly Journal of Economics*, 87(3): 355–374.

Spence, M. 1976. Informational aspects of market structure: An introduction. *The Quarterly Journal of Economics*, 90(4): 591–597.

Spicer, A., McDermott, G. A., & Kogut, B. 2000. Entrepreneurship and privatization in Central Europe: The tenous balance between destruction and creativity. *The Academy of Management Review*, 25(3): 630–649.

Turner, J. H. 2004. *Human institutions: A theory of societal evolution*. Lanham, Md.: Rowman and Littlefield.

Venkatesh, S. A. 2006. *Off the books: The underground economy of the urban poor.* Cambridge, MA: Harvard University Press.

Webb, J. W., Tihanyi, L., Ireland, R. D., & Sirmon, D. G. 2009. You say illegal, I say legitimate: Entrepreneurship in the informal economy. *Academy of Management Review*, 34(3): 492–510.

Weber, M. 1947. *The theory of social and economic organization.* New York: Macmillan Publishing.

Williamson, O. E. 1985. *The economic institutions of capitalism.* New York: Free Press.

Williamson, O. E. 1991. Comparative economic organization: The analysis of discrete structural alternatives. *Administrative Science Quarterly*, 36(2): 269–296.

6 Factors Influencing the Registration Decision in the Informal Economy

Bradley R. Skousen and
Joseph T. Mahoney

The central distinction of the informal economy vis-à-vis the formal economy concerns the legal status of economic activity. A common form of illegal activity is the failure of entrepreneurs to legally register and/or obtain business licenses, which enables the government to track and oversee economic activity (De Castro, Khavul, & Bruton, 2014; Nichter & Goldmark, 2009). Research on the informal economy has long explored the question of what prompts entrepreneurs and firms to register and has been largely examined from an institutional or legalistic perspective (De Soto, 1989; Webb, Bruton, Tihanyi, & Ireland, 2013; Webb, Tihanyi, Ireland, & Sirmon, 2009). The institutional perspective underscores that entrepreneurship is a socially constructed behavior conditioned by its social environment (Sine & David, 2010). This perspective posits that entrepreneurs are more likely to register when formal institutions facilitate registration through lower registration fees and less legal bureaucratic impediments, and when they offer higher levels of property rights protection and quality of services that benefit the entrepreneur (Marcouiller & Young, 1995; Nwabuzor, 2005; Thomas & Mueller, 2000). However, Godfrey (2011) notes that this perspective tends to over-emphasize the role and quality of regulatory institutional frameworks and neglects cognitive and normative institutions (Scott, 2008), which include the beliefs, values, norms, and customs that impact the registration decision.

Recent research in the extant management literature has begun to incorporate cognitive and normative institutions, which can be joined within the broad category of informal institutions (North, 1990). Within this perspective, the informal economy is defined as those "economic activities that are outside of formal institutional boundaries (i.e., illegal) yet fall within informal institutional boundaries (i.e., legitimate)" (Webb et al., 2009, 2013: 3). This definition adds clarity to the context of the informal economy, which is often referred to as an unregulated market even though the informal economy may be highly regulated by informal institutions that confer legitimacy to unregistered entrepreneurs. Research within this perspective focuses on the (potential and/or actual) interaction between formal and informal institutions and emphasizes that the decision to register is strategic in nature as rational decision-makers weigh the costs and benefits of registration (De Castro et al., 2014; De Mel, McKenzie, & Woodruff, 2013). However, this research gives little attention to the heterogeneity of micro-level attributes and strategies of entrepreneurs within the informal economy and how they may inform our current macro-and meso-level theories of the informal economy (Barney & Felin, 2013; Bruton, 2010; London & Hart, 2011; McGahan, 2012; Prahalad, 2005).

Drawing upon a variety of streams of literature, including entrepreneurship research on motivation, human capital, transaction cost economics, institutional theory, and family business, the current paper examines the impact of micro-level individual attributes and strategies of entrepreneurs on registration in the context of the base of the pyramid. Base of the pyramid markets are commonly defined as institutional environments characterized by formal institutional voids and where individuals often live in poverty (De Soto, 2000; London & Hart, 2011). Overall, the base of the pyramid comprises nearly 4 billion people, or 70% of the world's market (London & Hart, 2011; Prahalad, 2005; World Resources Institute, 2007). In many circumstances, the base of the pyramid is still growing in size. For example, it is estimated that there are over 200,000 urban slums comprising over 1 billion people (Davis, 2006). According to the United Nations, that number is expected to grow to over 2 billion people by the year 2030 (UN-Habitat, 2003). Specifically, we examine how an entrepreneur's motivation for starting a business and his or her level of education can influence the likelihood of registration. Next, we consider how the entrepreneur's strategic behavior may increase (the perception of) institutional pluralism and transaction cost hazards leading to a greater likelihood of registration. We conclude with a discussion of research implications and how our propositions may apply to other informal activity, along with potential avenues for future research.

Start-up Motivation

A large body of research in entrepreneurship has focused on understanding the extent to which personal attributes of the entrepreneur influence the entrepreneurship process and performance outcomes. Research suggests that an entrepreneur's motivation for starting a business is a salient attribute that influences behavior and how the entrepreneur navigates the entrepreneurship process (Shane, Locke, & Collins, 2003). While the stages of the entrepreneurship process of identification, evaluation, and exploitation are the same for registered and unregistered entrepreneurs, the nature and timing of activities, access to resources, and incentives of the entrepreneur may vary considerably based on whether the entrepreneur navigates the entrepreneurship process in a formal or informal institutional environment (Webb et al., 2013; Williams & Nadin, 2010). Institutions either facilitate or hinder the entrepreneur's ability to navigate each stage of the entrepreneurship process (Shane, 2000; Sine & David, 2010). At the earliest stage of the entrepreneurship process, institutions influence an entrepreneur's alertness to entrepreneurial opportunities as entrepreneurs are less likely to identify or be alert to the entrepreneurial opportunities that institutions define as illegal or illegitimate (Webb et al., 2009). Institutions not only influence the entrepreneur's alertness to opportunities but also the entrepreneur's ability to acquire and leverage resources to exploit entrepreneurial opportunities effectively and to grow the business (De Soto, 2000). Taken together, this research suggests that the entrepreneur's decision to register is driven by two overarching motivations: (1) the need to obtain legitimacy and other intangible benefits (e.g., trust, reputation), and (2) to more efficiently navigate the entrepreneurship process by gaining access to benefits (e.g., credit, property rights, training) from formal institutions for which informal institutions cannot act as an efficient substitute.

While both efficiency and legitimacy motivations may be present at the same time, the research literature is unclear concerning which motivation dominates the entrepreneur's registration decision and under what conditions. This literature suggests that entrepreneurs operating in informal institutional environments that are characterized by formal institutional voids (e.g., lack of property rights, access to credit, public infrastructure) (Webb, Ireland, & Ketchen, 2014) may seek to register their businesses in order to more efficiently navigate the entrepreneurship process independent of their concern for legitimacy and pressures from formal institutions. However, despite ample empirical findings that support a relationship between motivation and efficient behavior, little is known about this relationship in the context of the informal economy and lesser-developed institutional contexts (e.g., the base of the pyramid). To date, policymakers and the popular press have often conceptualized entrepreneurs at the base of the pyramid as a homogenous group of necessity-driven entrepreneurs that start businesses due to no other employment opportunities. Consequently, little is known about the heterogeneous motivations of entrepreneurs at the base of the pyramid and their relationship to business registration. Scholars working within the base of the pyramid context have long recognized the diverse nature and motivations of entrepreneurs at the base of the pyramid; however, there has been little research that has examined how such variation in motivations leads to the transition out of the informal economy through business registration.

The current paper follows prior research in conceptualizing an entrepreneur's start-up motivation by distinguishing between push and pull factors for starting a business (Kirkwood, 2009; Schjoedt & Shaver, 2007). Prior research has primarily used this categorization as an antecedent to specific entrepreneurial behavior and/or performance outcomes (Amit & Muller, 1995; Shapero & Sokol, 1982). Push factors refer to the conflict between one's current and one's desired occupational status that may push an individual into starting a business when other alternatives to achieve an individual's desired outcomes are unavailable. Common examples of push factors include unemployment and dissatisfaction with current employment. However, pull factors refer to the entrepreneur's expectation of potential rewards and being better off by starting a business. Examples of pull factors include autonomy, independence, money, need for control, and social status (Bhola, Verheul, Thurik, & Grilo, 2006; Uhlaner & Thurik, 2007).

Other research studies have built upon the distinction between push and pull factors to create similar constructs to measure an entrepreneur's motivation. Noteworthy is the distinction between necessity and opportunity-driven entrepreneurship recently advanced by the *Global Entrepreneurship Monitor* (GEM) (Reynolds, Camp, Bygrave, Autio, & Hay, 2001). Although, the nomenclature may differ, there is general consensus that necessity-driven entrepreneurs are considered to be motivated mainly by push factors, while pull factors form the basis of opportunity-driven entrepreneurs (Verheul, . Thurik, Hessels, & van der Zwan, 2010). The GEM survey has been utilized to examine the impact of an entrepreneur's start-up motivations on the level and type of entrepreneurial activity across nations. However, a significant limitation of comparative studies that have considered motivation as an antecedent to entrepreneurial behavior is the disregard of the registration status of the entrepreneur. Current estimates suggest that informal activity represents between 40%–60% of GDP in many emerging economies (Schneider, 2002, 2005). Therefore, our current understanding of differences between registered and unregistered entrepreneurs and their economic and social implications remains limited.

While differences in motivations between registered and unregistered entrepreneurs remains understudied, research has shown that push and pull motivations for starting a business tend to influence how entrepreneurs navigate the entrepreneurship process (Shane et al., 2003). For example, entrepreneurs motivated by pull factors tend to be financially more successful than entrepreneurs motivated by push factors (Amit & Muller, 1995). Other studies show that pull factors are associated with an entrepreneur's growth ambitions, risk tolerance, confidence to overcome obstacles, and a lower fear of failure compared to entrepreneurs driven by push factors (Bhola et al., 2006; Morris, Miyasaki, Watters, & Coombes, 2006). In sum, motivation theory suggests that entrepreneurs driven by pull factors are more likely to seek productivity and efficiency gains compared to entrepreneurs driven by push factors. As registration provides entrepreneurs with better access to benefits from formal institutions, entrepreneurs driven by pull factors are expected to be more likely to register.

Proposition 1: *Entrepreneurs driven by pull factors are positively associated with the likelihood of registration.*

Following this rationale, motivation theory suggests that entrepreneurs driven by pull factors may be more strongly associated with efficiency concerns rather than with acquiring legitimacy. However, entrepreneurs driven by push factors may be more strongly associated with legitimacy concerns as they seek to gain more respect, trust, and inclusion with customers and government agencies within the formal institutional environment without the intent to enhance the efficiency of their business.

> **Proposition 2**: *Entrepreneurs driven by pull factors are more strongly associated with efficiency concerns rather than legitimacy concerns obtained through registration.*
>
> **Proposition 3**: *Entrepreneurs driven by push factors are more strongly associated with legitimacy concerns rather than efficiency concerns obtained through registration.*

Human Capital

Entrepreneurship research also shows that an entrepreneur's level of human capital may be a key indicator of the entrepreneur's ability to success-fully identify, evaluate, and exploit entrepreneurial opportunities (Baum, Locke, & Smith, 2001; Chandler & Hanks, 1994). Human capital refers to "the skills and knowledge that individuals acquire through investment in schooling, on-the-job training, and other types of experience" (Unger, Rauch, Frese, & Rosenbusch, 2011: 343). Human capital theory (e.g., Becker, 1962, 1964; Schultz, 1961) suggests that entrepreneurs who have a greater stock of knowledge will have greater cognitive ability, which will lead to more productive and efficient activity (Block & Sandner, 2009). Hence, individuals with more knowledge or with a higher quality stock of knowledge are posited to be better at perceiving and exploiting entrepre-neurial opportunities than are individuals with less human capital (Davids-son & Honig, 2003; Shane, 2000). Unger et al.'s (2011) meta-analysis finds empirical support to further corroborate the positive relationship between human capital and entrepreneurial performance.

In the context of less developed institutional settings, human capital also plays a key role in sense making. Entrepreneurs in such settings deal with various sources of institutional ambiguity between legal rules and enforce-ment capabilities by government agencies and informal institutions that act as substitutes (Webb et al., 2013). As entrepreneurs seek to more effectively navigate the entrepreneurship process, they will become more aware of insti-tutional pluralism and competing pressures between formal and informal institutions (De Castro et al., 2014). Higher levels of human capital have also been shown to lead to greater willingness to engage with surround-ings, to search for new products or vendors, and transact with unfamiliar exchange partners (Kintgen, Kroll, & Rose, 1988; London, Esper, Grogan-Kaylor, & Kistruck, 2014; Rosa & Viswanathan, 2007). Thus, higher lev-els of human capital suggest that entrepreneurs in less developed contexts will have greater capacity to understand formal institutions and registration requirements.

While the concept of human capital is multi-dimensional in nature, the current paper focuses on the entrepreneur's education level as a key measure of productivity-enhancing human capital, which has been shown to be positively related to entrepreneurial performance (Murphy, Shleifer, & Vishny, 1991). Given that higher levels of education have been shown to be associated with more productive and efficient activity as well as sense making of the institutional environment, entrepreneurs with higher levels of education are expected to be more likely to register.

Proposition 4: As the entrepreneur's level of education increases, the entrepreneur is more likely to register.

Institutions and Entrepreneurship

In order for entrepreneurs to survive and thrive in their social environment they must obtain social acceptability and credibility (Scott, Ruef, Mendel, & Caronna, 2000). Scholars refer to these conditions by employing the concept of legitimacy (Scott, 2008). Legitimacy "is a generalized perception or assumption that the actions of an entity are desirable, proper, or appropriate within some socially constructed system of norms, values, beliefs, and definitions" (Suchman, 1995: 574). From an institutional perspective, legitimacy is not a commodity but rather "a condition reflecting perceived consonance with relevant rules and laws, normative support, or alignment with cultural-cognitive frameworks" (Scott, 2008: 59–60).

The entrepreneur's concern for obtaining legitimacy from others can rest among a variety of groups that can range from the broader society to smaller groups that share a collective identity (Bruton, Ireland, & Ketchen, 2012). The central tenet of recent management research that explains the rise and persistence of the informal economy is the concept of legitimacy and the institutions that confer it. This concept is articulated by the recently advocated definition of the informal economy as "economic activities that are outside of formal institutional boundaries (i.e., illegal) yet fall within informal institutional boundaries (i.e., legitimate)" (Webb et al., 2014: 3). Notably, this definition of the informal economy marks a clear distinction between formal and informal institutions, which is a defining feature of the institutional perspective.

Godfrey (2011) maintains that the informal economy is highly influenced by the entrepreneurs' interactions with and perceptions of formal institutions. As unregistered entrepreneurs interact with registered firms and other formal institutions, there may be increased pressure for the unregistered entrepreneur to conform to formal institutions by registering (DiMaggio & Powell, 1983; Meyer & Rowan, 1977; Scott, 1995; Webb et al., 2009). An unregistered entrepreneur who is detected by formal institutions has the potential to be delegitimized and shut down (Webb et al., 2013). As a consequence, the decisions regarding where to locate the business, with whom to interact, and the type of entrepreneurial opportunity the entrepreneur pursues have important strategic implications for the unregistered entrepreneur.

The likelihood of government detection may be influenced by how close and accessible the business is to formal institutions. Unregistered entrepreneurs operating their businesses within their own homes or outside of the home without a physical store-front (e.g., door-to-door salesman or street vendor) may limit their detection and pressure to comply with formal institutions; however, it may also reduce their ability to efficiently exploit entrepreneurial opportunities and grow their businesses. For example, entrepreneurs operating in the home may have limited ability to openly market their product and services and instead must rely more heavily upon word-of-mouth marketing (McPherson & Liedholm, 1996).

The likelihood of registration depends not only on the entrepreneur's physical location but also on whether or not the entrepreneur crosses into more formal institutional environments. Base of the pyramid markets are often clearly distinguishable from formal institutional environments. As unregistered entrepreneurs rely on clients and suppliers that operate in a more formal institutional environment, the unregistered entrepreneur may experience greater pressure to formally adopt business practices that are consistent with their clients and suppliers in order to obtain legitimacy (DiMaggio & Powell, 1983; Webb et al., 2009). Additionally, unregistered entrepreneurs venturing into more formal institutional environments may have greater interaction with or visibility by formal institutions than unregistered entrepreneurs that do not interact with clients or suppliers outside of their informal institutional environment. Hence, unregistered entrepreneurs who are more visible to formal institutions or cross institutional boundaries will be more likely to register their businesses in order to obtain legitimacy and to stay in operation as they may experience greater pressure to adhere to a different set of institutionalized rules and norms.

> *Proposition 5*: *Entrepreneurs operating within an informal institutional environment who are more visible to formal institutions are more likely to register.*
>
> *Proposition 6*: *Entrepreneurs who cross from informal institutional environments to more formal institutional environments to buy or sell goods and services are more likely to register.*

While we expect the relationship between crossing institutional boundaries and registration to be positive for entrepreneurs who either buy or sell goods and services, we suggest that interacting with suppliers (buying) may have a stronger positive association with registration than by interacting with clients (selling) because transactional hazards can be especially high with suppliers relative to those associated with clients. In the case of the base of the pyramid, where specialized assets may be low and transactions are generally small, carried out in cash, and occur more frequently, switching costs associated with changing suppliers may still be relatively high as unregistered entrepreneurs are resource constrained and may have neither sufficient capital nor ability to rely on formal institutions to rectify transactional disputes. Because the informal economy relies heavily on trust between exchange partners to overcome formal institutional voids and is supported by social networks that consider illegal activity legitimate, the costs of searching for and switching to a new network may be costly (Lyon, 2000; Rivera-Santos & Rufin, 2010; Webb et al., 2009). Such costs may be particularly relevant in the case of the base of the pyramid as transactions occur more frequently, and research has shown that repeated transactions lead to greater embeddedness within social networks (Uzzi, 1996).

As unregistered entrepreneurs seek to reduce transaction costs due to the high costs associated with the small size and frequency of transactions and lack of scale economies, unregistered entrepreneurs may seek to deepen their relationship (e.g., establishing credit) with a few suppliers. In other cases, only a few suppliers may be willing to work with unregistered entrepreneurs. Consequently, unregistered entrepreneurs may subject themselves to the costs associated with small-numbers bargaining, leading to strategic vulnerability as the supplier can engage in opportunistic pricing and other opportunistic behavior. While transactions that occur outside of government oversight can often be classified as pure market exchanges, the specifics of the transaction are largely governed by the firms with the stronger bargaining position of the two firms, which tends to be the registered firm if the transaction occurs between a registered and non-registered firm (Chen, 2007). This phenomenon places unregistered entrepreneurs at a significant disadvantage and subjects them to substantial transaction cost hazards, which may take the form of enforcement, monitoring, negotiation and searching costs to correct a transaction with suppliers that did not comply with ex-ante or ex-post expectations (Kistruck, Beamish, Qureshi, & Sutter, 2013). Taken together, one may expect this phenomenon to be amplified as entrepreneurs seek suppliers in more formal institutional environments as there may be fewer suppliers willing to establish a relationship with an unregistered entrepreneur.

Proposition 7: *The positive effect of crossing from informal institutional environments to more formal institutional environments on registration will be greater for entrepreneurs who buy rather than sell goods and services.*

Family Business

In addition to the entrepreneur's interaction with formal institutional environments and personal attributes of the entrepreneur, family ownership may be a salient predictor of registration. Recent management research posits that the informal economy is supported by groups of individuals sharing a collective identity upon which the entrepreneur can derive support and access to resources (Webb et al., 2009). One way in which entrepreneurs can benefit from such groups is to operate as a family business. Family business is a common ownership structure in the informal economy. However, it is difficult to define a family business operating in the informal economy based on legal ownership agreements, as is generally done in family business research in the formal economy (Khavul, Bruton, & Wood, 2009). In this research, a family business is defined as a business that is owned solely by family members or, in the case where there is only one owner, the owner employs family members and considers the firm to be a family business.

In the family-business literature, studies submit that family businesses have characteristics that differentiate them from non-family businesses and that such differences allow family businesses to accrue specific advantages compared to non-family businesses (Astrachan, 2010; Habbershon & Williams, 1999; Moores, 2009). For example, family businesses have the advantage of implicit contracting that can be enforced through informal control mechanisms such as creating a culture of compliance or clan-like behavior to reduce agency and monitoring costs (Daily & Dollinger, 1991; Kotey, 2005; Schulze, Lubatkin, Dino, & Buchholtz, 2001). Other research studies show that family businesses tend to have a longer term orientation as family business owners are particularly interested in the collective welfare of family members and the stability and longevity of the business so that the business can benefit future generations (Le Breton-Miller & Miller, 2006; Miller & Le Breton-Miller, 2006; Roberts, 1994). Collectively, these advantages often lead to higher levels of trust within family businesses compared to non-family businesses (Zahra, Hayton, & Salvato, 2004).

The extant research on family business suggests that the distinguishing features of family businesses have an important influence on how family businesses navigate the entrepreneurship process. For example, studies show that family businesses exhibit lower risk propensities, which leads to lower use of high-growth strategies and entrepreneurial orientation (Dertouzos, Lester, & Solow, 1989; Naldi, Nordqvist, Sjoberg, & Wiklund, 2007). Other studies have shown that family businesses differ in their resource accumulation strategies. In the context of the informal economy in Africa, Khavul et al. (2009) found that unregistered family businesses rely more heavily upon family resources to fund their businesses, therefore requiring less dependence on outside forms of capital. Similarly, Dyer and Mortenson (2005) found that family businesses operating in a hostile economic environment in Lithuania were more successful than non-family businesses due to their ability to draw on family resources, including both human and financial capital. These findings indicate that access to family resources may increase the family business's ability to survive and compete, particularly in institutional environments that lack well-functioning formal institutions (Sirmon & Hitt, 2003). Thus, family businesses are expected to be less likely to register compared to non-family businesses as family businesses tend to rely less on formal institutions as a control mechanism and have greater access to alternative resources in informal institutional environments. As a result, family businesses may be less likely to seek the benefits that formal institutions offer through registration compared to non-family businesses.

> **Proposition 8**: *Family businesses are negatively associated with the likelihood of registration.*

DISCUSSION

The purpose of this paper is to examine the relationship between the individual attributes and strategic behavior of entrepreneurs with registration in the context of the base of the pyramid. A summary of our propositions are presented in Table 6.1.

Entrepreneurs operating in competing formal and informal institutions environments face competing values, norms, and beliefs about registration, and we suggest that their response to such competing pressures can be partially explained by their individual attributes and strategic behavior. The complex nature of the interaction between registered and unregistered entrepreneurs and institutional environments provides ample opportunities

Table 6.1   Summary of Propositions

Proposition 1:	*Entrepreneurs driven by pull factors are positively associated with the likelihood of registration.*
Proposition 2:	*Entrepreneurs driven by pull factors are more strongly associated with efficiency concerns rather than legitimacy concerns obtained through registration.*
Proposition 3:	*Entrepreneurs driven by push factors are more strongly associated with legitimacy concerns rather than efficiency concerns obtained through registration.*
Proposition 4:	*As the entrepreneur's level of education increases, the entrepreneur is more likely to register.*
Proposition 5:	*Entrepreneurs operating within an informal institutional environment who are more visible to formal institutions are more likely to register.*
Proposition 6:	*Entrepreneurs who cross from informal institutional environments to more formal institutional environments to buy or sell goods and services are more likely to register.*
Proposition 7:	*The positive effect of crossing from informal institutional environments to more formal institutional environments on registration will be greater for entrepreneurs who buy rather than sell goods and services.*
Proposition 8:	*Family businesses are negatively associated with the likelihood of registration.*

for management scholars to further examine competing pressures from both formal and informal institutions (North, 1990; Scott, 1995) and to employ other theoretical lenses beyond institutional theory to examine the rise of the informal economy and an entrepreneur's transition out of it (Ketchen, Ireland, & Webb, 2014). Other theoretical perspectives that focus on the relationship between exchange partners and the nature of transactions (e.g., property rights theory, the resource-based approach, resource dependence theory, and transaction cost economics) may be informative lenses to explain the informal economy that to date have received little attention in informal economy research (Ostrom, 1990; Penrose, 1959; Pfeffer & Salancik, 1978; Williamson, 1985). Several research studies (Bruton, Khavul, & Chavez, 2011; Chen, 2007; De Castro et al., 2014) point out that unregistered entrepreneurs interact often with registered businesses as unregistered entrepreneurs often rely on and even provide registered businesses with raw materials and finished goods. This phenomenon suggests the need for more management research to understand how registered and unregistered businesses interact throughout their value chains and the nature of their transactions.

The current paper also calls for greater attention to the heterogeneous nature of start-up motivations and strategies in less developed contexts such as the base of the pyramid. The extant entrepreneurship literature on motivation suggests that push- and pull-driven entrepreneurs differ significantly in their ability to navigate the entrepreneurship process. The distinction between different motivations and their impact on the entrepreneurship process has not been adequately addressed in the context of the base of the pyramid or the informal economy and merits further examination. Future research studies may consider the heterogeneity of start-up motivations and types of entrepreneurs (e.g., subsistence versus transformative) within the base of the pyramid and examine their effects on the different stages of the entrepreneurship process and the transition out of the informal economy through registration. The current paper suggests that entrepreneurs are driven by two overarching motivations to register: (1) the need to obtain legitimacy and other intangible benefits (e.g., trust, reputation), and (2) to more efficiently navigate the entrepreneurship process by gaining access to tangible benefits (e.g., credit, property rights, training, etc.) from formal institutions for which informal institutions cannot act as an efficient substitute. We posit that these two overarching motivations to register may be associated with the push and pull factors for starting a business. Future research may consider whether the relationship between motives and registration is moderated by other factors such as institutional context (e.g., economic, political, social, cultural) and the interaction with and perceptions of government agencies that enforce regulations.

Another promising avenue for future research is to examine the ownership structure and agency issues of businesses in the informal economy and their influence on the entrepreneurship process and the likelihood of registration. While unregistered entrepreneurs are often self-employed, many unregistered businesses have multiple owners and employees (Bruton et al., 2012). However, little is known about how differences in ownership structure affect the entrepreneurship process and registration in the context of the informal economy. Family businesses are a common form of business in the informal economy, yet little is known about how family businesses differ from other businesses in informal institutional environments and if unregistered family businesses obtain similar benefits as those that are registered. Further, examining the ownership structure (e.g., family, non-family, mixed-family, partnerships), and how it influences each stage of the entrepreneurship process and the decision to register, will provide new insight into the motivations and underpinning mechanisms that sustain informal activity.

The focus of the current paper has been on identifying factors that influence the likelihood of registration. As noted by Godfrey (2011), the informal economy may be better conceptualized as residing on a continuum rather than being strictly dichotomous as either registered or unregistered, because unregistered entrepreneurs often comply with other legal requirements. Other common examples of informal activity may include the use of undocumented workers, off the books transactions, not paying taxes, skirting regulations (e.g., environmental), and infringing property rights. While we do not generate formal propositions on the relationship between other activities in the informal economy, the factors examined in the current study may also influence the decision to engage in other informal activity and may have a different directional effect. For example, in the current paper it is posited that pull factors will be positively associated with registration. However, pull factors may be negatively associated with other compliance requirements that entrepreneurs consider to be inefficient or unimportant. Many regulations are not as easily detectable as registration, and compliance with such regulations may also be highly associated with the entrepreneur's motivation.

From a policy perspective, several of the issues we raise are of relevance to policy makers, private agencies, and not-for-profits interested in the informal economy and the base of the pyramid. Unfortunately, access to quality education in informal institutional environments such as urban slums is limited. Because previous research indicates that higher levels of education lead to more productive and efficient behavior, education policy should be explicitly linked to entrepreneurship policy. In many cases, not-for-profit organizations and social entrepreneurs have made concerted efforts to fill this institutional void by providing entrepreneurship education, training services, and microfinance to underserved populations. This phenomenon is gaining importance in management research and to policymakers, yet much research remains to be done in order to understand the effectiveness of such organizations as substitutes for government agencies and programs.

Also of interest to policymakers is that there appears to be a relationship between industry and registration. For example, industries such as domestic services, seamstress services, confectionaries, and other basic service industries tend to not register compared to businesses in retail and more professional services (Skousen, 2014). These findings suggest that entrepreneurs that exploit entrepreneurial opportunities in specific industries may be unable to generate enough resources to comply with the costs of registration or may be able to rely less on formal institutions. As such, policymakers should be aware of the diverse nature of businesses and adapt registration and entrepreneurship policy to be more inclusive in an effort to encourage entrepreneurs who are weighing the costs and benefits of registration to register their businesses.

The informal economy, in part, arises as formal institutions are unable to provide basic services such as infrastructure. The prominence of urban slums in many developing economies highlights this phenomenon. Urban slums are often characterized by a labyrinth of alleyways and side streets that hinder the mobility of individuals and economic activity. Entrepreneurs who have limited access to such streets are constrained in their ability to draw on resources that require transportation. This reality points toward the inherit connection between urban planning and entrepreneurship policy. This connection, however, has remained largely absent in entrepreneurship and policy research and provides an opportunity for management scholars to bridge this important research gap.

CONCLUSION

The current paper suggests that management research would benefit from not only examining how informal and formal institutions interact and the quality of formal institutions but also how a micro-level perspective on individual attributes and strategies inform our current macro- and meso-level theorizing on the informal economy. As the informal economy remains an understudied and misunderstood phenomenon, management scholars are well positioned to add value to this stream of research. In an effort to guide future research, the current paper outlines important research areas that need further development to understand the registration decision and how entrepreneurs manage the entrepreneurship process in the context of informal institutional environments at the base of the pyramid. Focusing on these topics will add new value to management research and assist policymakers in improving the standard of living of the four billion people that live in underserved conditions throughout the world.

REFERENCES

Amit, R., & Muller, E. 1995. Push and pull entrepreneurship. *Journal of Small Business and Entrepreneurship*, 12(4): 64–80.
Astrachan, J. H. 2010. Strategy in family business: Toward a multidimensional research agenda. *Journal of Family Business Strategy*, 1(1): 6–14.
Barney, J., & Felin, T. 2013. What are microfoundations? *Academy of Management Perspectives*, 27(2): 138–155.

Baum, R., Locke, E., & Smith, K. 2001. A multi-dimensional model of venture growth. *Academy of Management Journal*, 44(2): 292–303.

Becker, G. 1962. Investment in human capital: A theoretical analysis. *Journal of Political Economy*, 70(5): 9–49.

Becker, G. 1964. *Human capital*. New York: Columbia University Press.

Bhola, R., Verheul, I., Thurik, R., & Grilo, I. 2006. *Explaining engagement levels of opportunity and necessity entrepreneurs*. Zoetermeer, Netherlands: EIM Business Policy & Research.

Block, J., & Sandner, P. 2009. Necessity and opportunity entrepreneurs and their duration in self-employment: Evidence from German micro data. *Journal of Industry, Competition and Trade*, 9(2): 117–137.

Bruton, G. D. 2010. Business and the world's poorest billion—The need for an expanded examination by management scholars. *Academy of Management Perspectives*, 24(3): 6–10.

Bruton, G. D., Ireland, R. D., & Ketchen, D. J. 2012. Toward a research agenda on the informal economy. *Academy of Management Perspectives*, 26(3): 1–11.

Bruton, G. D., Khavul, S., & Chavez, H. 2011. Microlending in emerging economies: Building a new line of inquiry from the ground up. *Journal of International Business Studies*, 42(5): 718–739.

Chandler, G. N., & Hanks, S. 1994. Founder competence, the environment, and venture performance. *Entrepreneurship Theory & Practice*, 18(3): 77–90.

Chen, M. A. 2007. *Rethinking the informal economy: Linkages with the formal economy and the formal regulatory environment*. DESA Working Paper No. 46. New York: United Nations.

Daily, C. M., & Dollinger, M. J. 1991. Family firms are different. *Review of Business*, 13(1): 3–5.

Davidsson, P., & Honig, B. 2003. The role of social and human capital among nascent entrepreneurs. *Journal of Business Venturing*, 18(3): 301–331.

Davis, M. 2006. *Planet of slums*. London: Verso.

De Castro, J. O., Khavul, S., & Bruton, G. D. 2014. Shades of grey: How do informal firms navigate between macro and meso institutional environments? *Strategic Entrepreneurship Journal*, 8(1): 75–94.

De Mel, S., McKenzie, D., & Woodruff, C. 2013. The demand for, and consequences of, formalization among informal firms in Sri Lanka. *American Economic Journal: Applied Economics*, 5(2): 122–150.

Dertouzos, M. L., Lester, R. K., & Solow, R. M. 1989. *Made in America: Regaining the productive edge*. Cambridge, UK: MIT Press.

De Soto, H. 1989. *The other path: The invisible revolution in the third world*. New York: Harper and Row.

De Soto, H. 2000. *The mystery of capital*. New York: Basic Books.

DiMaggio, P. J., & Powell, W. W. 1983. The iron cage revisited: Institutional isomorphism and collective rationality in organizational fields. *American Sociological Review*, 48(2): 147–160.

Dyer, W. G., & Mortenson, S. P. 2005. Entrepreneurship and family business in a hostile environment: The case of Lithuania. *Family Business Review*, 18(3): 247–258.

Godfrey, P. A. 2011. Toward a theory of the informal economy. *Academy of Management Annals*, 5(1): 231–277.

Habbershon, T. G., & Williams, M. L. 1999. A resource-based framework for assessing the strategic advantages of family firms. *Family Business Review*, 12(1): 1–26.

Ketchen, D. J., Ireland, R. D., & Webb, J. W. 2014. Toward a research agenda for the informal economy: A survey of the strategic entrepreneurship journal's editorial board. *Strategic Entrepreneurship Journal*, 8(1): 95–100.

Khavul, S., Bruton, G. D., & Wood, E. 2009. Informal family business in Africa. *Entrepreneurship Theory & Practice*, 33(6): 1219–1238.

Kintgen, E. R., Kroll, B. M., & Rose, M. 1988. *Perspectives on literacy*. Carbondale, IL: Southern Illinois University Press.

Kirkwood, J. 2009. Motivational factors in a push-pull theory of entrepreneurship. *Gender in Management: An International Journal*, 24(5): 346–364.

Kistruck, G. M., Beamish, P. W., Qureshi, I., & Sutter, C. J. 2013. Social intermediation in base-of-the-pyramid markets. *Journal of Management Studies*, 50(1): 31–66.

Kotey, B. 2005. Goals, management practices, and performance of family SMEs. *International Journal of Entrepreneurial Behaviour & Research*, 11(1): 3–24.

Le Breton-Miller, I., & Miller, D. 2006. Why do some family businesses out-compete? Governance, long-term orientations, and sustainable capability. *Entrepreneurship: Theory & Practice*, 30(6): 731–746.

London, T., Esper, H., Grogan-Kaylor, A., & Kistruck, G. M. 2014. Connecting poverty to purchase in informal markets. *Strategic Entrepreneurship Journal*, 8(1): 37–55.

London T., & Hart, S. L. 2011. *Next generation business strategies for the base of the pyramid*. Upper Saddle River, NJ: FT Press.

Lyon, F. 2000. Trust, networks and norms: The creation of social capital in agricultural economies in Ghana. *World Development*, 28(4): 663–681.

Marcouiller, D., & Young, L. 1995. The black hole of graft: The predatory state and the informal economy. *American Economic Review*, 85(3): 630–646.

McGahan, A. 2012. Challenges of the informal economy for the field of management. *Academy of Management Perspectives*, 26(3): 12–21.

McPherson, M. A., & Liedholm, C. 1996. Determinants of small and micro enterprise registration: Results from surveys in Niger and Swaziland. *World Development*, 24(3): 481–487.

Meyer, J. W., & Rowan, B. 1977. Institutionalized organizations: Formal structure as myth and ceremony. *American Journal of Sociology*, 83(2): 340–363.

Miller, D., & Le Breton-Miller, I. 2006. Family governance and firm performance: Agency, stewardship, and capabilities. *Family Business Review*, 19(1): 73–87.

Moores, K. 2009. Paradigms and theory building in the domain of business families. *Family Business Review*, 22(2): 167–180.

Morris, M. H., Miyasaki, N. N., Watters, C. E., & Coombes, S. M. 2006. The dilemma of growth: Understanding venture size choices of women entrepreneurs. *Journal of Small Business Management*, 44(2): 221–244.

Murphy, K. M., Shleifer, A., & Vishny, R. W. 1991. The allocation of talent: Implications for growth. *Quarterly Journal of Economics*, 106(2): 503–530.

Naldi, L., Nordqvist, M., Sjoberg, K., & Wiklund, J. 2007. Entrepreneurial orientation, risk taking, and performance in family firms. *Family Business Review*, 20(1): 33–47.

Nichter, S., & Goldmark, L. 2009. Small firm growth in developing countries. *World Development*, 37(9): 1453–1464.

North, D. C. 1990. *Institutions, institutional change and economic performance*. New York: Cambridge University Press.

Nwabuzor, A. 2005. Corruption and development: New initiatives in economic openness and strengthened rule of law. *Journal of Business Ethics*, 59(1): 121–138.

Ostrom, E. 1990. *Governing the commons: The evolution of institutions for collective action*. Cambridge, MA: Cambridge University Press.

Penrose, E. T. 1959. *The theory of the growth of the firm*. New York: John Wiley & Sons.

Pfeffer, J., & Salancik, G. R. 1978. *The external control of organizations: A resource dependence perspective*. Stanford, CA: Stanford University Press.

Prahalad, C. K. 2005. *The fortune at the bottom of the pyramid.* Philadelphia, PA: Wharton School.

Reynolds, P. D., Camp, S. M., Bygrave, W. D., Autio, E., & Hay, M. 2001. *Global entrepreneurship monitor 2001 executive report.* Kansas City, MO: Kauffman Foundation.

Rivera-Santos, M., & Rufin, C. 2010. Global village vs. small town: Understanding networks at the base of the pyramid. *International Business Review,* 19(2): 126–139.

Roberts, B. 1994. Informal economy and family strategies. *International Journal of Urban and Regional Research,* 18(1): 6–23.

Rosa, J. A., & Viswanathan M. 2007. *Product and market development for subsistence marketplaces.* Oxford, UK: Elsevier.

Schjoedt, L., & Shaver, K. G. 2007. Deciding on an entrepreneurial career: A test of the pull and push hypotheses using the panel study of entrepreneurial dynamics data. *Entrepreneurship Theory & Practice,* 31(5): 733–752.

Schneider, F. 2002. *The shadow economy: An international survey.* New York: Cambridge University Press.

Schneider, F. 2005. Getting beyond the training vs. work experience debate: The role of labor markets, social capital, cultural capital, and community resources in long-term poverty. *Journal of Women, Politics and Policy,* 27(3): 41–53.

Schultz, T. W. 1961. Investment in human capital. *American Economic Review,* 51(1): 1–17.

Schulze, W. S., Lubatkin, M. H., Dino, R. N., & Buchholtz, A. K. 2001. Agency relationships in family firms: Theory and evidence. *Organization Science,* 12(2): 99–116.

Scott, W. R. 1995. *Institutions and organizations.* Newbury Park, CA: Sage Publications.

Scott, W. R. 2008. *Institutions and organizations: Ideas and interests.* Thousand Oaks, CA: Sage Publications.

Scott, W. R., Ruef, M., Mendel, P. J., & Caronna, C. A. 2000. *Institutional change and healthcare organizations: From professional dominance to managed care.* Chicago: University of Chicago Press.

Shane, S. 2000. Prior knowledge and the discovery of entrepreneurial opportunities. *Organization Science,* 11(4): 448–469.

Shane, S., Locke, E. A., & Collins, C. C. 2003. Entrepreneurial motivation. *Human Resource Management Review,* 13(2): 257–279.

Shapero, A., & Sokol, L. 1982. The social dimensions of entrepreneurship. In C. Kent, D. Sexton & K. Vesper (Eds.), *Encyclopedia of entrepreneurship*: 72–90. Englewood Cliffs, NJ: Prentice-Hall.

Sine, W. D., & David, R. J. 2010. Institutions and entrepreneurship. In W. D. Sine, R. J. David (Eds.), *Institutions and entrepreneurship: Research in the sociology of work*: (21):1–26. Bingley, UK: Emerald Group Publishing Limited.

Sirmon, D. G., & Hitt, M. A. 2003. Managing resources: Linking unique resources, management, and wealth creation in family firms. *Entrepreneurship Theory & Practice,* 27(4): 339–258.

Skousen, B. R. 2014. *The informal economy: Predicting an entrepreneur's decision to legally register.* Champaign, IL: Dissertation proposal, University of Illinois at Urbana-Champaign.

Suchman, M. C. 1995. Managing legitimacy: Strategic and institutional approaches. *Academy of Management Review,* 20(3): 571–610.

Thomas, A. S., & Mueller, S. L. 2000. A case for comparative entrepreneurship: Assessing the relevance of culture. *Journal of International Business Studies,* 31(2): 287–301.

Uhlaner, L. M., & Thurik, A. R. 2007. Post-materialism: A cultural factor influencing total entrepreneurial activity across nations. *Journal of Evolutionary Economics*, 17(2): 161–185.

Unger, J. M., Rauch, A., Frese, M., & Rosenbusch, N. 2011. Human capital and entrepreneurial success: A meta-analytical review. *Journal of Business Venturing*, 26(3): 341–358.

UN-Habitat. 2003. *Slums of the world: The face of urban poverty in the new millennium?* Working Paper. Nairobi, Kenya: United Nations Human Settlements Programme.

Uzzi, B. 1996. The sources and consequences of embeddedness for the economic performance of organizations: The network effect. *American Sociological Review*, 61(4): 674–689.

Verheul, I., Thurik, R., Hessels, J., & van der Zwan, P. 2010. *Factors influencing the entrepreneurial engagement of opportunity and necessity entrepreneurs.* EIM Research Report, March.

Webb, J. W., Bruton, G. B., Tihanyi, L., & Ireland R. D. 2013. Research on entrepreneurship in the informal economy: Framing a research agenda. *Journal of Business Venturing*, 28(5): 598–614.

Webb, J. W., Ireland, D., & Ketchen, D. J. 2014. Toward a greater understanding of entrepreneurship and strategy in the informal economy. *Strategic Entrepreneurship Journal*, 8(1): 1–15.

Webb, J. W., Tihanyi, L., Ireland, R. D., & Sirmon, D. G. 2009. You say illegal, I say legitimate: Entrepreneurship in the informal economy. *Academy of Management Review*, 34(3): 492–510.

Williams, C. C., & Nadin, S. 2010. Entrepreneurship and the informal economy: An overview. *Journal of Developmental Entrepreneurship*, 15(4): 361–378.

Williamson, O. E. 1985. *The economic institutions of capitalism: Firms, markets, relational contracting.* New York: Free Press.

World Resources Institute. 2007. *The next 4 billion: Market size and business strategy at the base of the pyramid.* Washington, DC: World Resources Institute and International Finance Corporation.

Zahra, S. A., Hayton, J. C., & Salvato, C. 2004. Entrepreneurship in family vs. non-family firms: A resource-based analysis of the effect of organizational culture. *Entrepreneurship Theory & Practice*, 28(4): 363–381.

Part II
Empirical Research in the Informal Economy

7 Healthcare in the Informal Economy

John Ginther and Anita M. McGahan

Many nations struggle to establish health systems that adequately meet the needs of all citizens, and especially the poor. Informal healthcare providers emerge to address gaps in formalized healthcare offerings and often persist when formal systems continue to fail. Thus, the informal healthcare sector is large in many nations. Despite its importance and prevalence, research on the informal healthcare sector remains ill-developed. An accurate account of the nature and extent of informal health practices does not yet exist but is urgently needed as a prerequisite to good investment choices, managerial control, and health assessments. In this chapter, we seek to advance research on this topic. The goal is to elucidate several important issues that arise regarding healthcare in the informal economy: the range in quality, the health implications of non-registration, and the role of the informal economy in promoting healthcare innovation.

This study makes three contributions. First, we argue that the current definition of the informal economy does not fully capture the phenomenon of informality in the healthcare sector. We suggest an alternative that may also be applicable in other sectors. Second, we offer evidence from three case studies to explore the phenomenon of informality in the healthcare sector. Third, we introduce and develop the idea that informality may run on a spectrum rather than be dichotomous and, as such, gives rise to semi-formal providers. Lastly, we conclude by framing questions for further research.

DEFINING, SIZING, AND SCOPING THE INFORMAL HEALTHCARE ECONOMY

Assessing the size and scope of the informal healthcare economy requires defining its boundaries so as to identify the players involved in its delivery (Bruton, 2010; Bruton, Ireland, & Ketchen, 2012; McGahan, 2012). The "informal economy" has been broadly defined as encompassing business activities that are unregistered but otherwise considered legal (Godfrey, 2011; Hart, 2006). Implementing this definition in healthcare is challenging as the range of relevant registrations for health providers is difficult to assess. Registering authorities may be corrupt, unavailable, or even non-existent. By some criteria, the quality of care offered by informal providers may exceed that of formal ones. By others, the quality of care may be radically lower. Quackery is rampant. Unregistered health practitioners may engage in practices that are not strictly illegal but are harmful nonetheless. These difficulties are compounded by the inconsistencies in the literature in defining the appropriateness of various types of registration of informal providers.

Some progress has been made on developing an alternative definition of informality that describes the kinds of unregistered practices and practitioners that frequently arise in resource-limited settings, but which do not otherwise violate norms of health provision that are widely regarded as appropriate in resource-rich settings. An important study by Sudhinaraset, Ingram, Lofthouse, and Montagu (2013) reviewed 122 articles in the academic and non-academic literatures on healthcare informality in developing-market economies to identify the types of activities that occur in practice that meet this standard for informality. Commissioned by the Center for Health Market Innovations (CHMI), the study provides the most comprehensive profile of the current state of informal healthcare provision available today of which we are aware.

Sudhinaraset et al. (2013) seek to cultivate an understanding of informality from practice rather than to derive criteria for informality from theory. Their evidence points to four types of informality in the healthcare sector. These are:

1. *Lack of training.* Providers are not formally licensed, and may not have received formal training.
2. *Reliance on cash payments.* Providers require payment directly from patients (usually in cash) rather than through institutions such as governmental bodies or insurers.
3. *Absence of registration and/or regulation.* Providers are not registered or not required to register by governmental authorities when such registration is normally required by global practice.
4. *Absence of professional affiliation.* Providers do not belong to professional associations.

While a wide range of providers fall into these categories, Sudhinaraset et al. (2013) identified four groups that were prevalent in a large number of countries and settings that were classifiable as informal by several of the criteria outlined above:

1. *Drug sellers.* These include persons operating without or beyond their expertise, such as the selling of prescription drugs by retailers licensed to sell non-prescription drugs, the selling by pharmacists of counterfeit or non-regulated drugs, and the reselling by individuals of prescription drugs.

2. *Traditional birth attendants.* These include midwives and others involved in pre- and post-natal care as well as delivery.
3. *Village doctors and traditional healers.* These are people who provide health services without a license and/or formal training.
4. *Untrained community health workers (CHW).* These are unlicensed and/or untrained physician assistants, nurses, and/or attendants with responsibilities for implementing and/or following up on care as directed by a physician or person acting as a physician.

Little is known about the size of the informal healthcare sector either in resource-rich or resource-poor settings. The problem of the lack of clear criteria for identifying informal providers is compounded by the difficulty of applying the criteria, given that the lack of registration itself is consequentially illegal in many instances and thus drives informal providers into secrecy. Sudhinaraset et al. report on five studies estimating the relative size of the informal health sector as compared to the size of the entire health sector:

> [One] study found huge variations in the size of the informal provider sector (51% to 96%). . . In Bangladesh, researchers estimated that 87% of providers were informal, while in the rural region of Chakaria, 96% of all providers were informal. In India the informal sector was found to be between 51–55% of all providers. In Uganda, 77% of providers were found to be informal. (2013: 7)

Sudhinaraset et al. (2013) report that 9%-90% of citizens in countries under study use informal healthcare providers, with the breadth of the range attributed to, in part, the inconsistent methodologies applied in the 24 surveyed analysis. Despite the extent of the range in estimates, the studies suggest that informal providers are important as patients seek assistance. Reliance on informal health providers is especially common among low-income patients that perceive their health issues as not severe (Ahmed, Hossain, & Chowdhury, 2009; Kapoor, Raman, Sachdeva, & Satyanarayana, 2012).

The relative size and geographic base of each group of informal practitioners vary widely. For example, in Bangladesh, where most healthcare practitioners are classified as informal providers, Ahmed et al. (2009) assessed the relative prevalence of each type of informal provider and found that drug sellers comprise 8% of providers, traditional birth attendants 22%, and village doctors, traditional healers, and homeopaths 56%. Qualified allopathic professionals (physicians, nurses, and dentists) service about 5% of patients, and semi-qualified providers, including CHWs, treat about 8%; the remaining 1% accounts for circumcision practitioners, ear cleaners, tooth extractors, and other types of providers. Qualified medical professionals tend to live in urban areas, with only 16% of physicians based rurally (Ahmed et al., 2009).

Information about informal providers is not evenly distributed. More than a third of the papers in the systematic review by Sudhinaraset et al. (2013) mentions drug sellers, while informal CHWs were mentioned in only five papers. Ahmed et al. (2009) suggests the coverage does not match the relative prevalence of providers, as only 8% of providers in Bangladesh are classified as drug sellers although the estimated absolute number of unlicensed drug sellers is large: 80,000. Moreover, a significant portion of healthcare expenditures occurs at drug dispensers in the country accounting for 70% of out-of-pocket healthcare expenses (Ahmed et al., 2009).

Informal healthcare providers emerge, thrive, and persist where formalized healthcare offerings inadequately meet patient needs (Bloom et al., 2011; Sudhinaraset et al., 2013). Their presence can extend access to services and medications to those otherwise unable to access formalized healthcare offerings. Sudhinaraset et al. (2013) reported three main reasons cited by patients for seeking care from informal providers: convenience, affordability, and social and cultural effects. Many public healthcare systems are overburdened, and informal private alternatives are often seen as offering care closer to their home, maintaining longer hours, and more likely to stock needed medications (Sudhinaraset et al., 2013). The closer geographic proximity is an important consideration among patients opting for informal healthcare. Lower transport costs are commonly cited as a driver for their decisions for pursuing informal providers (Sudhinaraset et al., 2013). Even when public facilities offer treatment for free or at low cost, the patient may incur costs, such as for transportation, that create a barrier to access. These ancillary costs coupled with the perceived irregularity of medication stocks and the shorter hours of operation mitigate the attractiveness of lower prices. (Sudhinaraset et al., 2013).

Familiarity with informal providers also plays a critical role in the decision to seek care. One study found that people sought care from an informal provider due to familiarity with service and a track record of care: "we always go to Dr XX (also called locally as Bengali doctor) and recover quickly from our illnesses. He is wise and always has lot of patients in his clinic" (Kapoor et al., 2012: 2). The seriousness of symptoms also contributes to the decision to opt for informal providers (Center for Pharmaceutical Management [CfPM], 2008). Informal providers tend to operate in a specific geographic location and on a smaller scale than their public counterparts, increasing their perceived accountability (Sudhinaraset et al., 2013).

QUALITY OF INFORMAL HEALTHCARE PROVIDERS: THE CASE OF MALARIA TREATMENT IN NIGERIA

Staggeringly, little information has been developed about the performance of informal healthcare providers despite their size and importance in many country health systems. The sparse anecdotal evidence that is available suggests that informal providers generally deliver poorer quality of care than formal practitioners.

In this section, we examine how the incidence of malaria has been influenced by informality. Major progress has been made toward the elimination of malaria since 2000; however, strains of artemisinin-resistant malaria pose a direct threat to that progress. Artemisinin is a medication used in the treatment of uncomplicated malaria, with artemisinin-combined therapies (ACTs) as the recommended treatment for uncomplicated malaria according to the World Health Organization. Resistance to ACTs threatens progress to reduce the incidence of malaria as no alternatives to ACTs are currently available (World Health Organization, 2011). Cases of artemisinin-resistant malaria have been confirmed in Southeast Asia, but there are concerns for the emergence of cases elsewhere. One article noted possible artemisinin resistance in three cases in Nigeria (Ajayi & Ukwaja, 2013).

Consider the role of informal drug sellers in the treatment of uncomplicated malaria. About half of Nigerians with suspected malaria visit drug sellers (Peters & Bloom, 2012). Drug dispensaries are a major, and often only, point of contact for patients that present with symptoms. Four conditions must be met for the appropriate treatment of malaria: knowledge of and adherence to treatment protocols, appropriate diagnosis and referrals, patient education about malaria and treatment options, and availability of affordable ACTs (Kamal-Yanni, Potet, & Saunders, 2012). Inappropriate diagnosis can lead to missed opportunities for treatment and unnecessary deaths.

Evidence suggests that drug sellers fall short of these standards (Koh, Hedge, & Karamchandani, 2014). Knowledge across the board in Nigeria among both formal and informal pharmacists is inadequate, with only one in two public providers, who are required to be formally licensed, able to identify the first-line treatment for uncomplicated malaria; however, this figure pales in comparison with informal drug sellers—only 1 in 10 gave the correct statement (Kamal-Yanni et al., 2012). Informal drug sellers in Nigeria are not alone in their lack of knowledge. One study in Vietnam found that only 36% drug dispensers provided treatment in line with national guidelines (Sudhinaraset et al., 2013). The Rollback Malaria Partnership noted that informal providers have a poor record in the use of rapid diagnostic tests (RDT), and even compliance with negative results (i.e., selling anti-malarials despite negative results) (World Health Organization, 2011). Thus, drug sellers create extensive health problems in the country.

The drivers of this underperformance are multifaceted. Most drug sellers have little or no formal training in diagnosis or dispensing medication (Ahmed et al., 2009). Nigeria shifted to the present ACT-based guidelines for the treatment of malaria in 2005 (Ezenduka, Ogbonna, Ekwunife, Okonta, & Esimone, 2014); however, informal providers were not exposed to the policy change (Bloom et al., 2011). A study found most drug sellers were unaware of the policy change altogether (Bloom et al., 2011). Without knowledge of the proper course of treatment, non-ACT regimes remain commonplace. Despite government guidelines, non-ACT treatment was used by 27% drug sellers in Nigeria (Ezenduka et al., 2014). The study by Ezenduka et al. (2014) reported that even when drug sellers are aware of the importance and appropriateness of ACTs, they lack the requisite knowledge to prescribe in appropriate dosing. One study found that diagnostic testing for malaria by private providers was less common than in public facilities, although the examination of practices in six countries revealed troubling results in both cases (Kamal-Yanni et al., 2012). Patients prescribed and/or sold suboptimal doses of anti-malarial regimens have an increased chance of developing resistance to those medications.

Consumer preference is another factor undermining the receipt of proper treatment. Patients expressed skepticism when the Nigerian government announced a guideline shift to ACTs, because of the higher prices associated with the new approach (Bloom et al., 2011). Consumer preference for specific medications that are cheaper but less effective can sometimes drive transactions despite provider knowledge (Kamal-Yanni et al., 2012), especially in settings where drug sellers compete with each other and with formally licensed providers (Ezenduka et al., 2014). Even when tests are administered to patients, and malaria is shown to be absent, consumers sometimes nonetheless seek to purchase anti-malarials (World Health Organization, 2011). This creates a conflict of interest whereby providers stock cheaper but less effective medications and sell drugs that are detrimental to patient health in the short run because of their side effects and in the long run because they contribute to the emergence of drug-resistant strains of malaria (Kamal-Yanni et al., 2012).

Drug sellers also gain a toehold when patients cannot access the medications required for treatment through the public system or other formal channels. In Nigeria, only 9% of a sample of public drug stores stocked the recommended ACT while the majority had non-recommended anti-malarials available, and a third of shops offered a drug that governmental policy had banned because of its suspected contribution to drug resistance (Bloom et al., 2011). Thus, patients seeking treatment were compelled to turn to the informal sector to obtain desired medicine.

The case of malaria treatment by drug sellers in Nigeria demonstrates some of the problems associated with informality in healthcare provision. They emerge due to perceived and real shortfalls in the formal healthcare system. The responsibility for ensuring adequate treatment is primarily with providers, who are largely untrained, unregistered, and unregulated. Informal providers are typically unaware of guideline treatments, unequipped with diagnostic tools and antimalarials, and succumb when patients express willingness to pay for inappropriate treatment. These suboptimal interactions can contribute to poor health outcomes and long-term drug resistance.

THE RISKS OF REGULATORY DISENGAGEMENT: INADEQUATE MONITORING OF VALUE CHAINS

Regulation in the healthcare sector focuses on ensuring products and services "are safe, effective, and affordable at the point of use" (Bloom, Henson, & Peters, 2014: 4). Efficacy depends on managing the delivery of healthcare goods and services through a value chain that begins with patient diagnosis and continues through the administration of appropriate treatment protocols, the prescription of required medicines, and the administration of follow-up care. When any of the functions in this chain are performed by informal providers, regulatory oversight fails and the effectiveness of the entire chain is jeopardized (Bloom et al., 2014).

Non-registration heightens the risk that providers are ill-equipped to deliver quality care to patients. Informal providers operate in a diffuse system with often underdeveloped and inefficient referral networks and substandard clinical quality. Delays in seeing qualified medical professionals alone create adverse health consequences that, in some cases, may be life-threatening (Cross & MacGregor, 2010).

The fate of tuberculosis (TB) patients in India seeking care from informal providers demonstrates the problem. Poor and marginalized people in India seek medical care from informal providers in two-thirds of cases (Kapoor et al., 2012). Early TB symptoms are easily mistaken for less serious conditions; an accurate diagnosis of TB is frequently delayed when an informal provider is the first point of contact. While most patients in the study were eventually seen by qualified medical professionals and received directly observed treatment short-course (DOTS)—the best-practice treatment for TB—the delays experienced in obtaining necessary treatment led to worse patient outcomes (Kapoor et al., 2012).

The challenge is compounded when formally licensed providers sell drugs for which they are not licensed or when lax inspection leads to adverse practices. In Tanzania, the majority of recorded public and private healthcare facilities are drug dispensaries. Despite formal registration, only a small number are inspected, and the majority of those licensed to sell only non-prescription medication admitted to selling prescription drugs (CfPM, 2008). Thus, regulatory failure may contribute to poor health outcomes.

OPPORTUNITIES TO IMPROVE QUALITY OF CARE AMONG INFORMAL PROVIDERS

Informal sector providers exist because of gaps in formal healthcare offerings as well as by heritage of traditional practices. Unless and until formal providers can adequately meet the need of patients, informal sector providers will persist and play a role in the delivery of healthcare. As a result, there is opportunity for formal providers and administrators to engage their informal counterparts to improve the quality of care. We postulate that the extent of this engagement represents an alternative to the standard conceptualization of informality based on registration. A facet of the alternative that we offer is that informality may run on a spectrum from complete disengagement to nearly full engagement. We argue that conceiving of informality as running on a spectrum facilitates the implementation of policies and practices that acknowledges important differences between semi-formal providers and dangerous outliers. Such a conceptualization allows for policy frameworks that integrate the benefits of legitimate, valuable, and innovative activities in the semi-formal sector into the mainstream while, at the same time, pursuing illegal and harmful informal providers as illegitimate. A nuanced policy framework is essential for responding rapidly and effectively to opportunities for developing health systems.

The healthcare ecosystem is rapidly evolving, especially in resource-limited settings. Gathering the information required to assess high-performing initiatives remains challenging under even ideal circumstances. More information is needed on the opportunities to improve informal provider performance, isolating the approaches that can deliver the best catalytic improvement in healthcare quality. This will be no small challenge. Private enterprises operating within formal institutions closely guard their sensitive performance information (Bennett, Bloom, Knezovich, & Peters, 2014). Informal providers face an even greater disincentive for sharing their confidential information because of the legal and normative consequences of non-registration.

Bridging the performance gap to connect informal and formal institutions requires graduated sanctions that reflect the context. In some cases, semi-formal organizations may be made formal either through registration or through liberalization of registration requirements. In other cases, the practices of informal providers may become acknowledged positively. In yet others, informal providers may change their practices to achieve conformance. The literature discusses three main strategies for mitigating the risks associated with informal providers: education (training); oversight (regulation, enforcement, and registration); and market conditions (provider incentives).

Improving the knowledge base of informal providers is a necessary condition for improved health status outcomes, but education alone is insufficient. The most common recommendation in the literature for improving performance among informal providers is education (Sudhinaraset et al., 2013). Despite its frequency, Shah, Brieger, and Peters (2010) investigated the relative effectiveness of these interventions, finding those employing training alone resulted in positive outcomes in only 21% of cases.

Combining knowledge-based intervention strategies with market-based incentives appears to be more effective (Bloom et al., 2011; Shah et al., 2010; Sudhinaraset et al., 2013). For example, one of the reviewed studies demonstrated that training was insufficient because surrounding constraints continued to bind: "clinical quality trails behind knowledge due to lack of resources, access, and drug availability" (Sudhinaraset et al., 2013: 9).

Semi-formal providers have demonstrated interest in learning and improving their practices. An eHealth program operating in Bangladesh offers qualified medical advice via telephone to subscribers. While not designed for providers, the call center noted that a significant number of village doctors utilized the service to solicit advice from qualified physicians (Bloom et al., 2011). This same study noted that informal providers were interested in soliciting training on the treatment of common problems; however, the government did not offer that specific training despite the demand (Bloom et al., 2011). Action may have been barred because semi-formal providers are categorized similarly to dangerous, illegal, exploitative providers.

Some programs have been launched to engage informal healthcare providers in policy development and practice improvement. The Center for Health Market Innovations (CHMI) maintains a list of healthcare enterprises operating in low- and middle-income countries. The database contains 53 programs that include a component of engagement with informal providers (2013). One such program, Shasthya Sena, operates in Bangladesh to improve health outcomes among informal providers by addressing the knowledge and regulatory gaps present in the healthcare system. The approach has three pillars: training, networking, and monitoring. The training program focuses on diagnosis, treatment, and referral for 11 major diseases. Those trained through the program join a network whose membership employs principles of self-governance on quality. Shasthya Sena encourages unofficial regulation through committees formed to oversee the performance of informal providers. Members of the committees include program participants, government officials, and formal public and private providers (Center for Health Market Innovations [CHMI], 2014b).

The Accredited Drug Dispensing Outlets (ADDO) program exemplifies how inclusive engagement with informal providers can lead to improved health performance. This program takes a similar approach to Shasthya Sena, except with a focus on drug sellers in Tanzania. ADDO addresses each of the elements in the proper treatment of malaria: sufficient provider knowledge, availability of diagnostic tools, patient compliance with appropriate guideline treatments, and availability of medications for those treatments. Under the program, each provider is accredited based on regulations and standards put forward by the government. ADDO has developed a list of approved medications that includes non-prescription drugs and a select list of prescription medication (e.g., antibiotics) (CfPM, 2008; CHMI, 2014a). Providers receive training in diagnosis and treatment as well as in quality business management tools such as record keeping (CfPM, 2008). ADDO also distributes information pamphlets geared toward customers to raise their awareness on quality medicines (CHMI, 2014a). Lastly, the ADDO program monitors drug sellers accredited by the program. The overseeing of performance and regular record keeping improves compliance and limits stock-outs of medicines. The results are significant: Availability of tracked medicines was found to be 80% at the end of the study versus 53% in the control sample; patients rated the knowledge of their dispenser as higher after completing the program than did patients who worked with dispensers in the control group (CHMI, 2014a). Dispensers also showed lower incidence of inappropriate prescriptions. As a result, the program has been replicated in Liberia (CHMI, 2014a).

FRAMING THE INFORMAL HEALTHCARE SECTOR AND NEXT STEPS

Recognition of the spectrum of informality in health provision is an important step toward effective intervention in the informal sector. Discounting and disengaging informal providers is neither viable nor, in some cases of semi-formal provision, desirable. A health system perspective that does not include informal providers, especially in instances of significant informal healthcare prevalence, can undermine the establishment of quality health outcomes. When an inadequate and inequitable supply of qualified medical professionals coincide with a preference for informal providers among the poor and disadvantaged, as was found to be the case in Bangladesh (Ahmed et al., 2009), then the informal healthcare sector may be essential to the provision of care.

The focus of efforts to remediate informality should include addressing identified market failures rather than only seeking to integrate informal providers into formal healthcare systems. The case of uncomplicated malaria treatment in Nigeria demonstrates that market failures may arise within an enterprise, across a value chain, and at the broader ecosystem level—resulting in education, information, and access challenges. Addressing these shortcomings will likely require integration of informal providers into the formal health system.

Evidence suggests that established formal healthcare providers rely on semi-formal providers to improve health outcomes. Operation ASHA uses informal providers in TB treatment initiatives; CHWs operate the medicine pickup locations in local locations in accordance with DOTS guidelines. ASHA's results indicate both increased TB detection rates and decreased TB mortalities (CHMI, 2013).

Disregarding informal providers can worsen health outcomes. The role of drug sellers and the implications of artemisinin- resistant malaria development, as described above, highlight the consequences of excluding the informal sector in healthcare provisions. Drug sellers would have benefited from learning about changes in government treatment guidelines, yet no effort was made to inform them of the policy shift. Bloom (2014) argues for the inclusion of informal providers in conversations about health systems research by recognizing their value in expanding access to care and rectifying their substandard treatments and their consequences (e.g., artemisinin-resistant malaria). Poor linkages between informal and formal providers also delay referrals to qualified professionals (Bloom et al., 2011).

The complexity and heterogeneity of informal providers requires more research. Even if health systems administrators sought to include informal providers in their catchment areas, no protocol has been developed that represents best practice on how to accomplish this goal. Effective regulation requires continuity of care. Informal providers are the first and, in many cases, only point of contact for patients. Thus, comprehensive regulation necessitates their inclusion in the health system strategy. In notable cases, the integration and legitimation of semi-formal providers in the delivery of healthcare services has resulted in improved quality of patient care. With informal healthcare sectors accounting for substantial portions of health systems in many countries, opportunities to improve care are important.

Figure 7.1   Dentist, India, January 2014

REFERENCES

Ahmed, S., Hossain, M., & Chowdhury, M. 2009. Informal sector providers in Bangladesh: How equipped are they to provide rational health care? *Health Policy and Planning*, 24: 467–478.

Ajayi, N., & Ukwaja, K. 2013. Possible artemisinin-based combination therapy-resistant malaria in Nigeria: A report of three cases. *Revista da Sociedade Brasileira de Medicina Tropical*, 46: 525–527.

Bennett, S., Bloom, G., Knezovich, J., & Peters, D. 2014. The future of health markets. *Globalization and Health*, 10: 51.

Bloom, G. 2014. History, complexity and health systems research. *Social Science & Medicine*, 117: 160–161.

Bloom, G., Henson, S., & Peters, D. 2014. Innovation in regulation of rapidly changing health markets. *Globalization and Health*, 10: 53.

Bloom, G., Standing, H., Lucas, H., Bhuiya, A., Oladepo, O., & Peters, D. 2011. Making health markets work better for poor people: The case of informal providers. *Health Policy and Planning*, 26: i45-i52

Bruton, G.D. (2010). Business and the world's poorest billion—The need for an expanded examination by management scholars. *Academy of Management Perspectives*, 24(3): 6–10.

Bruton, G.D., Ireland, R.D., & Ketchen, D.K., Jr. (2012). Toward a research agenda on the informal economy. *Academy of Management Perspectives*, 26(3): 1–11.

Center for Health Market Innovations (CHMI). 2013. Highlights 2013. *Worldhealthpartners.org*. http://worldhealthpartners.org/Resources/Highlights2013.pdf, December 2013.

Center for Health Market Innovations (CHMI). 2014a. *Program profile—Accredited Drug Dispensing Outlets (ADDO)*. http://healthmarketinnovations.org/program/accredited-drug-dispensing-outlets-addo, October 25.

Center for Health Market Innovations (CHMI). 2014b. *Program profile—Shasthya Sena*. http://healthmarketinnovations.org/program/shasthya-sena, October 29.

Center for Pharmaceutical Management (CfPM). 2008. Accredited drug dispensing outlets in Tanzania strategies for enhancing access to medicines program. *Msh.org*. http://projects.msh.org/news-bureau/upload/SEAM-Tanzania_Final_ADDO.pdf

Cross, J., & MacGregor, H. 2010. Knowledge, legitimacy and economic practice in informal markets for medicine: A critical review of research. *Social Science & Medicine*, 71: 1593–1600.

Ezenduka, C., Ogbonna, B., Ekwunife, O., Okonta, M., & Esimone, C. 2014. Drugs use pattern for uncomplicated malaria in medicine retail outlets in Enugu urban, southeast Nigeria: Implications for malaria treatment policy. *Malaria Journal*, 13(1): 243.

Godfrey, P.C. (2011). Toward a theory of the informal economy. *Academy of Management Annals*, 5: 231–277.

Hart, K. 2006. Bureaucratic form and the informal economy. In B. Guha-Khansnobis, R. Kanbur & E. Ostrom (Eds.), *Linking the formal and informal economy*: 21–36. New York: Oxford University Press.

Kamal-Yanni, M., Potet, J., & Saunders, P. 2012. Scaling-up malaria treatment: a review of the performance of different providers. *Malaria Journal*, 11(1): 414.

Kapoor, S., Raman, A., Sachdeva, K., & Satyanarayana, S. 2012. How did the TB patients reach DOTS services in Delhi? A study of patient treatment seeking behavior. *PLoS ONE*, 7: e42458.

Koh, H., Hegde, N., & Karamchandani, A. 2014. *Beyond the pioneer: Getting inclusive industries to scale*. India: Deloitte Touche Tohmatsu India Private Limited. http://www.beyondthepioneer.org/wp-content/themes/monitor/Beyond-the-Pioneer-Report.pdf

McGahan, A. 2012. Challenges of the informal economy for the field of management. *Academy of Management Perspectives*, 26(3): 12–21.

Peters, D., & Bloom, G. 2012. Bring order to unregulated health markets. *Nature*, 487(7406): 163–165.

Shah, N., Brieger, W., & Peters, D. 2010. Can interventions improve health services from informal private providers in low and middle-income countries? A comprehensive review of the literature. *Health Policy and Planning*, 26: 275–287.

Sudhinaraset, M., Ingram, M., Lofthouse, H.K., & Montagu, D. 2013. What is the role of informal healthcare providers in developing countries? A systematic review. *PLoS ONE*, 8: e54978.

World Health Organization. 2011. *Global plan for artemisinin resistance containment*. http://www.who.int/malaria/publications/atoz/artemisinin_resistance_containment_2011.pdf, January 2011.

8 Informal Firms in China

What Do We Know and Where Does the Research Go

Xiaodong Yu and
Garry Bruton

INTRODUCTION

Transition economies are typified by informal businesses (Leng, 2001; Schneider, 2005; Sun, 2001; Webbet al., 2009). Yet not all transitional economies are the same (Huang, 2011; Schneider, 2002), with the role that government plays in seeking to control and address informal businesses varying widely. In this paper, we focus on China and informal firms to gain insight into what occurs in a system with strong governmental controls in which informality is not widely officially recognized (Zhang, 2005).

China is characterized by strong government at multiple levels, with a focus on state-owned companies (Chen, 2003 ; Liu, 1999 ; Lu, 1997). Often, even if a large private firm exists. it will have strong state relationships (Peng, 2000). The result is that the informal economy in China is largely ignored by the government despite employing up to 60% of the work force in certain urban settings (Huang et al, 2001). The government in China ignores informal firms despite generating extensive employment since informal firms generate minimal impact on the GDP of the nation. Additionally, the government recognizing informal firms can call into question the power of the party and state since such firms do not register with the government despite the state's strong control. However, semi-official neglect by the various levels of government in China does not mean scholars in the nation have ignored the existence of informal firms. Here we explore the Chinese literature on informal firms and the insights that can be gathered from this literature. We connect the resulting Chinese literature that we identify to that of the dominant international literature on informal firms.

This manuscript specifically draws on the sociological and economics foundations of the literature on informal firms in China published in Chinese journals. The insights gathered here will not only provide a foundation to better understand informality in China, but also inform scholars from other emerging economies that often look to China as a model of economic development. The chapter also connects the existing international literature to that in China so a more comprehensive understanding of informality can be developed by scholars around the world.

INFORMALITY LEVEL IN CHINA

In China, informal firms violate the law if they exist without registering with the government. While such actions are often tolerated in some societies, it could be considered unusual to allow such activities in China since the government keeps such strong control over so many things in the nation. Yet China today virtually ignores informal firms and keeps no official statistics on such firms since that would call into question the power of the state and the party (Gao, 1998; Xiao, 2001; Xu, 2004). This is despite the substantial size of the informal economy in China. This unique status of informal firms in China has inspired domestic scholars to examine the informal economy in the nation since it has been recognized as a significant part of the economy despite officially being ignored by the government (Lu, 2008; Wu, 2008).

The informal economy in China only began to appear after the economic reforms began in the late 1970s (Chen, 2006; Zhang, 2004; Zhou, 1999; Zhao, 2006). Prior to that time, an individual selling a few stalks of sugar cane could result in prison time; with such extreme penalties, there were effectively no informal firms. However, as the economy increasingly moved to market orientation, and state control on the economy lessened, the informal economy expanded to the extent that by the 1980s the proportion of informal economy as part of the nation's total GDP had increased to 3.51% (He, 2005; Zhang, Ding & Dan, 2004).

As economic reform continued in the nation, the level of informal firms began to rapidly expand in China, with approximately 25% of the nation's GDP coming from the informal sector in the 1990s (Hao, 2004; Liang, 2001; Sun, 2001; Xia, 2000, 2004; Xin, 2008). That level of informality has now declined as greater economic options have come about for individuals. However, a stable estimate of 15%–20% of the nation's GDP now comes from the informal sector (He, 2005; Li, 2008; Liang, 1999; Liu, 2002; Song, 2007; Xia, 2002, 2004; Xu, 2007).

The latest estimate, from 2012, is that approximately 15% of the nation's GDP is in the informal economy (Xu, 2014). It should be noted that a stable level of the informal economy means that informality is expanding in China as the economy itself expands. It is widely accepted that over the past 15 years China's GDP has expanded by approximately 800%, and the percentage of the economy that is informal has stayed relatively constant at 15%. At this level of informality, that means that at least 187 million people are directly involved in the informal economy and represent up to approximately 60% of the total labor force in some urban areas (Huang, 2011). Informal firms typically are found in wholesale and retail, catering, manufacture, and transportation industries in China (Lu, 2008).

It is well documented in other domains of Chinese research that there are significant geographic differences across China, with coastal regions far more developed than the inland regions (He, 2012). The same is true for the presence of informal firms (Ji, 1995). The more developed economy in coastal regions results in the informal economy being smaller in those areas. The greatest concentration of informal firms is in Western China, which is the least developed region of the country. Beijing, the center of political power in the nation, is the least active region for informal economy in China, followed by Tianjin, which is geographically close to Beijing.

METHOD

To examine literature on informal firms in China, we conducted a systematic review of a broad range of Chinese literature written in Chinese on the topic. To conduct the review, we employed the China National Knowledge Infrastructure database (CNKI) as the source of literature. The CNKI database is widely used in China and contains 7,985 journals listed in CSSCI (Chinese Social Sciences Citation Index). The result is over 100 million pieces of literature from China on a wide range of topics, including all major academic journal articles, doctoral dissertations, conference papers, books, and yearbooks.

The authors searched for all literature that appears under the key terms "informal economy," "underground economy," "shadow economy," and "hidden economy"; these terms have been recognized in China as synonymous with the term informal economy (Jiang, 2002; Wu, 1999; Xiao, 1999, 2001; Yan, 2000; Zeng, 2010). We initially identified the Chinese literature that used any of the four terms mentioned above as key words for the articles, which generated a total of 414 articles or other pieces of literature. To focus the analysis, we then targeted those articles or other academic publications that had been cited 10 times or more by other scholars, believing these articles the key ones driving the investigation of the topic in China. The result was 86 academic articles.

The earliest of the 86 articles was published in 1991, while the latest was in 2012. These articles were all empirically focused, with no theoretical development articles included in the 86 articles. There were 49 qualitative-based studies and 37 quantitative-based studies among the 86 articles. It should be noted that theory is not present in all articles, though historically Chinese articles have often been theoretical. The result is that 31 articles do not even mention theory in the article but just highlight the phenomenon of informal firms in China. We will initially review this Chinese literature along two dimensions: the reasons for informality in China and the impact of informality on the Chinese society and economy. We will conclude the paper with a discussion of the future research direction that should be taken by scholars.

REASONS FOR INFORMAL ECONOMY IN CHINA

The reasons for informality have been viewed from two broad perspectives: sociological and economic (Bruton, Ireland & Ketchen, 2012). Each of these two broad streams of literature connect with two broad theoretical perspectives on informality in the international literature, institutional theory and agency theory. We will examine the existing Chinese literature along each of those perspectives, connecting it to the relevant dominant international literature.

The sociological perspective on informality in China views broader societal pressures as leading to informality. The fact that the broader society is viewed as key is consistent with institutional theory perspective that has been widely employed in the research of informal economy in the international journals (e.g., Feige, 1999; Fernandez-Kelly, 2006; Portes & Haller, 2005). As noted above, typically in Chinese literature there is an absence of theory underpinning that research. More recently, scholars in China have sought to connect their research to well-recognized international theory, but often rather than testing theory they use theory to explain observations post hoc. Here we will draw on institutional theory to help better understand the Chinese literature and also connect it to the more widely recognized international research on the topic. However, we acknowledge that often the authors in China did not employ this theory themselves.

Institutional theory views the impact on firms as coming from either the macro or the meso level. At the macro level, one of the key issues that affects firms is the role of regulations and laws (legal institutions) (Scott, 1995, 2001). The central government of China has encouraged a massive movement of Chinese citizens from low-income, rural areas of the nation to urban centers in China (Huang et al, 2001). In large part, the government has encouraged this since it realizes that the nation cannot move forward as a rural nation (Wan, 1994). There is a strong willingness among rural farmers to move to urban centers since the life of rural farmers can be very hard and income limited. (Lin, 2007; Yang, 2010; Yi, Yan, & Xue, 2007). China has a registration system, hukou, which requires that individuals be registered in their original area of birth. If not registered in a given city, the person who has moved to that city can expect no social services. After moving into cities, many immigrants find it quite challenging to find jobs and survive since there are no social services (Li, 2002). Thus, while the government is encouraging the growth of the urban areas, it is not always ensuring that individuals have the right to work there. The result is that a third to a half of residents of Chinese cities are migrants who have no right to social services or education for their children. Without jobs or social services, the government typically allows individuals to operate informal businesses if they do not cause significant social disruption. If there is social disruption, the government can move aggressively to end the business activity. Thus, without social services or jobs, the people create ways to support themselves—informal businesses (Huang, 2011; Li & Tang, 2002). The government allows such informal firms to exist but does not in any way encourage them. Rather, it is more a setting of benign neglect since they officially should not exist (Li, 2002; Song, 2001; Zhang, 2008).

Institutional theory also provides valuable insights at the meso level of analysis. Meso institutions exist within small communities rather than at the broader macro or national level (DeCastro, Khavul, & Bruton, 2014). Within China, there is greater variance in economic development and culture within regions. Rather than a uniform nation such as the United States, China has been compared to the old European Common Market (the predecessor to the European Union), in which nations retained significant leverage and far greater cultural differences than the European Union of today, where free movement of people exists. The result is that there are distinct meso cultures in China today. Thus, within China there are regions that have been more accepting of informal firms than others. However, it has been found that once a region has established a strong history of informal firms, informal firms continue to resist the urge to register (Xia, 1997). The power of the local meso culture often discouraging registration when there are large numbers of informal firms (DeCastro, Bruton, & Khavul, 2014).

A strong element in the existing Chinese literature from a sociological perspective on informality that connects to the meso institutional literature in the international literature is how individuals in the informal firms network to overcome limits due to their informality (Ren, 2008; Tang, 2003; Wu, 2001). It has been recognized that strong networks are critical to informal firms building legitimacy (Khavul, Bruton, & Wood, 2009). In examining such networks, it has been found that in China people who share the same characteristics, such as hometown or hobby, often get together, making it easier to start a corporation (Ren, 2008). Thus, relationship networks also play an important role in gaining resource for informal economy (Wu, 2001). Raw material, customers and even information are available through personal networks of informal firm owners (Tang, 2003). The presence of such personal networks have been shown in international journals to play a key role in the power of meso institutions (Khavul, Bruton, & Wood, 2009). Some enterprises develop their businesses within the local community typically rooted in the community culture (Peredo, 2006). Research based on the urban informal economy in Africa shows that social networks have a significant positive impact on outcomes by facilitating access to a variety of useful resources for entrepreneurs (Berrou, 2012)

ECONOMIC PERSPECTIVE

Another key stream of Chinese literature on informality focuses on the economic perspective of informality. The key issue here is that entrepreneurs in China are informal to evade taxes and other forms of government regulation (Chen, 2007; Liu, 2002; Yan, 2000; Yang, 2007; Wu, 1999; Zhou, 2006). A key theoretical issue that often drives such economic analysis in international journals is agency theory. Here, in a manner similar to what we did when we looked at the sociological view of Chinese informality and connected the international literature on informality and institutional theory, we will connect the economic view of informal firms in China with the international literature and agency theory.

It has been recognized in international journals that when entrepreneurs start their businesses they need to allocate their limited resources into the most effective areas for success (Webb, et al., 2013). The same pressures appear to apply to Chinese firms. One key area of concern for Chinese entrepreneurs is that taxes can vary widely by province and city (Cui, 2012). There is evidence in the Chinese literature that the level of taxes has a positive relationship with the number of informal firms (Liu, 2002). In dominant international literature, tax and burdensome regulations are also regarded as antecedents to informality (Bruton, Ireland & Ketchen, 2012; De Soto, 1989), but scholars have also created a specific term, "stringency of policies,"—which includes tax, labor, trade, and other regulations—to measure the influence of policy on informal economy (Webb et al., 2013). Compared to these, Chinese literature focuses much more strongly on taxes, ignoring the importance of other aspects. In China, it is estimated that approximately 26% of total taxable earnings are lost due to tax evasion (An & Liang, 1999; Zhang, 2004; Zhang & Ruan, 2004). Thus, there are substantial levels of tax avoidance in the nation and the corresponding government regulation that goes with such avoidance.

It has been argued in the international literature that market liberalization within centrally controlled economies actually creates more informality because it fosters economic disruption (de Oliveira, 1994). A vein of Chinese research is consistent with this observation and has examined informality and economic reform (e.g., Hager, 2004 ; Qin, 2000; Wan, 1994 ; Xia, 1997; Yi, Yang, & Yi, 2004). The economic reform that began in the 1970s did not set a red line that prohibited the development of the informal economy (Wan, 1994). Instead, the initial main purpose of the economic reform was to improve life quality of the people, and any method that was effective in improving civilian's life quality was accepted. The result was that it was established early to ignore the informal firms that developed. This is especially true because it was recognized early that there is an employment benefit to allowing informal firms (Wan, 1994). Even today, it is officially estimated that China has an unemployment rate of over 10%, so allowing informal firms helps ensure that individuals have a means of income as social services, as noted above, are often limited. Such a policy was especially beneficial when inefficient state firms were being closed during the late 1990s. Allowing informal firms to exist also helped politically because it provided an outlet for the unemployed to ensure social stability (Liu, 2002; Lu, 2008).

INFLUENCE OF INFORMAL ECONOMY IN CHINA

Next, we will examine the influence of informality on the economy in China. Informal firms in China are seen by Chinese scholars as having both positive and negative social impact. We will first examine the positive benefits.

Positive Economic Benefits of Informal Firms

The most significant positive influence the informal firms have on the Chinese economy, as seen by Chinese scholars, is to provide employment while increasing the income of civilians (Jiang, 2005 ; Leng, 2001; Li, 2002; Wan, 1994). In 2006, a survey conducted by Labor Science Research Institute of China showed that about 80% of the 23,414 respondents in 10 large Chinese cities, such as Nanjing, Xi'an, and Changsha, were now, or previously had, pursued informal economic activities (Lu, 2008). The income generated by these informal firms helps many citizens live above poverty level (Li, 2002; Xu, 2010). It is important to note that the cities surveyed in this report were not cities along the coast, which have typically led the economic reform in the nation. Instead, they were cities that are important in the country but typically not viewed as part of the core of the nation's economic vitality. Thus, informality in such cities proved particularly useful as state firms closed but the growth of international firms or local private firms was not there to replace the jobs lost.

Also on the positive side, the informal economy is seen by local Chinese scholars as helping to balance the demand and supply of consumers in the society (Li & Tang, 2002). Often, a service or product is in short supply in the formal economy, and firms will not be able to meet the needs of the whole society. Informal firms are viewed as smaller and more flexible than formal firms by Chinese scholars. For example, informal firms are noted for their ability to meet this need (Yang, 2001). The ability of informal firms to complete the market by providing such services or products, thus increasing the utility of the society, is seen as a significant benefit to the society (Li & Tang, 2002). That view is consistent with the international research (Bruton, Ireland & Ketchen, 2012).

The benefit of informal firms does not only help to meet the needs of consumer but also often lays the foundation for the development of that industry (Yang, 2001). New product markets in China often first occur among informal firms, especially in rural areas in China (Lin, Zhang & Wu, 2002). After some development, the government ultimately creates regulation, and the previous informal firms finally move toward formalization. Thus, informality is seen by some scholars in China as a mere step in the industrialization process of the nation which, ultimately, will be naturally replaced.

Negative Economic Impact of Informal Firms
It is argued that one of the key negative impacts of informal firms is disruption to the government's macro control over the market economy (Liang, 1999; Xia, 1994). Some scholars who hold this negative view associate informal economic behaviors with hoarding and/or speculation that make macro control of the economy more difficult for the government (Xia, 1994). In addition, informal firms are seen by such Chinese scholars as disturbing the order of the market by disrupting the optimal allocation of economic resources (Ji, 1995; Liao, 1993 ; Xia, 1994; Zhang, 2004). These

scholars argue that the optimal allocation of social resources may involve a market mechanism, but it is the government that plays a major role in controlling this process (Liao, 1993). This view of the market is seen in contrast to informal economic behavior, which follows the principle of maximizing individual interest without concern for the society (Ji, 1995; Xia, 1997). From a macro policy perspective, the unknown nature of the informal sector also makes it difficult for government to control the economy (Ba, 2010 ; Dong, 2008 ; Ma, 2006).

Another negative impact on the Chinese economy is seen by some Chinese scholars as coming from the fact that the informal firms by their nature are illegal. As a result, the informal firms are often seen as breeding corruption since they often must provide small bribes to police to ignore them. (Cheng, 2006; Wu, 1996; Ji, 1995). Migrant labor will often strive for informal recognition and protection from formal municipal organizations, so they are not as vulnerable to bribe requests (You, 2001).

It is argued that one of the central reasons for informal firms is tax evasion (Yan, 2000; Yu, 2000). Some scholars view informal firms as free riders that do not pay taxes but take advantage of a society's benefits. The result is that the informal firms disrupts the fair competition environment of the market (Lv, 2000). Finally, it is argued that informal firms negatively impact consumers since such firms make it more difficult to guarantee quality and enhance service levels (Liu, 2005; Yi, 2003a; Yi, 2003b). It is interesting to note that this negative view of informal firms in the Chinese literature is in contrast to the dominant literature in international journals that stress informal firms can in fact increase the quality and degree of products offered to consumers (Khavul, Bruton, & Wood, 2009).

WHERE DOES THE RESEARCH GO IN THE FUTURE?

Chinese research opens up many questions for scholars as we look at both China and the world. Four key areas of research emerge as we consider the Chinese literature, including: how firms move from informal to informal; the relationship between the formal and informal economy; how to measure the nationwide scale of informal economy directly; and a need to push the study of Chinese informal firms toward a greater empirical and theoretical focus.

How to Move Firms from Informal to Formal

How to move firms from the informal to formal economy remains a key topic for Chinese scholars that is also important in the rest of the world. It is strongly argued in many international articles that firms will join the formal economy if taxes and regulation are reduced (Bruton, Ireland & Ketchen, 2012). However, as Katunakaran and Balasubramaniam (2012) highlight, there can also be an underlying institutional logic that drives firms to be informal. Webb et al. (2009) explained this issue by using a micro-level insight and presenting three methods for the informal economy participants: partial transmission, resisting transition, and fully transitioning. As already noted, there can also be meso institutional issues that impact these issues. To date. however, Chinese scholars have focused almost solely on macro-level concerns around issues related to the government for their research. For example, one of the most widely cited articles centers on the belief that if the tax burden of the whole society is lowered many firms will move to formal status (Liu, 2002; Yan, 2000). Such a view is centered on the belief by many that a high tax rate motivates firms to be informal (Chen, 2006). Consistent with this view of the role of financing in informality is the argument that if the social safety net is improved, and/or greater numbers of jobs are created in the nation there would be greater motivation for the informal firms to move to formal (Sun, 2001; Zhang, 2008). The nature of the Chinese government control is that such naturally occurring experiments in which variables such as taxes in a province or the social safety net can more easily occur if the government decides to change some of the these macro items in given areas of the nation. Thus, there is the potential for significant large scale social experiments in China.

However, future research on Chinese informality should be expanded to micro-level to better understand how these also impact informality in the nation and the movement to formal status. For example, one potential article that can guide Chinese scholars is Pisani (2012), which examined informal cross-border entrepreneurs at the South Texas–Northern Mexico border. He found that that the identity of those informal entrepreneurs is the key factor to informal activity. Another important article that Chinese scholars should look to for inspiration is Honig (1998), which examined the influence of human capital, social capital, and financial capital of informal business owners on profitability in Jamaica. Chinese scholars should look at these works and determine if the institutional setting of China results in similar or different results.

Relationship Between the Formal Economy and Informal Economy

Another key topic for future investigation is the relationship between the formal economy and informal economy. In the international literature, a paradox has been recognized in the relationship between the formal economy and informal economy—the two are often viewed separately but are in fact intertwined (Webb et al., 2009). For example, in Latin America it is known that the formal and informal economies work closely together (DeCastro, Khavul, & Bruton, 2014). Chinese researchers have recognized that the formal and informal economy grow at similar levels (Huang, 2004; Jiang, 2001; Li, 2005; Liu, 2003; Yang, 1996; Zhu, 2000). However, in a society in which informal firms are largely ignored, it is unclear what the nature of the interaction actually would be. For example, informal firms in many nations can still get financing from banks (Siquiera & Bruton, 2010), but it is unclear if this would also be the case in China since all banks are controlled by the government. Future research should expand this understanding of these inter-relationships between formal and informal firms, including financing in China.

Measure the Nationwide Scale of Informal Economy Directly

Most studies in China used indirect ways to evaluate the scale of informal economy in China, such as energy consumption and quantity of shipments (Xia, 2002 2004). Other Chinese scholars have imitated the international scholars by measuring the scale of informal economy through the use of currency demand (Schneider, 2002). However, each of these methods gives only a rough approximation. The Central University of Finance and Economics research group made the only nationwide survey of informal firms to examine the specific issue of informal finance. In a country where the government ignores informal firms, direct surveys of the scale of informal firms is difficult (Wang, 2008), but it is a domain in which future scholars should move as they seek more fully understand this rich topic.

Push to Move from a Phenomenon-Based to a Theoretical-Based Study

Until now, Chinese scholars have principally focused on the description of the general situation (Wang, 2008). What's more, scholars have not employed a theoretical insight to understand formal firms in China (Wang, 2008). Thus, the major challenge that faces Chinese scholars is how to push the study of Chinese informal firms toward one with a greater empirical and stronger theoretical foundation. Ignored by government, informal firms in China show specific and distinct characteristics, which can contribute to the improvement and development of theory by scholars that will benefit the world. Here we have focused on institutional and agency theories. As we highlight in our discussion, each of these theories offer scholars a rich foundation to explore Chinese informality. However, we hope these theories are not seen as exclusively relevant but as only a theoretical start to the investigation of this important topic.

CONCLUSION

Transition economies are typified by informal businesses. However, even though informal firms provide 15%–20% of the nation's GDP, neither international scholars nor Chinese scholars have paid the attention to the critical issue in China that it merits. It is clear, even as we review the literature here, that the existing Chinese literature does not pay the attention to the domain that it merits as a major component of the nation's economy. China has a strong government with a loud voice on domestic economy. In the future, scholars, both domestic and international, need to develop a far greater understanding of informal firms in China. The insights will benefit not only China but also the world as we seek to understand this important economic phenomenon.

Here, we specifically examine the sociological and economic foundations of the Chinese literature on the informal economy. Though informal firms have a positive influence on the employment rate, increase the income of civilians, balance the demand and supply of consumers in the society, and meet the needs of consumers, they are also regarded as the driving force to disrupt government's macro control, breed corruption, and evade tax in China. It is hoped that by opening Chinese research to international scholars, many questions will be generated both in China and around the world.

REFERENCES

(The articles starting with * indicates included in the 86 core articles on informal firms in China but not cited in this manuscript.)

An, T., & Liang, P. 1999. Thoughts about the research on tax erosion. *Taxation Research Journal*, 6: 22–28.

Ba, S., & Yan, M. 2010. The study on the indirect estimate of the external demand of Renminbi currency: 1999–2008. *Shanghai Journal of Economics*, 1: 20–25.

Berrou, J.P., & Combarnous, F. 2012. The personal networks of entrepreneurs in an informal African urban economy: Does the 'strength of ties' matter?. *Review of Social Economy*, 70(1): 1–30.

Bruton, G., Ireland, D., & Ketchen, D. 2012. Toward a research agenda on the informal economy. *The Academy of Management Perspectives*, 26(3): 1–11.

Chen, E. 2003. External condition analysis of SME in transforming countries. *Foreign Economies and Management*, 25: 33–38.

Chen, P. 2007. Private tax erosion model based on the behavior economics theory. *Finance and Trade Economics*, 11: 60–64.

Chen, X., & Yu, P. 2006. Impact factors and scale measurement of tax evasion. *Statistics & Decision*, 6: 69–71.

*Cheng, F. 2006. Street life and its suffering to Waifs: Based on the ethnography investigation. *Youth Studies*, 9: 1–9.

Cheng, Z. 2006. Summary on western corruption economy. *Social Sciences Abroad*, 5: 31–36.

Cui, W., & Wang, Z. 2012. Analisis on the efficiency of the local tax rate formulation mechanism. *Taxation Research*, 11: 54–59.

De Castro, J.O., Khavul, S., & Bruton, G.D. 2014. Shades of grey: How do informal firms navigate between macro and meso institutional environments. *Strategic Entrepreneurship Journal*, 8(1): 75–94.

de Oliveira, O., & Roberts, B. 1994. The many roles of the informal sector in development: Evidence from urban labor market research, 1940–1989. In C.A. Rakowski (Ed.), *Contrapunto: The informal sector debate in Latin America*: 51–71. Albany, NY: State University of New York Press.

De Soto, H. 1989. *The other path: The invisible revolution in the third world*. New York: Harper & Row.

Dong, J. 2008. The estimation of Renminbi currency demand abroad: 1999–2005. *Economic Science*, 1: 55–66.

Feige, E. L. 1999. *Underground economies in transition: Unrecorded activity, tax evasion, corruption, and organized crime:* 11–27. Brookfield, VT: Ashgate Publishing Company.

Fernandez-Kelly, P. 2006. Out of the shadows: Political action and the informal economy in Latin America: 1–22. University Park, PA: The Pennsylvania State University Press.

Gao, L., & Sun, S. 1998. Empirical method of informal economy measurement. *Statistical Research*, 5: 58–60.

Hager, P. 2004. Institutional change and economic development within transition period. *Comparative Economic and Social Systems*, 5: 1–11.

Hao, C. 2004. Estimation on the scale of tax losing in China. *Journal of Central University of Finance & Economics*, 11: 12–16.

He, H., & Zheng, S. 2005. The partition model of underground GDP: Discussion on the estimation of underground economy scale. *Statistics and Decision*, 1: 25–27.

He, T. 2002. Underground economy and control efficiency: Qualitative research on the issue of private lending legality. *Journal of Finance*, 11: 100–106.

Honig, B. 1998. What determines success? Examining the human, financial, and social capital of Jamaican microentrepreneurs. *Journal of Business Venturing*, 13(5): 371–394.

Huang, K. 2011. Specificity analysis of Chinese urbanization. *Urban Studies*, 18(8), 6–10.

Huang, D. 2004. Discussion on the sustainable development and construction of G-GDP. *Statistical Research*, 9: 46–49.

Huang, Z., Li, Q., Pan, Y., Liu, S., Guo, W. & Zhang, Y.,. 2001. Informal economy in China. *Opening Time*, 1: 5–31.

Ji, J. 1995. Underground economy in China. *Jiangsu Social Science*, 5: 37–41.

Jiang, G. 2001. On discriminating the efficiency of underground economic activities. *Research on Financial and Economic Issues*, 7: 75–79.

Jiang, P. 2002. National economy adjust accounts and statistical revolution of government. *Statistical Research*, 8: 28–31.

Jiang, P. 2005. Discussion on informal employment. *Statistical Research*, 6: 34–38.

*Jiang, X., & Ding, C. 2004. Analysis of private finance theory: Scope, comparison and institutional change. *Journal of Finance*, 8: 100–111.

*Jin, Y. 1995. Research on adjusting account of national economic welfare. *Statistical Research*, 5: 8–15.

Karunakaran, A., & Balasubramaniam, V. 2012. *Entrepreneurship within informal economies in rural India: A field study.* Presented at Academy of Management Conference, Boston, MA.

Khavul, S., Bruton, G.D., & Wood, E. 2009. Informal family business in Africa. *Entrepreneurship: Theory & Practice*, 33(6), 1219–1238.

Leng, X. 2001. Theoretical and practical trends of informal employment in foreign countries. *Social Science in Nanjing*, 5: 63–66.

Li, J. 2008. The size of non-observed economy estimated by the equilibrium model based on national accounts. *Journal of Central University of Finance & Economics*, 6: 24–28.

Li, L. 2005. Measurement on the scale of informal economy. *Corporate Economy and Science* (02S), 58-59.

Li, Q. 2002. Informal employment issue of the immigrants workers. *Expanding Horizons*, 6: 47–56.

Li, Q., & Tang, Z. 2002. Urban immigrants workers and informal employment. *Sociological Research*, 6: 13–25.

Liang, P. 2001. The scale of tax evasion: Based on the perspective of underground economy. *Journal of China Youth College for Political Sciences*, 1: 66–72.

Liang, P., & Liang, Y. 1999. Measurement and thought on scale of underground economy in China. *Finance and Trade Economics*, 5: 50–54.

Liao, H., & Wang, P. 1993. Underground economy: Cause and forming conditions. *Journal of Central University of Finance & Economics*, 3: 79–84.

Lin, Y., Zhang, S., & Wu, Y. 2002. Review on issue of Chinese residents income gap in recent years. *Economic Review*, 6: 57–62.

Lin, L. 2007. Correlation between income distribution and informal economy. *Business Research*, (24), 27–30.

Liu,B. 2002. The reason, harm and solution of underground economy in China nowadays. *Science, Economy, Society*, 20: 27–29.

*Liu, Q. 2003. A thinking on excessive money: Hypothesis of marginal propensity to consume. *Journal of Shanghai University of Finance and Economics*, 5: 32–39.

Liu, S. 1999. Research on non-governmental credit in China. *Journal of Jinan University*, 21: 7–18.

Liu, S., & Wang, Z. 2005. Economic monetization in China: Dynamic process and quantitative explanation. *Journal of Finance*, 3: 38–49.

Lu, M., & Tian, S. 2008. Explicit unemployment or recessive employment: Prove from the family investigation in Shanghai. *Management World*, 1: 48–56.

Lu, X. 1997. System factors of informal finance in China. *Finance and Trade Economics*, 5: 31–34.

*Luo, L. 2005. The basic estimation of the scale of informal economy in China. *Economic Science*, 3: 29–38.

Lv, J., & Zhuang, H. 2000. 'Huikou' and its consequence: Economics analyze on the negative effect. *Finance & Trade Economics*, 3: 30–34.

Ma, R., & Rao, X. 2006. The estimation of Renminbi currency demand abroad. *Economic Science*, 5: 18–29.

Peng, M. W., & Luo, Y. 2000. Managerial ties and firm performance in a transition economy: The nature of a micro-macro link. *Academy of Management Journal*, 43(3): 486–501.

Peredo, A. M., & Chrisman, J. J. 2006. Toward a theory of community-based enterprise. *Academy of Management Review*, 31(2): 309–328.

Pisani, M. J., & Richardson, C. 2012. Cross-border informal entrepreneurs across the South Texas–Northern Mexico boundary. *Entrepreneurship & Regional Development*, 24(3–4): 105–121.

Portes, A., & Haller, W. 2005. *The handbook of economic sociology* (2nd ed.). Princeton, NJ: Princeton University Press: 403–425.

Qin, R. 2000. Tax erosion and solution to underground economy in China. *International Taxation in China*, 12: 5–9.

Ren, S. 2008. Informal financing: Theory, reality and solution. *Finance & Trade Economics*, 8: 26–29.

Schneider, F. 2002. Size and measurement of the informal economy in 110 countries. Workshop of Australian National Tax Centre, ANU, Canberra, Australia.

Schneider, F. 2005. Shadow economies around the world: What do we really know? *European Journal of Political Economy*, 21: 598–642.

Scott, W. R. 1995/2001. *Institutions and organizations*. Thousand Oaks, CA: Sage.

Siqueira, A. C., & Bruton, G. D. 2010. High-technology entrepreneurship in emerging economies: Firm informality and contextualization of resource-based theory. **IEEE Transactions on Engineering Management**, 57(1): 39–50.

Song, X. 2007. Some issues and statistics about China's GDP economic research journal. *Economic Research Journal*, 8: 22–30.

Song, X., & Huang, Y. 2001. Informal economy and informal employment in Shanghai. *Urban Problems*, 2: 39–42.

Sun, J., & Zhu, J. 2001. Correlation analysis of the relationship between underground economy and income unfair. *Economic Review*, 11: 16–19.

Tang, L. 2003. Forming of network: A key case on the evolution of local black market. *Sociological Research*, 5: 95–106.

Wan, A. 1994. Theoretical thoughts about the situation of underground economy in China. *Journal of Central China Normal University (Philosophy and Social Sciences Edition)*, 1: 14–20.

*Wang, A., Zhang, Q., & Yu, X. 2004. The underground financial industry in China. *The Study of Finance and Economics*, 7: 35–38.

Wang, Y. 2008. Review on the underground economy issue in China. *Comparative Economic & Social Systems*, 4: 183–188.

Webb, J. W., Bruton, G. D., Tihanyi, L., & Ireland, R. D. 2013. Research on entrepreneurship in the informal economy: Framing a research agenda. *Journal of Business Venturing*, 28(5): 598–614.

Webb, J. W., Tihanyi, L., Ireland, R. D., & Sirmon, D. G. 2009. You say illegal, I say legitimate: Entrepreneurship in the informal economy. *Academy of Management Review*, 34(3): 492–510.

Wu, J. 1996. Research on the financial fraud problems. *Finance & Trade Economics*, 2: 45–49.

Wu, J. 1999. The unobserved economy: Scope, definition, style and method. *Statistical Research*, 11: 35–41.

Wu, J., & Zuo, Y. 2001. Several issues on the adjust accounts of informal sectors in China. *Statistical Research*, 5: 3–8.

Wu, Y. 2008. The measurement of taxation evasion scale in China. *Contemporary Finance & Economics*, 5: 38–42.

Xia, N. 1999. Discussion on the adjust accounts of the underground economy. *Statistical Research*, Additional Journal: 80–83.

Xia, N. 2000. Measurement model of underground economy and its sensitivity analysis. *Statistical Research*, 8: 38–41.

Xia, N. 2002. The estimating measurement of China's informal economy scale based on quantity of social shipments. *Statistical Research*, 2: 23–26.

Xia, N. 2004. The application of gray system model to the measurement of underground economy scale. *Academic Research*, 1: 40–43.

Xia, X. 1994. Macroeconomic control and its governance on underground economy. *Journal of Central University of Finance & Economics*, 1: 17–22.

Xia, X. 1997. Three topics on the underground economy. *Economist*, 5: 34–41.

Xiao, W., & Li, L. 2001. Underground economy: Underground economy: Reason, influence and measurement method. *Economy and Politics of the World*, 3: 58–63.

Xin, H., & Wang, T. 2008. The measurement of the taxation evasion of underground economy: Based on the improved currency radio method. *Modernization of Management*, 4: 50–52.

*Xing, C., & Han, L. 2001. Impact of the lever of finance and taxation on gink coefficient in China. *Modern Finance and Economics*, 9: 31–33.

Xu, A., & Li, J. 2007. The unobserved economy in China: New finding based on MIMIC model and economic census data. *Statistical Research*, 24: 30–36.

Xu, B. 2010. Underground economy and the first mover advantage of private enterprise. *Journal of Business Economics*, 1: 51–60.

Xu, B. 2014. Retest of the relationship between informal economy and formal economy. *Journal of Financial and Economy University*, 29(1), 4–11.

Xu, X. 2004. The measurement of domestic underground economy scale and analysis of its periodicity. *Statistics & Decision*, 10: 26–27.

Yan, C. 2000. Underground economy and taxation. *Taxation Research*, 8: 65–68.

Yang, C., & Sun, L. 2010. The scale, reason and influence of informal economy in different regions of China. *Economic Research*, 10: 34–43.

Yang, D. 2007. A study on individual factor's affecting tax payers' willingness to pay taxes. *Journal of Central University of Finance & Economics*, 9: 17–22.

Yang, M. 2001. Discussion on the issue of Green GDP adjusting account theory. *Statistical Research*, 2: 40–43.

Yang, M., & Song, J. 1996. Several theoretical issues on adjusting account of underground economy. *Statistical Research*, 5: 8–14.

Yi, X., & Xie, Z. 2003. Long-term trends and periodicity fluctuation of domestic monetary liquidity: 1978–2002. *Shanghai Economic Review*, 11: 17–24.

Yi, X., Xie, S., & Liu, Z. 2003. The long-term trend, level and fluctuation of China's ratio of M1 to M2: 1978–2002. *Journal of Central University of Finance & Economics*, 11: 10–14.

Yi, X., Yan, X., & Xue, D. 2007. Analysis and revelation of the informal: Sector related concepts. *World Regional Studies*, 11: 21–26.

Yi, X., Yang, B., & Yi, J. 2004. Calculation of the size of tax evasion in China and analysis of its effects on economy. *The Study of Finance and Economics*, 30: 31–40.

You, W., & Xiao, W. 2001. Study on the cause of formation of organized crimes. *Journal of the East China University of Politics and Law*, 17: 10–14.

Yu, W. 2000. Review on tax erosion economic model in foreign countries. *Economic Information*, 2: 72–75.

*Yuan, Z., & Lu, M. 1998. Theoretical analysis of the hidden employment. *Zhejiang Social Sciences*, 1: 11–16.

Zeng, W., & Xu, Y. 2010. Review of the researches on system of national accounts within the last 30 years. *Statistical Research*, 27: 35–41.

Zhang, D. 2004. Measurement of size of tax evasion. *Journal of Central University of Finance & Economics*, 1: 8–12.

Zhang, W., & Ruan, J. 2004. Remark on the frontier research on tax administration in western. *Public Finance Research*, 9: 60–62.

*Zhang, Y. 2001. Development trend of global underground economy. *Contemporary International Relations*, 3: 51–55.

Zhang, Y. 2005. Discussion on the definition of underground economy. *Statistical Education*, 4: 48–50.

Zhang, Y. 2008. Informal employment: Social recognition from the theoretical perspective a theoretical perspective. *Journal of Shanghai University of Finance and Economics*, 10: 18–24.

Zhang, Z., Ding, H., & Dan, F. 2004. The estimation of the scale of the underground economy in China. *Statistics & Decision*, 12: 22–23.

Zhao, L. 2006. Research and evaluation of the underground economy in China. *Statistical Research*, 9: 42–46.

Zhou, G. 1999. Summary on various methods and opinions of the measurement of informal economy in foreign countries. *Statistical Research*, 4: 48–51.

Zhou, Y. 2006. The taxation follows the scale measurement. *Taxation Research*, 4: 64–66.

Zhu, X., & Yang, M. 2000. Quantitative research on underground economy in China: 1979–1997. *Statistical Research*, 4: 32–37.

9 Subsistence Entrepreneurs and Formal Institutions
Semi-Formal Governance Among Ghanaian Entrepreneurs

Paul C. Godfrey and Gibb Dyer

Do subsistence entrepreneurs, whose businesses operate primarily in the informal economy, use formal institutions and legal mechanisms to enhance their business practices? Such a situation would run counter to received definitions of informal economic activities in both sociology and economics. Sociologists Portes, Castell, and Benton (1989: 12) define the informal economy as "characterized by one central feature: it is unregulated by the institutions of society, in a legal and social environment in which similar activities are regulated." Similarly, economists LaPorta and Schliefer (2008: 1) argue that "economic activity that [is] conducted by unregistered firms or by registered firms but hidden from taxation," belongs to the informal economy. To be unregulated and unregistered should mean that the benefits of regulation and legal standing lie outside the purview of informal entrepreneurs. Chen (2007) illustrates several interactions between actors in the formal and informal economies; some are based on a labor subcontracting model, others on arms-length buy-sell arrangements, even new forms such as micro-franchising (Fairbourne, Gibson, & Dyer, 2007). None of these interactions, however, consider the possibility that informal entrepreneurs have formal/legal institutional tools at their disposal.

This paper describes a group of subsistence entrepreneurs—operating at low scale, in labor intensive arenas, and earning small incomes—in Ghana who successfully use the legal mechanism of a trade association to further their business interests. The findings contribute to the literature on the informal economy by arguing for an expanded definition and model of informal economic activity. Several extant models build from the assumption that formal tools, organizations, and institutions are unavailable to informal entrepreneurs. For example, dualists (ILO, 2002; Ray, 1998) categorize economic activity as belonging to the formal or informal sector and argue that *either* formal/legal institutional *or* informal/social institutional structures regulate such activities (Webb, Tihanyi, Ireland, & Simon, 2009). Structuralists portray relegation to the separate sphere of the informal economy as a form of marginalization or oppression toward some groups by powerful interests in the formal economy (Portes et al, 1989; Venkatesh, 2006; Wallerstein, 2004). Legalists argue that a separate informal economy constitutes a rational response by entrepreneurs to avoid taxes or other regulations in their pursuit of wealth (LaPorta & Schliefer, 2008; Piggott & Whalley, 2001). This paper accepts and extends Hart's (2006) critique of modeling the formal and informal activity as separate sectors or economies and advances a more nuanced perspective, one that sees economic activities regulated by both formal (legal) and informal (social) mechanisms simultaneously, even when some of those activities may be strictly illegal. Such a perspective, we believe, can add a layer of rich understanding that replaces an "artificial landscape" of the theorized informal economy (Polanyi, 1957: 257) with a more nuanced and informative model.

This paper contributes to the management literature by investigating these issues within a subsistence marketplace context. Webb et al. (2009) theorize about the role of the informal economy for entrepreneurs seeking to grow new businesses in the developed world, Spicer, McDermott, and Kogut (2000) examine the role of informal economic organization in the transition from communism to capitalism in Eastern Europe, and London and Hart (2004) focus on issues germane to Western Multi-National Corporations; however, little management scholarship bases inquiry from the perspective of subsistence entrepreneurs at the bottom of the economic pyramid. The perspective of those at the bottom of the economic pyramid matters for business leaders at the top considering how, when, and why to do business in subsistence marketplaces.

THEORY DEVELOPMENT

Economic activities consist of those physical, mental, social, and organizational actions involved in the production and exchange of goods and services. Economic activities do not cut at the joints between the formal and informal economy as enterprises in both economies engage in production and exchange. The institutional mechanisms and tools (e.g., legally enforceable written contracts, law enforcement agencies, courts, and forums for mediation or shared heritage and culture, common meanings, ties of friendship of kinship) that structure, limit, and regulate economic activities cut at the joint between the formal and informal economies. The formal economy has been defined as those economic activities supported and/or proscribed by the institutional and legal apparatus of the nation-state (LaPorta & Schleifer, 2008; Webb, Tihanyi, Ireland, & Simon, 2009). Venkatesh (2006) describes the essence of the formal economy as the combination of *licit* processes *and* outputs of production and exchange while *illicit* processes *or* outputs define the informal economy[1]. Webb et al. (2009) amplify this distinction by modeling the formal economy as licit and legitimate, the informal economy as illicit but legitimate, and the criminal economy as both illicit and illegitimate. Licit and illicit, as well as legitimate and illegitimate, will be defined by local actors and institutions, meaning that the exact contours of what constitutes formal and informal economic activity will vary. Godfrey (2011), however, offers a more nuanced approach that includes a semi-formal sector, one that uses both formal and informal mechanisms to regulate transactions.

Toward a New Model of the Informal Economy

Most definitions presume that choosing illicit means or illicit ends excludes those individuals or entities from legal regulation and/or protection. Becker (2004: 13) notes that informal employment "is *not recognized, regulated, or protected* by existing legal or regulatory frameworks (emphasis added)." Dualists, structuralists, and legalists all accept this logic as fundamental to the nature of the informal economy, extending it to the bundle of activities engaged in by informal actors. Substantial evidence exists—and the empirical study reported below buttresses this evidence—that entities competing informally (illicit means or ends) account for legal regulations and garner legal protections as they do business. Consider Napster, the exemplar of Webb et al.'s (2009) portrayal of the informal economy. While Napster pursued illicit ends (illegal transfers of copyrighted material), it did so as a legally registered corporation capable of being sued (e.g., *A&M Records, Inc. v. Napster*, 2001). Similarly, one can reflect on the number of building contractors utilizing the illegal practice of undocumented workers who operate as licensed contractors and pay into workers' compensation funds for those workers (Webb et al., 2009). Subsistence entrepreneurs occasionally use legal processes such as bank accounts or wire transfer facilities, and formal firms operating in the developing world may make facilitating payments or engage in other illicit processes in order to get business done. Evidence exists that firms engaged in illicit processes or products use legal organizations, structures, and regulations while doing business.

The paradox of formal/ legal protections for illegal economic activity arises from at least three sources. First, most constitutional states offer residents some blanket protections to citizens. Freedoms such as expression or the right to collective organization may supersede regional or local regulations. Ventakesh (2006) describes an underground economy in Chicago's urban South Side in which actors opportunistically invoked their right to police protection and public safety to intervene in community affairs while simultaneously putting at risk their off-the-books businesses. Similarly, a country's meta-institutional orientation (Friedland & Alford, 1991) may create classes such as labor, capital, or ethnicity (e.g., indigenous peoples) that grant special rights to all members of the protected class.

Second, the formal institutions of the state exist as separable organs; each one will focus on their own work and interests and have only limited contact or overlap with other bureaucratic organs. Weber (1947) outlines how the division of labor and clear lines of reporting and authority characterize efficient professional bureaucracies. Tax collection falls under one department, employment regulation a second, and workplace safety a third. Each agency, tasked with its own mission, authority, and objectives, finds little reason, and even less incentive, to notice and report activities outside their official scope. Entrepreneurs seeking advantage from one branch of the state need only ensure that they meet the requirements of that agency. Bureaucratic separability may be particularly characteristic of the impoverished nations filled with poor, subsistence entrepreneurs (Easterly, 2006). and government officials working in their own silos may afford protection to enterprises duly registered even as those entities violate other laws.

Finally, the advantage provided by formal organization and legal standing helps informal economy participants create and maintain order in their world. Specifically, formal organization and legal registration encodes certain baseline rules of behavior or procedures such as compliance with basic health practices or standards. Formal organizations make plain the social contract that often underlies informal activities (Durkheim, 1933). Formalization—and legal registration—also provides for a legitimated authority structure with roles, hierarchies, and procedures to enforce rules and contracts. Such a structure provides informal entrepreneurs with legitimacy when they must violate unspoken social norms. Put differently, formal structures and legal backing provides this group of entrepreneurs with a set of mechanisms that reduce the risk of transacting business, both risks from state intrusion but also market imperfections or vagaries.

Godfrey (2011) offers a revised model of economic activity that incorporates formality and informality into a semi-formal economy. Based on the dimensions of legal registration and bureaucratic administration (each as a yes/no response), four different types of economic activity appear. Formality (a yes on both dimensions) and informality (a no on both dimensions) account for the types of organizations most prevalent in the economics and management literature (see Guha-Khansnobis, Kanbur, and Ostrom (2006), Portes and Sensenbrenner (1993), Venkatesh (2006) for examples of research around informal economic activity). The relational economy— legal organization but non-bureaucratic administration—has received substantial attention by scholars working to understand transactional governance (e.g., Lazzarini, Miller, & Zenger, 2004; Poppo & Zenger, 2002).

Relational governance provides firms with substantial advantages in times of uncertainty and change. The final form, unregistered but formal, bureaucratic administration, should be an empty set; however, as noted above, evidence suggests that such activity takes place. This chapter highlights a set of entrepreneurs operating in this semi-formal economy and selectively using legal structures to enhance their operations.

Research Questions

Venkatesh (2006) observes that actors invoke formal/ legal structures to solve short-term challenges and crises such as outlandish gang-related drug sales or violence, but rely on social network resources to solve longer term community issues. Barnard (1938), alternatively, sees long-term benefit from relying on the security and regularity of formal institutions to supersede informal, social organization. The first research question considers timing and circumstances: In a subsistence environment, when do entrepreneurs use formal or legal structures to solve short-term crises or manage longer term challenges?

Invoking legal protections in some part of a business opens other aspects of the business to possible scrutiny and discovery by other organs of the state bureaucracy; going to the law jeopardizes the illegal parts of the operation. Sitkin and Roth (1993) write about the risks and challenges of blending legal and social governance forms. The movement to legal sanction, for example suing a supplier, may poison valuable relationships of trust that guide day-to-day transactions; conversely, failing to enforce breeches of contract in the name of building trust may perpetuate negative behaviors into the future. The second research question examines this issue: When do formal and legal tools reinforce the socially constituted norms of the market and when do they weaken those norms?

EMPIRICAL RESEARCH

Data

The research project from which the data are drawn began in 2004 with an invitation from the Dean of the authors' business school to become involved in research around poverty alleviation. Consistent with that goal, the lead author selected Ghana as a research site, given its relative political stability, record of sustainable economic growth, and the location of an affiliated nongovernmental organization (NGO) in the country to provide logistical support. The original investigations aimed to understand the determinants and definitions of success among micro-entrepreneurs, specifically individuals who created successful businesses without outside assistance such as microcredit.

Theoretical sampling (Rynes and Gephardt, 2004; Suddaby, 2006) principles guided the site selection process, and four urban craft and food markets in and around Accra, Ghana, fit the criteria because they contained a variety of micro-entrepreneurs. The lead researcher and a research assistant identified a core set of successful micro-entrepreneurs based on the stability of location and observed sales and income as well as a willingness to participate in a series of interviews[2]. The research assistant used the same criteria to expand the sample. Data collected in summer of 2005 come from repeated semi-structured interviews, observation, and participation in market activities (purchase of goods and services). The initial sample consisted of multiple visits with 24 interviewees. Two follow-up rounds of interviews in 2008 and 2009 expanded the sample to 27 micro-entrepreneurs plus local academics, NGO leaders, and World Bank personnel. A final visit to Ghana in 2012 allowed the researchers to see the longer term impacts of informal and formal organization on these markets. The entire research data base consists of over 90 single-spaced pages of field notes as well as photos and collected artifacts. Table 9.1 contains descriptive information on the complete set of entrepreneurs.

Table 9.1 Descriptive Data on Interviewees in the Research Process, Names Disguised

Name	Born	M/F	Education	Hometown	Business	Emp.	Income Group
Aba	1958	F	SSS	Kumasi	Art and Craft Shop Owner (5 Shops)	4	High
Adelle	1963	F	JSS	Osu (Accra)	Consumer Products Shop Owner	0	Low
Akanke	1958	F	JSS	Accra	Shop Owner, Fabric Maker	2	Middle
Alike	1960	F	N/R	Accra	Banana Stand Owner	2	Middle
Agu	1964	M	JSS	Bokuruwa-Kwahu	Hardware Store Owner	0	Low
Bantu	1978	M	JSS	Kwame-Krum	Carver, Art and Craft Shop Manager	0	Low
Baako	1944	F	PRI	Volta Region	Fabric Shop Owner	20	N/R
Cecia	1963	F	B.S. Econ	Accra	Cosmetics Shop Owner	0	Middle
Enoch	1955	M	Technical School	Volta Region	Weaver	2	Middle
Fineas	1976	M	Metal engineering	Accra	Carver and Art Shop Owner (3 Shops/Internet)	2	High
Freddie	1979	M	JSS	Jamestown	Shirt Seller	0	Low
Keon	1971	M	PRI	Accra	Clothing Shop Owner	0	Middle
Kilara	1980	M	JSS	Cape Coast	Art and Craft Shop Employee	N/A	Low
Myuna	1967	F	N/R	Eastern Region	Beautician and Doll Maker	23	Middle

(Continued)

Table 9.1 (Continued)

Name	Born	M/F	Education	Hometown	Business	Emp.	Income Group
Maka	1955	M	SSS	N/R	Hotel, Transportation, Building Materials Owner	UNK	High
Naeem	1979	M	JSS	Upper East Region	Carver, Weaver, and Art Shop Owner (3 shops)	4	Middle
Panyin	1937	M	SSS	Accra	Baker	4	High
Pilan	1977	M	Administration	Kumasi	Research, Property Management Company Owner	20	High
Raphael	1954	M	Polytechnic	Central Region	Construction Company Owner	36	High
Razi	1969	M	JSS	Osu (Accra)	Store Owner and Telecom Shop	0	High
Tabari	1984	M	JSS	Adenta (Accra)	Video Game Rental Business	0	High
Taree	1975	M	Electrical Engineering	Volta Region	Electrician and Art and Craft Shop Owner	0	N/R
Vinita	1972	F	SSS	Mountain Region	Consumer Goods Shop Owner	0	Low
Vonni	1958	F	SSS	Labadi	Fish Smoker and Trader	0	High
Vanessa	1951	F	SSS	Winnebe	Rabbit Raiser	0	N/R
Warner	1981	M	JSS	Volta Region	Cigarette Vendor, Art and Craft Shop Manager	0	Middle

The research design allowed the researchers to follow grounded theory principles (Glaser & Strauss, 1967; Suddaby, 2006), including a focus on emic (respondent centered) understanding and constant comparison between the data and extant/ emergent theoretical constructs that resulted in an iterative data collection strategy in which subsequent interview topics built on insights and analysis of previous data. All interviews invited respondents to share their own histories of success, views of the current environment, and challenges. The researchers did not use theoretical terms or suggest categories of responses; follow-up questions generally sought to better understand why the participants felt and thought as they did.

The researchers identified themselves at the outset as university researchers and described the goals of the project and purpose of the interviews. As a part of the work, the researchers purchased items from a number of these vendors; however, the researchers tried to decouple purchases from participation in the interview process in order to avoid biased responses by the interviewees. A single research assistant conducted the initial interviews in 2005 and the primary author and another research assistant conducted the 2008 and 2009 interviews together. The lead author made the 2012 visit unaccompanied.

Current Sample

The data for this paper come from a theoretically driven sample based on the research questions outlined above. The authors reviewed coded field notes for instances of informal entrepreneurs utilizing legally constituted and recognized organizations and institutional structures in their activities. The classification of informal entrepreneur depended on whether, although the products sold were all legal, the means of production and sale contained a preponderance of off-the-books or illicit elements (Venkatesh, 2006). These individuals either hired or paid employees extra-legally or failed to record and report revenue to the taxing authority.

The selected data constitute a multiple-holistic case study design (Yin, 2002) considering multiple events or issues within a single site or level of analysis, in this case a trade association operating at the Airport Market (a pseudonym). The Airport Market consisted of about 60 shops in 2005 and over 100 by 2008. The market, about 100 yards long and 40 yards deep, lies just down a slight hill off a road connecting three of Ghana's largest cities. The Airport Market, although populated by informal entrepreneurs, utilizes both legal and bureaucratic structures.

Trade associations are legally recognized workers collectives (unions) organized under the Ghanaian Industrial Relations Act of 1958, enacted a year after Ghanaian independence (TUC, 2011). Any economically oriented collective group can organize a trade association—even business owners—and gain labor protection and formal political voice with the Trade Union Council (TUC).[3] Formed in 2000, the Airport Market Trade Association (AMTA) represents the dues-paying members of the Airport Market (dues run about $1/ month, and the AMTA had over 130 members as of 2009), maintains a written constitution and by-laws, and has a regularly elected chair, vice chair, secretary, and treasurer (Fineas, 2005, 2008).[4] The AMTA places all dues in a formal bank account. The AMTA acts as a mutual aid society as well as trade association: AMTA funds can be used to help out members in distress, such as providing assistance for funeral expenses or fires (Fineas, 2005).

Method

The analysis for this article combined the grounded theory used in the overall project with accepted analytical methods for case study research (Eisenhardt, 1989; Miles & Huberman, 1994; Yin, 2002). Given the strictures of this chapter, we selected four discrete business challenges in which the AMTA played or failed to play a role. The cases consider two short-term and two long-term challenges, thus providing ample opportunity to examine the research questions.

Within-case analysis constitutes the first step in good case study research, and the researchers wrote narrative cases to capture each event based on the field notes (Miles & Huberman, 1994; Yin, 2002). The construction of each case allowed the researchers to move to theory and identify relevant constructs in each case. Cross-case analysis provided the opportunity to triangulate these findings and revealed new patterns and constructs to elaborate the analysis and strengthen conclusions. Table 9.2 provides key data for each of the four cases, and the ensuing analysis builds upon the data described here to investigate the research questions. The four cases have been labeled *Accra Beautification*, *Market Regulation*, *Flood Cleanup*, and *Infrastructure Upgrades*.

Data and Analysis

Accra Beautification. The Accra beautification case captures an all-too-common problem faced by subsistence entrepreneurs without titled land: "Cleaning the streets" represents a common action by government leaders to assert control and project a positive image to outsiders (Alike, 2009). Table 9.1 describes the key events that took place during this successful use of the AMTA mechanism. The AMTA succeeded because it provided substantive advantages and relief to the entrepreneurs. The AMTA gave the entrepreneurs legal status and standing through the TUC to press its claims when other bureaucratic agencies offered no relief; indeed, the lack of titled property gave rise to those seeking to evict the traders. The AMTA afforded the owners a legitimate political voice to employ in the fight to maintain their shops, and the pooled funds allowed the group to retain an attorney and attract politically powerful individuals to visit the market, something no individual could have afforded on their own.

Table 9.2 Four Cases Involving the Airport Market Association

Dimension/Case	Accra Beautification	Market Rules	Flood Cleanup	Infrastructure Upgrades
Date	2007	Ongoing	2008	2009
Triggering Event	Soccer tournament, UN Conferences	Strategic differentiation	Major storm causes flooding of canal	Opening of new mall across the roundabout
Key Events	• Metropolitan Authority moves to evict shop owners • Market Association provides money for lawyer • Fineas (Market Chair) works with TUC and initiates letters to officials • Member of Parliament (MP) visits site, notes Association • Shops allowed to remain, non-AMTA shops close	• Market focuses on low-pressure selling environment and high-quality, genuine goods • Clear rules formalized in association documents • Association Chair initiates disciplinary actions toward violators • Market association has formal committee to enforce violations of rules	• Canal flood damages shops; mud, garbage, and debris abound in common areas • Shops had between 12–15 inches of water inside • Insufficient sandbagging exists, no later sandbagging occurred (2009) • Individuals team up to clean shops, no work on common areas • No coordinated cleanup effort of common areas	• Mall filled with foreign goods raises competitive bar for amenities • 4-way interchange replaces roundabout and reduces traffic • Need for common area improvements seen by leaders and participants • Shop owners lack formal title to their land and shops, which discourages investment • Sales eroding
Primary Data Sources	Interviews with Alike, Aba, Naeem, Fineas, and others	Fineas, Warner, and others	Observation by researchers, lack of mention in interviews	Interviews with Aba, Fineas, Naeem, Warner, and others
Time Frame	Short term	Long term	Short term	Long term
Success of Market Association	Successful	Successful	Unsuccessful	Unsuccessful

Market Regulation. The Airport Market caters to Ghana's expatriate population; the historical majority of visitors to the market come from Accra's expatriate community of Chinese, Indian, American, and European nationals purchasing for their own needs, to provide unique gifts to visitors, or to send home (Warner, 2008). The market's strategy aims to create a sales culture of high-quality and genuine Ghanaian (and West African) handicrafts coupled with a low pressure sales atmosphere. Coleman (1988) notes that social capital and collective norms set and enforce market regulatory structures; however, here the formal rules and structure of the AMTA articulate, codify, police, and enforce the selling culture as described in Table 9.2. The AMTA does not control prices at the market; one interviewee, Fineas (2008), indicated that the needs of individual shop owners control their own pricing in the market and no seller wants to infringe on another's right to earn as they see fit. While the AMTA controls selling behaviors, an attitude of individual owner rights and laissez-faire seems to permeate the business approach of the market.

The AMTA constitutes a tool these entrepreneurs can use to supplement and enforce informal, socially generated rules and sanctions through both substantive means (e.g., the ability to encode norms and beliefs into formal rules) and symbolic structures. The formal authority of the Chair, derived from his legitimate election by members (Weber, 1947), in enforcing the market rules provides a mechanism whereby rules can be enforced without rupturing the good will and mutual trust that arises from the informal nature of the market.

Flood Cleanup. A substantial rainstorm greeted the researchers in Ghana for the 2008 round of data collection; in fact, all landings were delayed due to the energy driving the storm. The research visit to the Airport Market the next morning revealed that the canal running alongside the market had flooded the shops and common areas, as described in Table 9.2. Approaching the market from the road proved a difficult and dirty task, which seemed of little concern to market participants.

The researchers came to the market with the goal of a better understanding of the nature and functioning of the AMTA; hence, both researchers took notice of the lack of coordinated activity at the canal to mitigate flooding or in cleaning the common areas. In subsequent interviews *no one* remarked on the lack of collective action regarding the flooded common areas, and Fineas did not talk about flooding as either a short-term crisis for which the AMTA could coordinate joint activity or a long-term issue for remediation. Interviewee Aba (2008) noted in a later interview a recognized need for concrete flood control of the canal to prevent flooding; an examination of the canal bank revealed one row of sandbags (about 3 ft in height). This lack of action constitutes a case of the dog that didn't bark (Doyle, 1892/2003).

Why did AMTA leaders fail to use the organization to require, or at least coordinate, cleanup of the common areas of the market? Why didn't they even talk about the potential of the AMTA to contribute to this issue, even when the researchers asked about the structure and advantages of the

AMTA? Unlike the case of market rules, it appears that emergency procedures have not been incorporated into the explicit rule of the market (Aba's comments seem consistent with this interpretation) and so the AMTA lacks a substantive mandate to act in this case. The lack of a formal rule may also constrain the symbolic authority of the chair to intervene; the case of cleaning the common areas appears to be treated like pricing in the market, left to the discretion of individuals. Paradoxically, the AMTA succeeds in regulating common behavior but fails in coordinating physical spaces.

Infrastructure Upgrades. The Accra Mall, located about one-half mile from the Airport Market just across a newly built highway interchange, opened in 2007 to celebrate the 50th anniversary of Ghanaian independence and as a symbol of the increasing prosperity and sophistication of the country (Accra Mall, 2011). The researchers systematically scoured the mall looking for Ghanaian-made handicrafts and found none—the mall features European, Nigerian, and South African imports; nevertheless, the mall constitutes a long-term competitive threat to the Airport Market in the eyes of market participants. Fineas (2009) explained that the mall had "raised the bar" of competition for the level of the shopping experience expatriates wanted and would tolerate, and Aba (2009) called the Airport Market "an eyesore" in comparison with the new mall. Market participants failed to effectively respond to this threat.

Fineas and Aba both viewed the future of the market as dismal absent major upgrades to the market layout and common areas. Fineas (2009) saw the creation of parking facilities and a redesign of the physical layout as essential; Aba (2009) argued that toilet facilities and more differentiated merchandise would help the market compete. Because of their collective nature, many improvements would need the approval of, if not formal coordination through, the AMTA.

Aba believes that such improvements would prove difficult without formal, legally recognized property rights, the lack of which obviates AMTA from stewarding effective improvements. Given the risk to their current survival—business dropped between 50%–75% at most shops in the market since the mall opened—few participants saw extensive investments in their own infrastructure, let alone substantial outlay for common areas, as prudent. The legal structure of the AMTA facilitated substantive relief when the shops faced closure during the beautification episode; the limited benefit and the lack of concomitant property rights precludes similar action in the case of long-term decline.

When do entrepreneurs use formal institutional structures to solve short-term crises or manage longer term challenges? The entrepreneurs at the Airport Market used the AMTA to solve both short- and long-term business issues; however, they also failed to use the AMTA to solve other crises and long-term issues. The answer to this conundrum seems to lie in the answer to the second question: When do formal and legal tools reinforce the socially constituted norms of the market and when do they weaken those norms?

It appears that these entrepreneurs invoke the formal and legal structure of the AMTA only when its use complements, rather than contradicts, the underlying social norms in the market. Survival of their businesses, threatened during the Accra beautification, quickly became a shared value among market participants, and the low-key sales culture that the AMTA reinforced appeared deeply engrained among all the interviewees. The lack of use of the collective machinery of the AMTA to clean up short-term flood damage or coordinate common-area improvements puzzled the researchers, particularly since the interviewees themselves appeared not to perceive the AMTA as a viable contributor (as evidenced by their lack of talking about it). It seems plausible to assume that control of the common areas of the market—the focus of both cases—falls under the laissez-faire culture that permeates much of the market. An alternative explanation for the relative success and failure of the AMTA considers the role of the AMTA in solving collective action problems at the market.

Collective Action Problems

The concepts of legal substance and symbolic organization help explain how and why the entrepreneurs at the Airport Market use the AMTA to benefit their business activities. Mancur Olson's (1965) theory of collective action furnishes another lens through which to view the uses and successes of the AMTA. Olson observed that many projects that would benefit members of a community fail to happen because of the following problem: the collective benefits of the action fall to every member regardless of their contribution to bringing that benefit about; rational actors will allow someone else to incur the costs of action and then enjoy the associated benefits. Simply put, free riding dooms many efforts at collective action.

Collective action works in two instances. In those situations where the benefits of collective action are high (e.g., the evictions threatened in the beautification episode) but the individuals incur few costs, few barriers exist to collective action due to the gap between private benefits and cost (Libecap, 1989). Interviewees Warner (2008) and Naeem (2008) both noted that their actions were limited to paying their AMTA dues; Fineas, acting as AMTA Chair, did all the work to save the market. Collective action also works when shirking and free riding can be controlled through monitoring (Olson, 1965). The AMTA has formally encoded a clear set of acceptable behaviors, and the organizational structure of the AMTA provides an enforcement mechanism. The behavioral observability of these rules and the close proximity of the participants allow for efficient monitoring of shirking and facilitate effective collection action. The AMTA works in those instances with low collective action problems or a high degree of monitoring and enforcement capability.

Collective action fails, however, when the benefits of action accrue to the larger group but may not devolve directly to individuals, and the anticipated costs to each individual prove substantial. Upgrading the market's infrastructure by changing the layout (Fineas's solution), building a toilet (Aba's recommendation), or other enhancements of the common areas exemplify this case. The expected individual benefits of improved amenities that would come to the market appear not to exceed the individual costs, which would be substantial—far greater than the $1 per month dues. The case of flood control operates under the same logic; the benefits of clean and tidy common areas—or flood mitigation efforts—simply do not outweigh the individual costs. Under this condition, most rational entrepreneurs would wait for someone else to make the investment and then enjoy the benefits at no cost (Olson, 1965); thus, the machinery of the AMTA should remain idle. The leaders of the AMTA may be loath to intervene because the costs of its own action in terms of legitimacy or enforceability may be less than the collective benefit.

DISCUSSION

Limitations

As with all empirical research, the present study suffers from limitations and shortcomings. First, as with most qualitative enquiries, the authors opted for the precision and insight offered by a few cases at the expense of the generality of a larger sample size (Weick, 1979), and the reported findings should be considered both exploratory and tentative given the small number of cases. Second, the data come from one country, with a single historical trajectory and a set of unique institutions (Thelen, 1999). The market association form may be country, and time, specific, which suggests that future researchers focus on both within-country *as well as* cross-country research to gain a richer picture of the deep structures that provide the opportunity for legal and formal governance in the developing world. Third, our research focused exclusively on an urban environment, and significant differences exist between urban and rural conditions. Finally, the initial project sought to understand these entrepreneurs in their own frames and terms and how they saw the environment they competed in. While the emic basis of the interviews offers the perspective of the subsistence entrepreneurs themselves, the method leaves theoretically relevant holes; indeed, the picture of the AMTA relies as much on when actors did not use the structure as when they did.

Implications

This study indicates that subsistence entrepreneurs in the developing world, much like their counterparts in the developed world (e.g., those studied by Venkatesh (2006)), have access to and utilize formal economy structures to govern transactions and solve business problems. The gap between understanding subsistence entrepreneurship in the developing versus the developed world may be narrower than one would initially think. On a related note, the study indicates that developing country subsistence entrepreneurs act as economically rational actors, contrary to some extant models that view informal entrepreneurs as possessing inferior human capital compared to those in the formal economy (LaPorta & Schliefer, 2008). The Ghanaians in this study desired as much legal/formal structure as they could reasonably obtain and would like to obtain more in terms of property ownership and rights. They also seem to engage in a sophisticated cost-benefit analysis when employing the AMTA and balance the advantages of relying on formal and legal authority with the risks of unsettling the underlying set of norms, relationships, and attitudes that provide so much of the market's governance.

These findings suggest that business executives doing business in subsistence markets, and those charged with creating public policy for those markets, should focus on helping these entrepreneurs overcome barriers to collective action. DeSoto (2000) argues that policymakers focus on making the tools of formalization more available and easier to obtain through efforts such as expedited business registration. This study suggests, along with McMillan (2002) and Portes and Sensenbrenner (1993), that policymakers focus on making formalization more beneficial in the day-to-day lives of subsistence entrepreneurs. When the private and collective benefits of formalization/ legalization exceed the private costs, then subsistence entrepreneurs should prove more willing to symbolically and substantively move toward formalizing their operations.

We suggested at the outset that studying the informal economy from the perspective of those at the bottom, the subsistence entrepreneurs themselves, would add value to the literature. Prahalad (2005) emphasizes the rationality, intelligence, and acumen of consumers at the bottom of the pyramid; this research helps both scholars and executives understand that the same intelligence, rationality, and acumen apply to those engaged in production at the bottom of the pyramid. This study begins to answer Karnani's (2007) call to understand production at the bottom of the pyramid; indeed, the current findings illuminate the institutional governance mechanisms available to those creating wealth at the bottom of the pyramid.

Our argument at the outset claimed that revising and expanding the definition of the informal economy would aid scholarship and further research. Weick (1979) notes that scholars must choose between generality and precision in their study, and the presumption toward parsimony raises the question of whether an expanded definition of the informal economy gives up more in the explanatory simplicity of generality (illegal enterprises lack access to legal protection, which is obviously true in many cases) than it gains in the explanatory richness of a detailed and nuanced description. If the results were limited to a group of Ghanaian entrepreneurs, then we would gladly cede the point and argue for explanatory simplicity; however, the results of this study confirm the episodic use of formal structures and legal protections among entrepreneurs in the undeveloped world, both the subsistence type studied by Venkatesh (2006) and the growth type targeted by Webb et al. (2009). Occam's razor favors simplicity over complexity, but the razor wants to parse real landscapes, not artificial ones designed simply for elegance and simplicity's sake (Polanyi, 1957).

The expanded view of the semi-formal economy presented here shows that the condition of non-legal registration but formal administration (through the AMTA) is not an empty set but filled with actors and activities. This enriches the field's understanding by providing an opposite quadrant to relational governance, a topic of interest to strategy and management scholars (e.g., Poppo & Zenger, 2002). The extant view in this literature models trust and informality as a replacement for legal and formal governance when the latter fail, with the presumption being that formality will always provide superior governance. Our work suggests that reliance on legal and formal structures for governance may be the replacement for the failure of informality, with the proviso, however, that legal structures may only be invoked when consistent with informal goals, norms, and attitudes. Similarly, the risk of relational governance lies in the traditional hazards of breach of contract while the risk of legal governance may be the potential destabilization of the underlying social and informal governance structures.

Finally, a redefinition of economic activity as being governed by a mix of both formal and informal institutions and structures moves the literature on the informal economy in the direction suggested by Hart (2006). Hart's concern with the notion of an informal economy or informal sector lies in the tendency of researchers to bifurcate a real, nuanced, and complex world into simplistic categories that obscure more of reality than they reveal. He suggests thinking about informality as an organizing mechanism available to structure different types of activities and not informality as some separate place or state.

CONCLUSION

Do subsistence entrepreneurs, whose businesses operate primarily in the informal economy, use formal institutions and legal mechanisms to enhance their business practices? Yes. The evidence presented in this paper, based on qualitative research in subsistence marketplaces in Ghana, indicates that informal entrepreneurs have access to, and utilize, formal and legally recognized organizational forms in pursuit of their business goals. Such a finding suggests that the current view of the relationship between formal and informal economic governance—the view of two separate and distinctive sectors—should give way to a richer, more nuanced version of economic activity governed by both formal and informal mechanisms.

NOTES

1. The informal economy means illicit means or ends; the criminal economy consists of illegal means and ends. The current paper excludes the criminal economy from consideration.
2. Most entrepreneurs fit the description of subsistence entrepreneurs' earlier, small-scale, labor-intensive, and low-income-producing businesses. These entrepreneurs, through our interviews, saw themselves as operating in the informal economy, given local norms and standards.
3. The right to organize as a trade union came from a pro-socialist oriented government at Ghanaian independence in 1957, thus conforming to the theorized driver of legal governance arising from citizenship rights.
4. Although we use the author-date format to cite interview data, the author refers to the respondent and the year to the year in which the interview took place or other data were collected.

REFERENCES

A & M Records, Inc. v. Napster, 239 F.3d 1004, 2001.

Accra Mall. 2011. http://www.accramall.com/, February 10.

Barnard, C.I. 1938. *The functions of the executive.* Cambridge, MA: Harvard University Press.

Becker, K.F. 2004. *The informal economy: Fact finding study.* Swedish International Development Agency.

Chen, M.A. 2007. *Rethinking the informal economy: Linkages with the formal economy and the regulatory environment.* New York: Economic and Social Affairs, DESA Working paper # 46.

Coleman, J.S. 1988. Social capital in the creation of human capital. *American Journal of Sociology*, 94: S95–S120.

De Soto, H. 2000. *The mystery of capital : Why capitalism triumphs in the West and fails everywhere else.* New York: Basic Books.

Doyle, A.C. 1892/2003. *The silver blaze.* The memoirs of Sherlock Holmes. New York, NY: Bantam Classics.

Durkheim, É. 1933. *The division of labor in society.* New York: Macmillan.

Easterly, W. 2006. *The White Man's burden: Why the west's efforts to aid the rest have done so much ill and so little good.* New York: Penguin books.

Eisenhardt, K.M. 1989. Building theories from case study research. *The Academy of Management Review*, 14(4): 532–550.

Fairbourne, J.S., Gibson, S.W., & Dyer, W.G. 2007. *MicroFranchising : Creating wealth at the bottom of the pyramid.* Northampton, MA: Edward Elgar.

Friedland, R., & Alford, R.R. 1991. Bringing society back in: Symbols, practices, and institutional contradictions. In Powell, W. W. and DiMaggio, P. J. (Eds.), *The new institutionalism in organizational analysis*: 232–266. Chicago: The University of Chicago Press.

Glaser, B.G., & Strauss, A.L. 1967. *The discovery of grounded theory : Strategies for qualitative research.* Chicago: Aldine de Gruyter.

Godfrey, P. C. 2011. Toward a Theory of the Informal Economy. *The Academy of Management Annals*, 5(1): 231–277.

Guha-Khansnobis, B., Kanbur, R., & Ostrom, E. 2006. Beyond formality and informality. In B. Guha-Khansnobis, R. Kanbur, & E. Ostrom (Eds.), *Linking the formal and informal economy: Concepts and policies*: 1–18. Oxford: Oxford University Press.

Hart, K. 2006. Bureaucratic form and the informal economy. In B. Guha-Khansnobis, R. Kanbur, & E. Ostrom (Eds.), *Linking the formal and informal economy*: 21–36. Oxford: Oxford University Press.

International Labor Organization (ILO). 2002. *Women and men in the informal economy: A statistical picture*: 64. Geneva, Switzerland: International Labor Organization.

Karnani, A. 2007. The mirage of marketing to the bottom of the pyramid. *California Management Review*, 49: 90–111.

LaPorta, R., & Shleifer, A. 2008. *The unofficial economy and economic development*: 1–75. Working Paper Series, National Bureau of Economic Research, Washington, DC.

Lazzarini, S. G., Miller, G. J., & Zenger, T. R. 2004. Order with some law: Complementarity versus substitution of formal and informal arrangements. *Journal of Law, Economics, & Organization*, 20(2): 261–298.

Libecap, G. D. 1993. *Contracting for property rights*. New York: Cambridge University Press.

London, T., & Hart, S. L. 2004. Reinventing strategies for emerging markets: Beyond the transnational model. *Journal of International Business Studies*, 35(5): 350–370.

McMillan, J. 2002. *Reinventing the bazaar : A natural history of markets*. New York: Norton.

Miles, M. B., & Huberman, A. M. 1994. *Qualitative data analysis : An expanded sourcebook*. Thousand Oaks: Sage.

Olson, M. 1965. *The logic of collective action: Public goods and the theory of groups*. Cambridge, MA: Harvard University Press.

Piggott, J., & Whalley, J. 2001. VAT base broadening, self supply, and the informal sector. *The American Economic Review*, 91(4): 1084–1094.

Polanyi, K. 1957. The economy as instituted process. In K. Polanyi, C. M. Arensberg, & H. W. Pearson (Eds.), *Trade and market in the early empires*: 243–270. Chicago: Henry Regnery Company.

Poppo, L., & Zenger, T. 2002. Do formal contracts and relational governance function as substitutes or complements? *Strategic Management Journal*, 23(8): 707–725.

Portes, A., Castells, M., & Benton, L. A. 1989. *The informal economy : Studies in advanced and less developed countries*. Baltimore, MD: Johns Hopkins University Press.

Portes, A., & Sensenbrenner, J. 1993. Embeddedness and Immigration: Notes on the Social Determinants of Economic Action. *American Journal of Sociology*, 98(6): 1320–1350.

Prahalad, C. K. 2005. *The fortune at the bottom of the pyramid*. Upper Saddle River, NJ: Wharton School Pub.

Ray, D. 1998. *Development economics*. Princeton, NJ: Princeton University Press.

Rynes, S. L., & Gephardt, R. P. 2004. Qualitative research and the "Academy of Management Journal." *Academy of Management Journal*, 47: 451–462.

Sitkin, S. B., & Roth, N. L. 1993. Explaining the limited effectiveness of legalistic "remedies" for trust/distrust. *Organization Science*, 4(3): 367–392.

Spicer, A., McDermott, G. A., & Kogut, B. 2000. Entrepreneurship and privatization in Central Europe: The tenuous balance between destruction and creation. *The Academy of Management Review*, 25(3): 630–649.

Suddaby, R. 2006. What grounded theory is not. *Academy of Management Journal*, 49: 633–642.

Thelen, K. 1999. Historical institutionalism in comparative politics. *Annual Review of Political Science*, 2: 369–404.

TUC. 2011. *Ghana Trades Union Congress*. http://www.ghanatuc.org/. Accessed 2011.

Venkatesh, S. A. 2006. *Off the books : The underground economy of the urban poor*. Cambridge, MA: Harvard University Press.

Wallerstein, I. M. 2004. *World-systems analysis : An introduction*. Durham: Duke University Press.

Webb, J. W., Tihanyi, L., Ireland, R. D., & Sirmon, D. G. 2009. You say illegal, I say legitimate: Entrepreneurship in the informal economy. *Academy of Management Review*, 34: 492–510.

Weber, M. 1947. *The theory of social and economic organization*. New York: Simon and Schuster.

Weick, K. E. 1979. *The social psychology of organizing*. New York: Random House.

Yin, R. K. 2002. *Case study research : Design and methods*. Thousand Oaks: Sage Publications.

10 An Individual's Unique Identity as a Missing Link in Research on the Informal Economy

Learning from India's Aadhaar Project

Vijay Sathe and Urs Jäger

Developed countries provide each individual with an official birth certificate, on the basis of which are issued other official ID documents such as a passport and a driver's license that provide a unique identity (UID) for each individual. Those who live in developed countries take the UID for granted and use it to open bank accounts, buy and sell products and services, receive government services and benefits to which they are entitled, and transact the business of everyday life in myriad other ways in the formal economy.

However, such a "simple thing" as a formal identity is anything but simple in many informal settings. In fact, one of the reasons why informality may persist is because, without an identity, transition to the formal economy may be impossible. So this is an important issue in understanding how the informal economy really functions and the barriers to exiting it.

The work of Nobel laureate Amartya Sen (2010) highlights the importance not only of food, clothing, housing, and other basic human needs but also of *access* to education, nutrition, healthcare and other services to enable people to lift themselves out of poverty and flourish. It is an obvious but often ignored fact that one cannot get access to the services that one is entitled to if one does not have any verifiable identification to prove who one is. While informal identification worked to some extent when most of the population lived in small villages, it cannot help those who wish to leave—or escape—their local context to access the resources and opportunities available in the modern economy.

Many of the world's poor at the base of the pyramid (BoP), estimated at 4 billion in a world population of 7 billion (Hammond, Kramer, Tran, Katz, & Walker, 2007), do not have a birth certificate (for example, 50% of the population of India does not have a birth certificate) or a UID that is based on it. Many of these people live and work in the informal economy, and they can increase their incomes either if they become more productive in the informal economy or if they can get jobs in the formal economy where the wages are higher because of its greater productivity (Kotwal, 2011a). However, the poor are trapped because it is difficult for them to do either for a variety of reasons, including lack of knowledge, skills, awareness, connections, and a UID.

The term "unique identity" may conjure up for the reader a wide variety of images and meanings, including the rights of those who feel excluded from work or even from society because of their social status or ethnic or sexual orientation, but our use of the term UID is limited to an economic perspective based on whether a person has an official, unique identification and whether, on the basis of such identification, he or she can gain access to the formal economy and to the resources and services to which he or she is entitled. It is for this reason that in this chapter we will refer to individuals operating in the informal economy—with or without a UID—as "market actors."

We argue that the concept of a UID is missing in research on the informal economy and its links to the formal economy, and we explore how the possession of a UID by market actors in the informal economy influences their ability to access the formal economy. We also review some of the important research questions to be addressed once the UID is included in scholarly work on the informal economy.

UIDs IN TRADITIONAL AND MODERN SOCIETIES

In traditional societies, such as in the half a million villages of India, "everybody knows everybody" whereby an individual's ID is defined informally only. Such an "informal ID" may be sufficient to work and live in the informal economy of the local community, but it does not automatically enable a market actor to access the informal economies of other communities or the formal markets, whether they are local, regional, national or global.

In some developing countries, like India, that have state governments within a federal structure, a local government may provide an official ID that is accepted within its jurisdiction, including in all the villages and other traditional communities within it. Such "regional IDs" enable a market actor to access government services and benefits and the formal markets in the region, but they do not guarantee similar access to the formal markets beyond the region and the benefits and services offered by the national government.

In modern societies, with the increasing influence of the Internet, mobile phones, and similar technologies on people's everyday lives, a market actor may create and use multiple IDs—with usernames and passwords—in order to get access to different online services. More and more people who live and work in the world's informal economies also now have this opportunity to create and use such "online IDs" to access information via the World Wide Web, communicate electronically with those they know as well as with those they do not know, and get work done that does not require a UID.

Although providing people in informal markets with "online IDs" through the use of new technologies sounds promising, this is only a first step. The critical question is what kinds of opportunities this opens up for market actors in informal economies and how new technologies can help them get access to formal economies and government services and benefits to which they are entitled but which they often do not receive due to graft and corruption and because they do not possess a UID. To motivate this discussion, we now introduce an ambitious and controversial UID project currently underway in India.

INDIA'S LARGE-SCALE "NATURAL EXPERIMENT": AADHAAR, THE WORLD'S MOST AMBITIOUS UID

This large-scale "natural experiment" in India provides an unusual opportunity for research on the informal economy, specifically the neglected question of how a UID can influence the lives of those who live and work in the informal economy.

In early 2009, the Prime Minister of India invited Mr. Nandan Nilekani, co-founder of Infosys, one of the world's largest software companies, to lead the Indian government's audacious plan to issue to each of the country's 1.2 billion residents an IT infrastructure-enabled UID that could be readily authenticated online, thus circumventing the familiar problems of duplicate ID cards and fake identities (http://uidai.gov.in/). This UID has been branded as "Aadhaar," which means "foundation" in many Indian languages, because its aim is to provide for every resident of India the freedom to pursue whatever direction in life he or she seeks as well as to ensure that the benefits intended for the poor actually reach them instead of being siphoned off by corrupt intermediaries (Sathe, 2011). The project is controversial because of concerns about data privacy and the risk that it might make it more difficult for the poorest of the poor living in remote areas without Internet access to secure its benefits.

As of October 2014, over 650 million people in India possess this UID, and most of them live in the informal economy. The newly elected Prime Minister of India, Narendra Modi, not only supports the Aadhaar project championed by the rival Congress party that his party trounced in the Indian national elections held in May 2014 but also has decided to expand enrollment to 1 billion UIDs as soon as possible (Sathe, 2014).

Of significant theoretical interest is the following point made by Nandan Nilekani (in an email communication with the authors in 2012), who brought India's UID from concept to 650 million people in possession of it in five short years (2009–2014)—that "identity rights" are more basic to economic empowerment than the acknowledged importance of "property rights":

Hernando de Soto (2000) has argued that "property rights" is what distinguish western capitalism and is what the developing countries need. Our belief is that "identity rights" precede property rights as without a formal identity a person cannot even stake his claim in a society—for his rights, his entitlements, access to products and services, a bank account etc. This "formalization" of participation of a nation's residents has political, economic and social consequences.

India's Aadhaar enables the market actors in the informal economy to open and use bank accounts, obtain credit and insurance, buy property or other assets, and get health, education, and other benefits that they are entitled to but do not receive because they lack proof of identity. Also, although the 73rd amendment to India's constitution was passed some time ago with great fanfare because it devolved greater authority to local levels, these levels have now become more bureaucratic and corrupt (Kotwal, 2011b). UID-enabled transactions via transparent electronic media can help to reduce the power of the local elite to obstruct individual initiative and extract illegal "rents" via "hold-up." For example, in places where land records can now be registered at a kiosk electronically, the local bureaucrats cannot intervene and take bribes (Nilekani, 2009). By providing identity rights to hundreds of millions of people, the UID has the potential to create positive change on a massive scale, which scholars have argued is needed to match the enormity of the task (Hart, 2010).[1]

But some critics have argued that India's Aadhaar UID may also lead to breach of individual privacy and national security (Sathe, 2011, 2014). Others have objected that the proposal to transfer cash benefits directly into their UID-enabled bank accounts in order to prevent leakage to corrupt intermediaries (Kotwal, 2011b) may not be on balance a better alternative than the present, albeit corrupt, system of in-kind benefit transfers via the public distribution system of subsidized products and services such as food grains and LPG gas cylinders for home cooking (Adhikari et al., 2011). Concerns also have been raised about the unintended consequences of UIDs—for example, although UID enrollment is voluntary, it could become the *de facto* requirement for identification in ways not intended or beneficial to the individual (Chacko & Khanduri, 2011).

The technological, political, bureaucratic, and behavioral challenges involved in issuing 1.2 billion UIDs are immense (Sathe, 2011, 2014), but these issues are beyond the scope of this discussion. Instead, we will consider how India's UID, already issued to over 650 million residents of India, will impact the lives of the market actors in the informal economy both positively and negatively and whether or not the UID will facilitate their entry into the formal economy. Ultimately, the aim is to discover what this example can teach us about the impact of the UID on both the market actors in the informal economy and on the corporation seeking to do business in the informal economy (Rangan, Quelch, Herrero, & Barton, 2007). The lessons will be relevant for market actors in informal markets—not only in India and the other BRIC countries (Brazil, Russia, China) but also in other developing countries and the developed world.

Learning from Aadhaar I: Challenges in Moving from the Informal to the Formal Economy

The work of Kotwal (2011a) provides the relevant facts on the informal economy in India for this discussion. With the informal economy defined as all those employed in enterprises with less than 10 people, 92% of those employed in India are in the informal economy, and only 8% of all employees are in the formal economy! It has been estimated that the contribution of the informal sector to India's GDP is 55% (Raveendran, 2006), but the formal economy grows much faster due to the availability of credit and technology transfers from more advanced economies. In short, the benefits of bringing even a fraction of the 92% of workers in the informal sector into the formal economy are significant.

Kotwal has provided a detailed explanation of how there is both a demand problem and a supply problem that makes it difficult for people in the informal economy to enter the formal economy (Kotwal, 2011a). The supply problem is easy to understand—many of the poor in the informal economy simply do not have the knowledge and skills required by the formal economy. But the composition of aggregate demand is also a problem. Despite high unemployment, the shortage of the talent required by the high productivity formal sectors of the economy (such as software and business services) leads to higher wages for people employed there, who already possess the basic necessities of life. So their additional income goes into purchase of discretionary items such as expensive imported goods and high-end services that can be generally provided only by those already in the formal sector—which is why the benefits of India's growth have not trickled down to the poor in the informal sector but instead have led to those already well off in the formal sector becoming even better off. To increase the income of the poor, the productivity of the informal sector must be increased.

Most of the workers in India's informal economy are in the agricultural sector, which accounts for almost 60% of total employment but only 20% of the value added by the total economy. So even though the "green revolution" from hybrid seeds and fertilizers has enabled India to reach self-sufficiency in food grains and other staples, agricultural productivity is still very low compared to other developing countries. Improvements in the productivity of agriculture can lift the incomes of the majority of the poor who depend on it by enabling them to plant and harvest higher value added crops.

Kotwal has argued (in personal communications with the authors in 2012) that UID will help the poor farmers to become more productive by: (1) giving them access to bank accounts and credit, which would enable them to make the necessary investments and take the risks of adopting better technology without having to pay sky-high interest rates (typically 60%) that money lenders charge or fear physical abuse if they default; (2) enabling them to legally own property and other assets; (3) allowing them to take the necessary business risks, if personal risks can be covered via UID-enabled health and life insurance; and (4) improving their knowledge and skills via UID-enabled access to better education and training. Some of these improvements should be visible within a short period of time; others will take much longer. Kotwal concluded with the observation that Aadhaar is not a panacea. It cannot solve all of India's social and economic problems that its critics expect it to. The purpose of India's UID is to give the disenfranchised their identity rights, and this can empower them to improve their lives.

Learning from Aadhaar II: The Challenges of Doing Research on UID in the Informal Economy

Kotwal has also provided the following account of the challenges of doing field research in the informal economy (personal communication with the authors in 2014). With his approval, we include his commentary in full below:

> Last year we launched our project in India in rural Maharashtra to investigate if the UID could be used to improve the efficiency and to reduce the graft in government's poverty alleviation schemes such as the National Rural Employment Guarantee Scheme. The wage payments were often delayed and sometimes the funds meant for wages even got siphoned off on the way. The idea was to change the wage payment mechanism; instead of channeling the funds allotted to wages through the local bureaucratic structure they would be directly transferred into the bank accounts linked to the workers' unique identification numbers. The plan was to see if the scheme made a difference.
>
> As expected, the project proposal received enthusiastic support from Nandan Nilekani—the chairman of the autonomous government agency charged with creating a database of UIDs for all the residents of India. He had been given the rank of a cabinet minister in the central government and assigned the responsibility for the success of the UID. The project would be meaningless if the database did not find good applications that solved some real problems. Our project would clearly be considered an ideal application.
>
> Nilekani's office sent down instructions to the Maharashtra State level office of UID Administration to cooperate with us. We were able to coordinate with the state level officials and the District Collector's office to set things in motion. However, we soon discovered that the major roadblock was in getting the local banks to cooperate. We needed the banks to open accounts in the names of the targeted beneficiaries in our treatment area and link them to their UID numbers. The banks had no incentive to do so. The targeted beneficiaries were poor and they would not leave the cash transferred into their accounts there for very long. The banks did not view this as a moneymaking opportunity and were reluctant to move.

One lesson we learned through this experience was that in this sort of informal setting where markets are yet to make inroads, you need a coordinating agent to get things moving. People are poor and don't use banks. Banks stay out because people don't use them. Access to amenities depends very much on whom you know—your connections. The local elites have power because of the connections they have. The impasse could be broken if the poor were free of their dependence on the local elite, and that in turn would be possible if cash could be directly transferred into their accounts. But that cannot happen when the banks see no incentive in doing so. It is a Catch-22.[2]

An informal economy is caught in such mutually reinforcing logjams. We managed to bring in a lot of pressure (through connections!) to get the banks to cooperate and get the project started. However, data gathering in an informal economy poses a whole other set of problems.

We had to survey a large number of laborer households to see if their experience had undergone a noticeable change. We had to also find out what the variation across individuals depended on. In order to get uncontaminated data, we preferred to talk to every individual in isolation, and this included talking to wives separately from their husbands. There was no harder challenge to overcome.

First, there is little sense of privacy in Indian villages. Every time our team rolled into a village, a crowd greeted us and then followed us wherever we went. There is no hostility, just idle curiosity about what these city folks are doing in our village. Everyone knows everyone and when we entered a household, half a dozen other people would crowd in and participate. Unless we found a way to tactfully ask them to stop, a question to a household member would be answered in a chorus sometimes after an intense public debate.

The challenge of interviewing the woman in the household without allowing her husband to answer all questions on her behalf was almost insurmountable. "Why would she say anything different from what I am saying?" We had to be culturally sensitive to deal with it. It helped to have a female interviewer to deal with such a situation but we often did not have enough females in our team. This too was in some sense a cultural issue. It was difficult to recruit women in rural areas for a job that took them away from home for a prolonged period.

Even getting objective facts like who owns how much land was a challenge as it was difficult to see well-kept records. It was rare that the local record keeper ("talathi") was available when we needed him. In this informal economy, all information was also informal. We needed multiple sources of information to verify whatever we had garnered.

Despite all this, I would say that one would not have any sense of the village reality and the heart-wrenching poverty without walking through these villages.

An Ethical Dilemma for Researchers

Since the Aadhaar UID "natural experiment" is underway in India, consider the philosophy of Mahatma Gandhi, the father of the nation, who believed strongly in cottage industries and self-sufficient villages as the path to individual prosperity and happiness. If so, a UID is far less important. What does a researcher say to the villager who says, "we are quite happy with the way we live, so please leave us alone"? Or what does he or she say to a market actor in the informal economy who says, "I live below the radar of police scrutiny; a UID will make me more visible and vulnerable. So please leave me alone"? Is it ethical to "leave them alone" if having a UID is the key to accessing opportunities and benefits that they don't know they can get with it?

We believe the answer to this ethical dilemma for researchers—concerning people's free will and perception of their self-interest on the one hand, and their inability to perceive and comprehend the economic opportunities that might open up for them with a UID on the other hand—are two liberating forces: *education* and *choice*. Researchers should create the empirical evidence needed to educate people so they understand what is available along with the associated pros and cons, and give them the freedom to decide what they wish to do for themselves. In that spirit, we now introduce five building blocks of an empirical research program for understanding how UIDs influence market actors in the informal economy and their ability to participate in the formal economy.

BUILDING BLOCKS OF AN EMPIRICAL RESEARCH PROGRAM TO UNDERSTAND HOW THE UID INFLUENCES MARKET ACTORS IN INFORMAL ECONOMY AND THEIR ABILITY TO PARTICIPATE IN THE FORMAL ECONOMY

Building Block I: Micro Perspective on the Informal Economy

Godfrey (2011, 2014) has argued that the work on poverty alleviation has focused on what he refers to as the "big P"—whether it is the work of development economists interested in raising the income of the market actors in the informal economy above the commonly used benchmark of $1.25 per day per person at purchasing power parity (PPP), or the work of the institutional theorists such as Douglass North on the need for strong institutions and property rights to lift people out of poverty, or work that views poverty alleviation initiatives that don't "scale up" as "failures." In contrast, Godfrey argues, there has been little research on what he refers to as the "little p," by which he means a focus on understanding how the market actors at the BoP live in their everyday life, what they value, what their daily lives and constraints and opportunities actually are, and how they in fact lift themselves out of poverty (Godfrey, 2014).

We are in agreement with Godfrey's observation that research on the informal economy is biased toward "big P," and we also agree that more research on the "little p" is needed. As we see it, studying "little p" includes trying to understand market actors in the informal economy from a holistic point of view. Taking the "little p" perspective, an economic point of view would not be enough to understand the whole complexity that market actors in the informal economy have to deal with. The following example can explain what we mean: In the Amazon region of Peru, the son of the community teacher followed a socially defined career, as he was expected to follow his father's work from birth onward. He grew up with the status of the "future community teacher." He did not need to get a university degree to attain the professional status of a teacher assigned by his community, as is the case in modern societies. In addition to this, these market actors work in informal organizations and often run their own small businesses. Their environment as market actors is characterized by the following challenges: they have no access to social services of the local or national government; their market rules are often unpredictable, which is why their business focus is mainly on the short term; market practices are based on community traditions and other non-economic social practices; effective market practices depend on local values (tradition, culture, religion, etc.); other challenges such as despotism and corruption. All of these elements include more than just the economy.

To cover this complexity, including economic and social phenomena, we follow Drucker (2003, 2003/1950) and assume that market actors in the informal economy are characterized by their status and function, just like market actors in the formal economy are. An example can explain what we mean: On an island in Indonesia, near Bali, a market actor in the local community had a very low income but a high religious status. His function was to judge conflicts in the community. For this work, he received food and accommodation for his whole family from the community. In that sense, he had the status of a community judge and his function was to trade his judgments for food and accommodation. From this perspective, it makes sense to assume that people who live and work in the informal economy are capable market actors. To understand a market actor's status and function, we need to set aside the assumption that trade works within functioning money markets only. It is more helpful if we take a sociological point of view and assume trading to be a basic human behavior that is based on a market actor's status and function.

Building Block II: Inclusion Capital as a Conceptual Entry Point

Godfrey's book *More than Money* (2014) analyzes the complex living structure of market actors at the BoP based on five forms of capital. Similar to Godfrey, we deploy the concept of "inclusion capital" to structure the analysis of opportunities that a UID might provide market actors in the informal economy.[3]

The notion of inclusion capital is based on research about career capitals (Jäger, Höver, Schröer, & Strauch, 2012; Mayrhofer et al., 2004). It refers to different modes of support that market actors in the informal economy have at their disposal to get access to formal markets (Mayrhofer & Schneidhofer, 2009; Mayrhofer et al., 2004). For instance, the leader of a poor, indigenous community in Costa Rica worked as a tourist guide for some time and one day decided to study agronomy. He remembered one of the tourists he met, called her, and got an invitation to apply for a scholarship that she supported. He got the scholarship, studied, and returned to his community. His studies changed his perspective on his community's life: Before his studies, he called it a natural lifestyle; afterward, he called it the life of poor people.

Just as in this example where the community leader used relations built in the past, inclusion capital is rooted in past work experiences (Iellatchitch, Mayrhofer, & Meyer, 2003). It is also based in internal perceptions (like being a market actor in the informal economy or not) and external issues (like the fact that this community leader did not have the money to pay for his studies) (Iellatchitch et al., 2003). Inclusion capital arises from social interactions between market actors in the informal economy and other actors. Those interactions influence the market actor's successful access to formal markets. In comparison with motivations, inclusion capital is thus situational and contextual; in this sense, it is socially-derived, not individually-driven like motivation is (Inglis & Cleave, 2006). Inclusion capital can become internalized and thus potentially determine what one wants and what one needs from one's working life.

Building Block III: Research Questions on Inclusion Capital and Market Actors in the Informal Economy

Following Iellatchitch et al. (2003) and Godfrey (2014), we assume inclusion capital to be a multi-level phenomena located at the intersection of the organizational context and individual biography, thus linking micro- and macro-frames of reference (Grandjean, 1981; Schein, 1978). The concept of inclusion capital reflects an effort to structure this complexity along three main lines. First, an inclusion field is a field of actors, such as the market actors in an informal economy who intend to enter a formal economy. Referencing Bourdieu (1994), we define an inclusion field as a patterned set of practices. These practices suggest competent action in conformity with rules and roles. The field is a "playground or battlefield in which agents try [. . .] to maintain or improve their place in the given and unfolding network of work-related positions" (Iellatchitch et al., 2003: 732), hence, to support the inclusion of actors from the informal into the formal economy.

Further, actors in a specific inclusion field value particular types of inclusion capital, which refer to "the different modes of support the individual obtains and has at his/her disposal and may invest for his/her further" inclusion success (Iellatchitch et al., 2003: 733). For instance, a market actor in the informal economy is better off when she has good personal relations with representatives of the local government than when she does not. She might ask them for support when she leaves her farm and needs help to take care of the cows.

Every agent in the field has a unique portfolio of capital. The starting point is the set of genes everybody gets when entering life. There is a complex interplay between genetic disposition and social context throughout a person's life. During personal, educational, and professional development, this interplay leads to a constantly changing and partly stable portfolio of capital assets. The individual invests this capital in his/her career not as the result of rational decision-making processes but rather as a result of what Bourdieu calls habitus (Iellatchitch et al., 2003). This is a unique mixture of external determinants and emerging strategies—a strategy without strategic intention (Bourdieu, 1990). To put the inclusion capital approach simply, an individual entering an inclusion field strives to embody the capital that is valued in that field. By the "intentionless" strategy of the habitus one "invests" the acquired capital in one's process to become included in the formal economy. As a product of this investment, the individual reproduces the capital valued in the field.

In the field of market actors in the informal economy, we are interested in inclusion capital that supports access to the formal economy. We do not take a psychological perspective to analyze social motives of market actors in the informal economy. We take a sociological viewpoint by following Bourdieu's concept of career capital and distinguish between four types of capital:

Cultural capital. Cultural capital designates education (Bourdieu, 1994); this might be knowledge gained by formal or informal education, such as traditional knowledge about naturopathy, knowledge about nutrition, and cultural habits in protecting traditional communities from external forces (Iellatchitch et al., 2003). That knowledge is also durable in times when market actors at the BoP become challenged by external changes such as crime. Some development specialists, in particular from the non-profit world, argue that market actors in the informal economy are under the threat of an economic or political colonization. The market actors in the informal economy would be in danger of being compromised by the rationalities of governments or markets. But taking a "little p" perspective might show that many market actors in the informal economy are competent in using those forces for their own benefit. In some cases, they even learn to use the word "poverty" at the right moment to get money and help from international development organizations!

With respect to the main focus of this article—the UID—we deduce the following guiding question from the explanations about cultural capital: How would a UID such as India's Aadhaar, affect a market actor's ability to build cultural capital? We offer the following proposition: By enabling access to education opportunities not previously available and opportunities to pay for such education via access to bank accounts and credit, possession of a UID would have a positive influence on a market actor's cultural capital.

Social capital. Most of the market actors in the informal economy work and live in strong community bonds with informal UIDs and what can be characterized as social capital (Bourdieu, 1994). Social capital involves relationships of mutual recognition and acquaintance and resources based upon social connections and group or class membership (Iellatchitch et al., 2003). This social capital seems to be strongly related to market rules in informal economies. In many cases, these rules are strongly embedded in their community bonds. For instance, one poor community that produced and sold organic bananas did not have a truck to transport them. Some of the growers were well off and could afford to buy their own truck. But they did not buy one because they knew that the community leaders traditionally decided such issues. From a market perspective, this decision of the market actor might appear to be irrational, but from the perspective of community rules, it makes sense.

With respect to social capital and UID, we introduce the following guiding question: How would a UID such as India's Aadhaar affect a market actor's ability to build social capital? We offer the following proposition: To the extent that UID enables access to people who were not previously in the market actor's network of contacts, a UID would have a positive influence on the market actor's social capital.

Symbolic capital. Symbolic capital is something that is perceived or socially recognized as legitimate (Iellatchitch et al., 2003). For instance, in a poor region of Argentina, a gynecologist worked in one of the most popular local hospitals. His colleagues and the public celebrated him as one of the best doctors. One day he resigned from his well-paid job. The public system was too corrupt and inefficient. The poor did not get the health services to which they were entitled, and the rich bought services from a private healthcare system. This doctor started to work directly with the poor communities and created a private healthcare system for the poor. The poor immediately accepted the doctors work, as the hospital he worked for before had a positive reputation in poor communities. This symbolic capital supported the doctor to enter the poor communities with his new services.

We propose the following guiding question for symbolic capital and UID: How would a UID such as India's Aadhaar affect a market actor's ability to build symbolic capital? We offer the following proposition: By providing official and unambiguous identification—leaving no doubt about who is who—the possession of a UID would have a positive influence on a market actor's legitimacy and, hence, his or her symbolic capital.

Economic capital. In addition to cultural, social, and symbolic capital, economic capital is key for market actors in the informal economy (Bourdieu, 1994) who are challenged by a structural gap between the formal and the informal markets.

This gap is mostly characterized by the difficulties of the actors in the informal markets to get access to the economic capital of equity investors, banks and the credit they offer, and knowledge about reducing their costs and how to reach international customers (London, Anupindi, & Sheth, 2010).

We propose the following guiding question for economic capital and UID: How would a UID such as India's Aadhaar affect a market actor's ability to build economic capital? We offer the following proposition: By enabling access to education opportunities not previously available and opportunities to pay for such education via access to bank accounts and credit, possession of a UID would have a positive influence on a market actor's economic capital.

Building Block IV: Market Actors With and Without a UID

Research remains to be done on the opportunities and challenges facing market actors who have or do not have a UID in situations in which they are operating in the informal or the formal economy. Consider the four basic situations (Table 10.1).

No UID in informal economy. The opportunities and challenges for market actors in this situation are:

- No access to social services of the local or national government
- Unpredictable market rules
- Market practices based on community traditions and other non-economic social practices
- Effective practices depend on local values (tradition, culture, religion, etc.)
- Challenges include despotism and corruption

No UID in formal economy. The opportunities and challenges for market actors in this situation are:

- Inequality—lack of formal power—in business relations when negotiating with formal actors
- No access to social services of government

Table 10.1 Operating in Formal or Informal Economy?

		Operating in Formal or Informal Economy?	
		Informal	Formal
Individual has a UID?	Yes	UID in informal	UID in formal
	No	No UID in informal	No UID in formal

- Risks of being abused
- No access to formal rights

UID in informal economy. The opportunities and challenges for market actors in this situation are:

- Exit option to leave informal economy
- Inequality—formal power—in business relations when negotiating with informal actors
- Access to social services of government
- Access to formal rights
- Access to formal market institutions and their services

UID in formal economy. The opportunities and challenges for market actors in this situation are:

- Transparent market rules
- Predictability of market actions
- Access to social services of government
- Access to formal rights
- Access to formal market institutions and their services

Some important research questions that emerge out of this typology are as follows: First, why do people in the informal economy remain there? For instance, Hernando de Soto (2000) has noted an important hurdle that the market actors face in moving out of the informal economy: Even with property rights in hand—but without a UID—the power of the local elite and the dominant culture can stifle initiative. Second, will the UID enable the market actors in the informal economy to overcome such hurdles? Or will the formal economy remain a bridge too far—for a variety of personal and social reasons, including family, status, and caste as well as intimidation and exploitation by thugs and the powerful elite? Third, some market actors may wish to remain in the informal economy because they *prefer* its cost-benefit trade-offs. If so, will the UID give them the freedom *not* to move to the formal economy?

Building Block V: Why Business Firms Are Interested in Having Market Actors in the Informal Economy Participate in the Formal Economy

Scholars disagree on why business firms are interested in having market actors in the informal economy participate in the formal economy. The two main positions are well represented by the work of Karnani versus Prahalad and Hart.

The Karnani position. Some scholars, including many from the non-profit field, are skeptical about for-profit firms that do business in informal markets. They argue that firms of this kind focus on profit and are likely to abuse people in need. Business school professor Karnani, for example, strongly supports this view and points out that it is naive to assume that large and even medium-size companies will not take advantage of market actors in the informal economy, given their far greater economic power. In the end, he argues, companies likely use this advantage to meet their financial goals, in some cases to the disadvantage of market actors in the informal economy. Therefore, according to Karnani, market actors in the informal economy need help; they do not need markets (Karnani, 2010).

The Prahalad and Hart position. Prahalad and Hart introduced an alternative point of view. Instead of considering the poor as a weak and a disadvantaged group of society, they view market actors in the informal economy as "clients" or "producers" (Prahalad, 2007). These authors remind us that poverty is also a matter of perception. If we, for instance, assume that those who earn less than $1.25 USD a day, wearing dirty clothes, having unhappy faces, and complaining about their unmet needs yearn to live like middle-class North Americans, we will surely see these types of people as "poor." But it would be as ignorant to assume that all of these people need solidarity and help as it would be ideological to assume they were all capable of effectively participating in formal markets.

We would argue that solidarity-based approaches such as Karnani (2010) and market-based approaches such as Prahalad (2007) alone do not address the complex reality of the very diverse and huge informal economies. Our knowledge of how these markets work will advance when both these perspectives and others get incorporated into research, when co-creation of innovative business solutions—as Ted London and Stuart Hart have put it—between market actors from informal economies and businesses from formal economies takes place (London & Hart, 2011).

CONCLUSION

Management scholars view informal economies as one of the most challenging environments for firms (Karamchandani, Kubzansky, & Lalwani, 2011). This is mostly because our perceptions of highly developed societies do not support a broad and deep understanding of how informal markets actually work.

Research on the informal economy invites serious consideration of how it differs from the formal economy and, just as important, how it is linked to it. In this chapter, we argued that one of the missing links that can illuminate the connection between the informal and the formal economy is the concept of "identity rights" and its implementation in the form of a UID.

The term "identity rights" has a wide variety of meanings, including the rights of those who feel excluded from work or even from society because of their social status or ethnic or sexual orientation, but our use of the term is limited to whether a person has a widely accepted official identification (starting with a certificate at birth that enables the issuance of other forms of official ID such as driver's license or passport) and whether, on the basis of such identification (as in the case of India's Aadhaar UID), he or she can gain access to the resources and services to which he or she is entitled as a market actor.

NOTES

1. For example, India has for years provided subsidies for purchase of LPG gas cylinders (used for home cooking) via its "fair price shops" which could be pocketed by unscrupulous intermediaries. *The Economic Times* reported on December 25, 2014, that "the ambitious scheme of giving cash subsidy on cooking gas *directly to consumers* has become the world's largest direct benefit transfer" scheme (bigger than similar schemes in Brazil and China) with 25 million households getting about $90 million USD via direct benefit transfers into their bank accounts since November 15, 2014. Consumers who did not have a bank account could readily open one via their Aadhaar UID number after authentication by the bank. The price of a subsidized LPG gas cylinder was Rs 417 per 14.2-kilogram bottle while its market price was Rs 752, the difference being the subsidy component. This direct subsidy scheme, called PAHAL for Pratyaksh Hanstantarit Labh, already covered 75% or more of the population in the 54 districts of India (from a total of 600) which had the highest Aadhaar UID enrollments. The PAHAL scheme was to be rolled out to the rest of the country starting January 1, 2015. See "Cash subsidy on LPG world's largest direct benefit transfer scheme" (accessed on December 31, 2014): http://articles.economictimes.indiatimes.com/2014–12–25/news/57395688_1_54-districts-dbtl-cash-subsidy
2. There were over 50 million Aadhaar UID-linked bank accounts in India as of March 2014, but most banks showed little interest in opening new Aadhaar accounts for micro-deposits and withdrawals because they made little money on such accounts. To provide the banks with a fair incentive, the state of Andhra Pradesh offered the banks a 2.5% commission on all benefits payments deposited into Aadhaar-linked bank accounts, to be deducted from the beneficiary's benefits, and this worked well enough that the Aadhaar organization recommended it become national policy.
3. We are guided by Bourdieu's (1994) integrated concept of four capitals. Godfrey's typology of five capitals is based on empirical observations and a different theoretical discussion. It would be interesting and instructive to compare Bourdieu's four capitals with Godfrey's five capitals, but that is beyond the scope of this discussion.

REFERENCES

Adhikari, A., et al. 2011. Food entitlements: An open letter to the Prime Minister of India. *Economic & Political Weekly*, July 23: 22–23.
Bourdieu, P. 1990. *In other words: An invitation to reflexive sociology*. Stanford, CA: Stanford University Press.

Bourdieu, P. 1994. *Raison pratiques. Sur la théorie de l'action.* Paris: Éditions du Seuil.

Chacko, S., & Khanduri, P. 2011. *UID for Dummies.* New Delhi, India: Jawaharlal Nehru University.

De Soto, H. 2000. *The mystery of capital: Why capitalism triumphs in the West and fails everywhere else*: Basic Books.

Drucker, P. F. 1950/2003. *The new society.* New Brunswick, London: Transaction Publisher.

Drucker, P. F. 2003. *The new realities.* Brunswick, London: Transaction Publisher.

Godfrey, P. C. 2011. Toward a theory of the informal economy. *The Academy of Management Annals,* 5(1): 231–277.

Godfrey, P. C. 2014. *More than money: Five forms of capital to create wealth and eliminate poverty.* Stanford, CA: Standford Univesity Press.

Grandjean, B. D. 1981. History and career in a bureaucratic labor market. *American Journal of Sociology,* 86(5): 1057–1092.

Hammond, A., Kramer, W. J., Tran, J., Katz, R., & Walker, C. 2007. *The next 4 billion: Market size and business strategy at the base of the pyramid.* Washington, DC: Worls Resource Institute, March.

Hart, S. L. 2010. *Capitalism at the crossroads: Next generation business strategies for a post-crisis world.* Upper Saddle River, NJ: Prentice Hall Pearson.

Iellatchitch, A., Mayrhofer, W., & Meyer, M. 2003. Career fields: a small step towards a grand career theory? *International Journal of Human Ressource Management,* 14(5): 728–750.

Inglis, S., & Cleave, S. 2006. A scale to assess board member motivations in nonprofit organizations. *Nonprofit Management & Leadership,* 17(1): 83–101.

Jäger, U., Höver, H., Schröer, A., & Strauch, M. 2012. Career capitals of executive directors in German faith based organizations. *Nonprofit & Voluntary Sector Quarterly,* 42, (5): 1026–1048.

Karamchandani, A., Kubzansky, M., & Lalwani, N. 2011. The globe: Is the bottom of the pyramid really for you? *Harvard Business Review.*http://hbr.org/2011/03/the-globe-is-the-bottom-of-the-pyramid-really-for-you/ar/1.

Karnani, A. 2010. Failure of the libertarian approach to reducing poverty. *Asian Business & Management,* 9(1): 5–17.

Kotwal, A. 2011a. Economic liberalization and indian economic growth: What's the evidence? *Journal of Economic Literature,* 49(4): 1152–1199.

Kotwal, A. 2011b. Perspectives on cash transfers: PDS forever? *Economic & Political Weekly,* September: 3–5.

London, T., Anupindi, R., & Sheth, S. 2010. Creating mutual value: Lessons learned from ventures serving base of the pyramid producers. *Journal of Business Research,* 63: 582–594.

London, T., & Hart, S. L. 2011. *Next generation business strategies for the base of the pyramid. New approaches for building mutual value.* Upper Saddle River, NJ: Financial Time Press.

Mayrhofer, W., Iellatchitch, A., Meyer, M., Steyrer, J., Schiffinger, M., & Strunk, G. 2004. Going beyond the individual. Some potential contributions form a career field and habitus perspective for global career research and practice. *Journal of Management Development,* 23(9): 870–884.

Mayrhofer, W., & Schneidhofer, T. M. 2009. The lay of the land: European career research and its future. *Journal of Occupational and Organizational Psychology,* 82: 721–737.

Nilekani, N. 2009. *Imagining India.* London: Penguin Press.

Prahalad, C. K. 2007. The BOP debate: Aneel Karnani responds. *NextBillion.net.* http://nbis.org/nbisresources/sustainable_development_equity/bottom_of_pyramid_debate_with_prahalad.pdf.

Rangan, K. V., Quelch, J., Herrero, G., & Barton, B. 2007. *Business solutions for the global market actors at the BoP: Creating social and economic value.* San Francisco, CA: Jossey-Bass.

Raveendran, G. 2006. *Estimation of contribution of informal sector to GDP.* New Delhi, India: National Commission of Enterprises in the Unorganized/Informal Sector, May.

Sathe, V. 2011. The world's most ambitious ID project: India's project Aadhaar. *Innovations*, 6(2): 39–66.

Sathe, V. 2014. Managing massive change: India's Aadhaar, the world's most ambitious ID project. *Innovations*, 9(3–4): 85–111.

Schein, E. H. 1978. *Career dynamics: Matching individual and organisational needs.* Reading, MA: Addison-Wesley.

Sen, A. 2010. *The idea of justice.* London: Penguin Books.

11 Informal Financial Services
A Proposed Research Agenda

Les Dlabay

Business skills of entrepreneurs and workers in the informal economy provide the foundation for their financial success and improved quality of life. Efforts to enhance this human capital is strongly connected to the availability of financial resources. Individuals and enterprises operating with an extralegal status usually require borrowing and other financial transactions through informal activities. Bruton, Ireland, and Ketchen (2012) bring forth this issue with an emphasis on the trust that must exist when extending and repaying a non-legally binding loan. An initial viewing of the informal financial services environment indicates consumer credit transactions as the primary activity. However, as a result of the need for other services, various financial product offerings have developed. As noted by Collins, Morduch, Rutherford, and Ruthven (2009), informal services are used since the need to save often exceeds demand for borrowing. Beyond loans, various savings vehicles allow informal business proprietors and households an opportunity to smooth erratic cash flows and accumulate funds for large expenditures. To reduce uncertainty from varied financial risks, insurance schemes are created. Informal networks for transfers of funds, including remittances, may include traditional exchanges along with expanded use of mobile technology.

Despite charging higher rates and having inconsistent service quality, informal financial services are often preferred over the more formal providers available in a community. Through extensive use of financial diary methodology in Bangladesh, India, and South Africa, Collins et al. (2009) note an array of motivations for using alternative banking services, ranging from the flexibility of loan terms from friends and family to saving time when not traveling to formal financial institutions. Informal financial service clients also expressed a greater sense of security when borrowing from a local moneylender since the person is someone they know and see regularly. The informal financial services ecosystem is a diverse, complex interaction of individuals and institutions in varied cultures and economic settings.

As a result of the great diversity of informal financial activities, Adams and Fitchett (1992) advocate use of a continuum to communicate this market phenomenon. As shown in Table 11.1, informal financial service providers may be viewed in three major categories with progressions of informality attributes among these groupings.

Table 11.1 Sources and Attribute Degrees of Informal and Quasi-Formal Financial Services

Individual Financial Service Providers	Community-Based Financial Service Providers	Quasi-Bormal Financial Service Providers
• Family members, friends • Market trade moneylenders • Shop owners, loan sharks • Deposit collectors (moneyguards) • Informal currency traders	• Self-help groups (SHGs) • Rotating savings and credit associations (RoSCAs) • Accumulating savings and credit associations (ASCAs) • Village savings and loan associations (VSLAs) • Remittance networks	• Credit unions, cooperatives • Pawnshops • Postal service • Non-governmental organizations (NGOs) • Informal microfinance institutions (MFIs) • Mobile phone banking
A. FINANCIAL REGULATORY STATUS		
None	None	Nominal
B. NUMBER OF PARTICIPANTS		
Few	Several	Numerous
C. GEOGRAPHIC PROXIMITY		
Localized clients	Wider community participation	Regional participation
D. DEGREE OF TRUST (Social Collateral)		
Extensive	Significant	Considerable
E. SOURCE OF CAPITAL		
Individual	Group	Group/external
F. ADMINISTRATIVE MECHANISM		
Negligible	Minimal	Some presence

Factors that may be used to distinguish among the varied degrees of informal financial service provider categories include:

A. **Financial regulatory status.** Individual and community-based providers are unregistered business enterprises. Quasi-formal providers are those that have a legal business status within a society but are not subject to the country's laws, regulations, and supervision for formal financial institutions.

B. **Number of participants.** Most individual providers interact with only a few clients, while community-based and quasi-formal providers involve a larger number of participants.

C. **Geographic proximity.** The location of activity ranges from very localized, such as a village market, to regional coverage for quasi-formal financial service providers. A credit cooperative in India, for example, may have outlets throughout a state and perhaps across the country.

D. **Degree of trust.** With social collateral being an essential factor contributing to the effectiveness of informal services, trust-based network connections are fundamental. Screening by individual lenders may rely exclusively on personal knowledge of the borrower or recommendations from previous clients. Group consensus regarding personal character is the basis for community-based financial groups. Quasi-formal service providers may use some type of primitive credit reporting system.

E. **Source of capital.** While most funds are from within a community, slight variations exist. As the number of clientele increases and geographic coverage expands, external funds from nonprofit donor organizations and formal financial institutions may be used for lending and to cover operating costs.

F. **Administrative elements.** Documentation and operating procedures are very nominal for individual and community-based service providers, with a greater degree of paperwork for quasi-formal market participants.

INDIVIDUAL FINANCIAL SERVICE PROVIDERS

Family members and friends are the foundation of informal financial services for providing loans and money storage. Beyond these personal acquaintances, informal financial entrepreneurs fill gaps in demand for borrowing, saving, and other financial service needs.

Market Trade Moneylenders

In most informal economic settings, for centuries, individuals have been lending for personal and business needs. While most moneylenders provide loans for small amounts, typically using their personal funds, some indigenous bankers have been known to lend more substantial sums. While the loans are usually unsecured, based on a personal acquaintance or recommendation, assets such as gold, jewelry, or land may serve as collateral. In various regions of India, moneylenders are called *shroffs*, *seths*, *sahukars*, *mahajans*, and *chettis*. Their activities technically come under control of the

Money Lenders Act, which requires a license for moneylenders to conduct business and sets forth loan terms. However, compliance is rare since most moneylenders disregard the regulation (Srinivas, 2015a: Moneylenders).

In the Philippines, a type of informal financier is the *5–6 moneylender* who operates in village markets and trading areas. Borrowing five pesos, a person pays back six, which is a 20% interest rate for the agreed time period (usually a week, but sometimes just a day). Annual interest rates easily exceed 1,000%. However, most loans are for a relatively short term, to bridge the time between current expenses and expected future income. Two types of 5–6 moneylenders are common. First, *community insiders* are Filipino moneylenders who lend to operators of small, informal business enterprises. Second, *unwelcome outsiders* are moneylenders who obtain funds through informal channels originating in India (Kondo, 2003).

Instead of legal documents, 5–6 borrowers sign a pledge to pay in notebooks, on calendars, or on plain paper. These records may be kept by the lender or with the customer. Since entries are in the lender's handwriting, the customer is not able to tamper with the document. Daily collections are fundamental for the success of 5–6 businesses. Indian moneylenders often conduct collections in the early morning, especially in "wet markets" (vegetable stalls) to obtain funds from vendors during high cash-flow times. For other stores and clients, collections occur in the late morning or early afternoon. Indian lenders use motorbikes to facilitate collections over a wide area of locations. This transportation mode is less costly than an automobile and allows ease of navigation through narrow streets (Kondo, 2003).

A variation of the market moneylender exists in Indonesian fishing communities. Traders provide loans to fishermen for various personal and business needs. Although no interest is charged, the traders buy some fish from the borrower at 5%–10% below market price. This allows the trader to obtain a profit when the fish are processed and sold. Loans are repaid by the fishermen when they sell their remaining catch to other traders (Mohammad & Yunaningsih, 2014).

Shop Owners and Loan Sharks

Retailers, both formal and informal, frequently extend credit to shoppers. For centuries, local store owners allowed regular customers to buy on account. The amounts owed are paid back, perhaps with interest, usually within a week or at the end of the month. *Warungs* (small, family-owned stores) in West Java sell fishermen diesel fuel for their boats and other household necessities, charging prices 10%–15% higher for the goods bought on credit. This arrangement with the store owner is often preferred since no documentation is required and the amount owed can be repaid when fish are caught (Mohammad & Yunaningsih, 2014).

In most regions, exploitive lenders, often referred to as *loan sharks*, charge excessive rates. In China, customers may pay interest as high as 70%

to these underground lenders due to limited access to state-controlled banks (Barboza, 2011). Loan sharks in South Africa continue to exploit borrowers, especially in low-income communities, sometimes forcing payment by taking personal property to cover an amount owed (Micro Finance Regulatory Council in South Africa, 2015). In Thailand, despite a program to reduce use of loan sharks, an estimated 700,000 Thai borrowers are paying about 3% a day, or about 1,000% a year (Thai Intel ASEAN News, 2015). In many settings, the creation of microloan programs has been a response to the exploitive actions of moneylenders and loan sharks.

Deposit Collectors

To avoid the many requests for financial assistance or loans from family and neighbors or the lure of peddlers, storing cash is a vital service for those without access to a formal financial institution. The use of *deposit collectors*, or *moneyguards*, who hold another person's funds, is a tradition among many indigenous savers. Family members or friends will not likely charge for their service. However, local entrepreneurs will charge a fee for holding funds, which can be as high as 10% of the balance. *Susu collectors* in Ghana, serving traders in market areas, provide a method by which clients accumulate capital—a valuable service since most banks do not have low-balance accounts. Also, in many cultures, funds kept at home are subject to access by family and friends, so the moneyguards allow capital to build up elsewhere. As reported by Collins et al. (2009), using financial diary data, moneyguarding was a service commonly used by households in Bangladesh, India, and South Africa.

Money storage services allow a person to keep money safely out of reach without spending time on travel. Deposit collectors often meet customers at their homes or business location. In contrast, moneyguards usually expect clients to come to them. Using a deposit collector is not without risk since a saver may not be able to access funds when needed, or a collector may depart a community with the savings (Ledgerwood, 2013).

Informal Currency Traders

Lawful retail enterprises often serve as a front for unregistered foreign exchange activities. These informal currency traders compete with the currency services offered at banks, hotels, airports, and rail stations. A survey of U.S. embassy representatives by Dlabay and Reger (2007) concluded that nations with lower levels of economic development tended to experience greater levels of informal foreign-exchange activities. The unregistered currency exchange services usually operated in small, locally owned shops, with the retailer providing non-government-sanctioned exchange activities. Border areas involved a greater level of informal exchange activities, including acceptance of a neighboring country's currency. This parallel currency-exchange market was especially prevalent in southern Africa.

COMMUNITY-BASED FINANCIAL SERVICE PROVIDERS

Beyond family members, friends, and individual shop owners exists community-based groups providing financial services within a village or region. These locally formed and self-managed groups adapt to cultural norms and regional business practices, and may be referred to as "informal credit markets" (Ghate, 1992).

Self-Help Groups

Most common in India and in other areas of South Asia and Southeast Asia, *self-help groups* (SHGs) are village-based assemblies involving 15 to 20 women, usually in rural areas, who come together to form an informal savings and credit organization. Also called savings and credit groups (SCGs) or self-reliant groups (SRGs), members are committed to financial and business development activities benefiting all involved (US AID, 2008). Serving to facilitate entrepreneurial activities, SHGs also provide women with social and economic empowerment. The funds collected from the group may be used for small interest-bearing loans to the members. Group interactions develop a collective environment with a primary focus on savings. Loan rates and borrowing terms are established by the group with a commitment to fund borrowing with the accumulated savings of the participants. These SHG activities help to overcome a lack of financial services, thus creating confidence and economic self-dependence, particularly among women who are often invisible in the social structure.

Studies report the benefits of self-help groups for women, especially in India, through enhanced financial security and improved self-confidence as well as increased literacy. Women are treated with more respect and attain an improved social status (Sinha, 2010). Self-help groups are the basis for the creation and operation of other community-based finance groups such as rotating savings and credit associations (RoSCAs) and accumulating savings and credit associations (ASCAs) (Nokia Research Center, 2015).

Rotating Savings and Credit Associations

With names such as *arisans, chit funds, ekub, osusu,* and *tandas,* (Bouman, 1995), rotating savings and credit associations (RoSCAs) exist in over 70 countries. These community-based, informal finance service tradition allow people otherwise unable to save or obtain credit to pay for medical bills or to buy a water buffalo or oxen for a family business. Ardener and Burman (1996) describe the RoSCA as "an association formed upon a core of participants who make regular contributions to a fund which is given in whole or in part to each contributor in turn."

At each RoSCA meeting, funds are collected from each member and distributed to one person. Two common methods are commonly used to determine who will receive the money: (1) a *random* RoSCA distributes funds based on an arbitrary drawing, with the process repeated with previous recipients excluded until all members have received the money once. (2) With a *bidding* or *auction* RoSCA, participants present offers for the money. At the next meeting, members who still haven't received the fund bid to receive it (Food and Agriculture Organization of the United Nations, 2002). RoSCAs dissolve after each group member receives the money once. At which point, another group may be formed, sometimes with different terms, rules, and members. RoSCAs serve as a support system for each other, providing economic and social empowerment, especially among women.

Cultural differences among RoSCAs vary greatly. Referred to as a *tontine* (in French-speaking areas) or *njangi* (in English-speaking communities) of Cameroon, these socio-economic associations serve as a microfinance provider at all levels of society. Three forms of tontines are common in Cameroon. First, the strictly financial association, or contribution club, is the most basic type, with collected funds distributed to one or two members for their personal financial use. Second, the financial and social tontine has the added element of social responsibility with the creation of a "trouble bank." These savings funds are used for expenses associated with illnesses, births, or deaths in the families of the group members. Third, the financial and social work-group tontine, which operates mainly in rural areas. While similar to the other two types in its purpose of collecting and saving money, the group also engages in manual work for their members and sometimes non-members. Group members work together for farm activities to clear or hoe a parcel of land. This group effort makes the task easier and faster since farm equipment is usually not available. These rural associations are also a source of entertainment for group members using funds for food, drinks, music, and dance (Etchu-Njang, 2007).

Many RoSCAs also operate in immigrant communities of industrialized societies. *Kye* is the Korean version used in the Los Angeles area. Many of South Asian descent participate in RoSCAs in Oxford. This trend was also observed among Somali women living in the United Kingdom (Ardener & Burman, 1996). Tandas, also called *cudinas*, are common among Latino and Chicano populations in the United States (Thompson, 2014). Regardless of the form taken, the purpose of these groups is fundamentally the same: to promote the economic and financial welfare of their members.

Accumulating Savings and Credit Associations

As an extension to the services provided by RoSCAs, accumulating savings and credit associations (ASCAs) emphasize savings among group members. Depositing varying amounts at each meeting, group members may or may not borrow these funds depending on their personal and business needs. Earnings from interest on loans made is ultimately paid to the members who deposited funds. In contrast to RoSCAs, ASCA funds are not all distributed at each meeting. Instead, the ASCA makes loans, as requested by group members, charging interest and setting a repayment plan (Rutherford & Arora, 2009). ASCAs may also have a separate loan fund for use in the event of a disaster (natural or personal), serving as an insurance feature. ASCAs are often "time-bound," with members saving, borrowing, and repaying for a predetermined amount of time, usually six to 12 months. These cycles are usually adopted to address the seasonality of rural cash flows. However, given the diversity of indigenous ASCAs, the cycle can vary in length, with some choosing to operate indefinitely (Chipeta, 2011).

Village Savings and Loan Associations

Created as a more formalized community-based financial service group, village savings and loan associations (VSLAs) involve a time-bound model for borrowing and the accumulation of funds. Group members save and request loans from the monetary pool. After a set time period, the *share out* occurs, when amounts saved are returned to group members. Participants also receive a share of the loan interest earned in proportion to the amount saved during the cycle, usually nine or 12 months. At this point, group members have the option to re-form the group, which often occurs. A new cycle of the VSLA for savings and lending starts. The independent and self-managing nature of VSLAs also includes strong transparency and accountability. Savings and loan payment transactions occur at the group meeting in the presence of all members, creating witnesses for each financial exchange. VSLA members are often relatively well off and well educated, as reported by Anyangoet al. (2007) in their study in Zanzibar-Tanzania. Participants in the research experienced sustainable savings and lending programs in areas poorly served by more formal financial service providers. Expanded use of VSLAs were also reported in Angola, Burundi, Côte d'Ivoire, Eritrea, Haiti, India, Kenya, Lesotho, Malawi, Mozambique, Rwanda, Uganda, Zambia, and Zimbabwe.

While generally exempt from regulatory barriers, some countries require VSLAs to register with a local authority. Variations of VSLAs are commonly facilitated by microfinance and development organizations in an attempt to avoid excessive savings fees and serve the need for saving among the poor. The savings groups of the Aga Khan Foundation are called community-based savings groups (CBSG), and the savings and internal lending community (SILC) is the program of Catholic Relief Services. Saving for Change (SfC) is a cooperative effort between Freedom from Hunger and Oxfam, while CARE makes use of the VSLA model (Allen & Panetta, 2010). Several of these programs combine the savings groups with development activities to distribute social products, such as solar lanterns, and to expand the availability of agricultural inputs, such as seeds and fertilizer (Rippey & Fowler, 2011). Community Managed Savings and Credit Association (CoMSCA) is the designation used by World Vision for its VSLA-type program.

The VSLA program of World Relief is Savings for Life (SfL), designed to empower the most vulnerable in communities lacking access to basic financial services. SfL groups range in size from 10 to 25 self-selected members, which ensures a high level of trust and results in a 99% loan-repayment rate. Groups are self-managed, writing their own constitution and policies and electing a five-person leadership committee. Savings are kept in a three-lock box with all transactions occurring in front of all group members when the three key holders and box keeper are present. Groups also develop a "social fund," a form of insurance to assist members. At the end of the group cycle, members receive all their savings from the past nine to 12 months plus interest, usually a rate of return of 30%–60%. Groups may then disperse, although almost all start a new cycle and continue as a savings group (World Relief, 2012).

As a faith-based organization, World Relief builds on the VSLA methodology with program implementation through the local church. Volunteers serve as field agents to organize and train the savings groups along with an emphasis on spiritual transformation. Since its inception, the SfL program has empowered more than 100,000 participants in six African countries (Roenigk, 2015) The village of Gahanga, in Rwanda, started a savings group called *imbereheza*, which means "better days ahead." Group meetings start with prayer, singing, and dancing. After six months, the group collected 58,000 francs (about $100 USD), in a community where the average person earns less than $2 a day. The funds are borrowed by group members to pay medical bills, to buy sugar and flour to bake food items to sell, and to start small manufacturing businesses. SfL also assists with other services, including volunteers who bring life-saving health messages to mothers and guidance for buying better seeds and fertilizer for greater crop yields. (World Relief, 2015)

Remittance Networks

A variety of informal money-transfer systems exist around the world, such as *hundi in* South Asia, fei-chen in China, hui kwan in Hong Kong, *padala* in the Philippines, and *phei kwan* in Thailand. The majority of these networks, especially those in African mineral exporting nations, developed to finance trade and transfer funds against the movement of goods. (Isern, Deshpande, & Van Doorn, 2005). Most commonly used by migrant workers in the Middle East and Asia, *hawalas* are informal remittance networks. The movement of funds across continents occurs through brokers around the world who have developed a mutual trust among network participants. The brokers not only earn a commission but also may profit from differences in exchange rates. In recent years, hawalas have been scrutinized as a possible funding source for terrorist activities (Faith, 2011). The process starts with a person who wants to send money to another country contacting a hawala dealer, or broker. After negotiating the fee and exchange rate, the dealer (A) contacts (by phone, fax, or e-mail) another dealer (B) in the country where the money is to be sent. Dealer B arranges for the payment to be made in the local currency and will eventually settle this transaction with Dealer A when money needs to be sent back to the originating country.

QUASI-FORMAL FINANCIAL SERVICE PROVIDERS

A more formalized version of the village savings and loan association is the credit cooperative. These financial service providers are subject to general and commercial laws, but not usually under formal bank regulation and supervision. These include credit unions, credit cooperatives, and financial non-governmental organizations (NGOs) (Pagura & Kirsten, 2009; Ritchie, 2015).

Credit Unions and Credit Cooperatives

Although not conforming to financial institution regulations of a country, credit unions and credit cooperatives serve many financial service needs in a community. These quasi-formal financial service providers accept savings and extend credit to targeted community members, who become member-owners. These nonprofit microfinance institutions (MFIs), sometimes organized using a *village banking model*, usually involve a smaller geographic reach than more formal financial institution, and are organized for maintaining the cooperatives sustainability. The social collateral among the group serves to improve repayments and reduce operating costs.

The cooperative financial services model is prevalent in Asia. The savings and credit cooperatives (SACCOs) in Nepal are small, indigenous lending groups that may or may not be registered with local authorities. The Small Farmers' Cooperatives Limited (SFCLs), also in Nepal, are rural-based, member-owned and controlled groups that provide financial and non-financial services (Mercy Corps, 2008). India has a long history of rural credit cooperatives that include the State Cooperative Banks (SCB), District Central Cooperative Banks (DCCB) and Primary Agricultural Credit Societies (PACS) for short-term credit, and Primary Cooperative Agriculture and Rural Development Banks (PCARDB) for long-term credit. Rural cooperative foundations in China have a "quasi legality" status due to ambiguity as to the government agency assigned with the regulation of these financial institutions (Tsai, 2004).

Pawnshops

For centuries, pawnshops, often with exorbitant interest rates on loans, have had a market presence in most countries. Pawnbrokers are characterized by high-volume, short-term, small loans secured by taking possession of a physical asset. Loan amounts are notably smaller in value than the item held as security. Despite high costs associated with the processing and storing of collateral, no time is used to evaluate the borrower or to collect the past-due amounts. Loans are made on the value of the collateral, which often consists of gold, jewelry, or high-demand, high-value consumer goods. The item may be later sold to recover any past-due loan amount. Pawnbrokers often operate a retail store to sell goods that are not redeemed (Ledgerwood, 2013). Some countries have established regulations and required registration. In India, these lenders are subject to the Pawn Brokers Act of 1962, which requires a pawnbroker to register and regulates the rate of interest that may be charged along with other loan terms. Compliance has only been at about 35%–40% of pawnshop operators (Srinivas, 2015b: Pawn Brokers).

Postal Service

Operating outside the formal banking system, post offices offer a range of financial services in Asian and African countries previously under British rule. While having a legal business status, they are not subject to formal banking regulations. Many unbanked people use this financial service provider. In India, for example, the postal service has been a major provider of banking and other financial services since 1854. Using the brand name "India Post," this government-operated enterprise offers savings accounts, money transfers, money orders, life insurance, and mutual funds through more than 150,000 offices.

Non-Governmental Organizations (NGOs) and Informal Microfinance Institutions (MFIs)

In contrast to community-based financial service providers, most NGOs fund their programs with external funding from donors or grants. These relief and development organizations often serve as intermediaries between donors and clients in informal economic settings. They operate locally as well as globally (through a physical or an online presence), and are sometimes referred to as financial intermediary non-governmental organizations (FINGOs). These MFIs are usually licensed to offer limited financial services such as savings plans and loans (Mercy Corps, 2008).

MICROINSURANCE PROGRAMS

Death or illness of the household head, funeral costs, crop failure, and livestock loss are common risks faced by entrepreneurs and households operating in the informal economy. The financial stress of these losses are especially burdensome due to irregular income and limited capital accumulation. A variety of microinsurance programs have been created to cover potential hazards in exchange for small premium payments; life and health-care coverage are most common. Informal microinsurance programs may also surface within a community-based financial service provider or a sav-ings group. Contributions of participants above the amount saved create a small fund to cover emergencies encountered by group members. Insurance products for the cost of funerals, medical expenses, and education fees if the main household provider dies are a component of some VSLAs (Allen & Panetta, 2010).

Burial societies involve a community-managed savings fund, usually in urban areas, created to cover funeral costs of family members. Households make weekly or monthly payments to participate in the program. Some burial societies may lend out funds to earn additional revenue for the group. *Stretcher clubs*, most often in rural areas, are informal insurance programs for health emergencies. Contributed amounts cover the costs of transport and medical care at a health center. The name is derived from the tradition in which patients were carried on stretchers to receive medical service.

Informal microinsurance programs provide the benefit of creating prod-ucts closely adapted to serve the needs of their clientele. However, these schemes are limited by their small size and scope of operations, which can result in a high risk of financial adversity if the same calamity occurs for a large number of participants at the same time. Some, but very few, commu-nity-based microinsurance plans develop coalitions with other groups in an effort to increase efficiency and reduce risk (Ledgerwood, 2013). Microfi-nance development organizations, such as ACCION and Opportunity Inter-national, are engaged in microinsurance activities. Others are assessing the feasibility and cost effectiveness of using existing financial service delivery channels or are establishing partnerships with existing MFIs as well as alli-ance models, such as through mobile phone networks.

MOBILE BANKING TECHNOLOGY

Financial data with manual recordkeeping systems are evolving toward electronic documentation, especially mobile phone banking. Low-income and rural consumers receive funds, pay bills, and transfer payments to oth-ers. Remote locations without access to banks, cash machines, and credit cards are often served by mobile phone banking technology. Cell phone financial transactions, while sometimes connected to a bank account, may bypass banks in the future with a summary on phone bills. Informal entrepreneurs and consumers are increasingly connected to cell phones for banking and other services. M-PESA, in Kenya and elsewhere in Africa, has built an extensive mobile money system for domestic remittances along with expanded access to financial services for many not previously served. (Mas & Radcliffe, 2010) While several barriers exist for financial inclu-sion of currently unbanked populations, Singh (2013) notes the need for regulatory balance between allowing new business models and protecting consumers. Branchless banking, through existing and emerging technology, is advocated by businesses and governments with caution expressed by development organizations.

SUGGESTED RESEARCH FOR INFORMAL FINANCIAL SERVICES

Bruton et al. (2012) note significant gaps in management research related to informal business activities. They call for "an indigenous examination of the firms and managers in institutional settings where informal firms dominate." This research agenda should include the sub-discipline of informal financial services. With the major portion of human activity in informal settings, a need exists for expanded scholarship that provides evidence and insight in relation to various elements of management research.

Environmental Influences and Contingency Theory

The *organic organization*, as identified by Burns and Stalker (1961), sets forth the need to assess the creation and operation of informal financial services in light of environmental influences. The cooperative systems of people is especially relevant for community-based financial service providers. Further, as noted by Lawrence and Lorsch (1967), matching internal organizational characteristics to environmental requirements results in improved performance. As with the array of informal financial services, community members adapt to cultural and economic circumstances to create savings and credit programs for varied environmental needs.

With regard to environmental influences on informal financial services, researchers might consider these topics:

- What cultural factors influence the creation and operation of community-based financial service providers such as SHGs, RoSCAs, ASCAs, and VSLAs?
- How do volatile economic conditions and unstable political environments create circumstances affecting development and implementation of alternative financial services?
- What analogies exist among institutional models of informal financial service providers?
- What metrics are most relevant to measure the effectiveness and social impact of alternative financial service providers?
- How can social collateral be assessed and enhanced among a range of informal financial service providers?
- How might training programs of community-based financial service providers be developed for increased economic and social benefits, such as improved financial literacy?

- How does the physical and social infrastructures of a society create the need for and effectiveness of informal financial services?
- What digital finance regulations are appropriate for the existing and evolving informal financial service market environment?

Organizational Structure and Linkages

As informal and formal financial services blend to better serve traditionally underserved clients (both entrepreneurs and households) several strategic issues should be assessed for effective implementation. While individual loans are common in developed economies, the use of the *trust group* lending model is prevalent in informal market settings. This group lending approach evolved from the cultures of SHGs and RoSCAs. The groups, involving 10 to 30 people, seek loans for microenterprise activities and household expenditures. Group members assure each other's loans. This social collateral ingredient results in repayment rates of over 90% (Opportunity International, 2015).

McGahan (2012) advocates collaborative innovation between formal and informal economic actors. While advances have occurred in the delivery of financial services to underserved entrepreneurs, coverage continues to lack in most rural and low-income areas. As a result, a "mutually beneficial partnership between a formal and a less formal institution that results in the expansion of rural financial services" is supported (Pagura & Kirsten, 2009). These informal-formal connections for financial services exist in varied formats.

Horizontal linkages, an alliance among similar financial enterprises, have the potential benefits of reduced transaction costs, improved economies of scale, and shared technical assistance. Fundacion para Alternativas de Desarrollo (FADES) is an unregulated microfinance institution in Bolivia. The horizontal linkages of FADES with other informal financial service providers resulted in additional funding, increased numbers of clients, and an expansion of financial services offered (Quiros & Gonzalez-Vega, 2007).

Cooperative efforts among financial intermediaries at different levels of the value chain, *vertical linkages*, represent another informal-formal collaboration. Formal financial institutions providing subsidized funding to an informal moneylender who lends to rural borrowers creates this connection. With banks offering a wider array of services more efficiently than most nonprofits, vertical linkages provide the unbanked populations served by MFIs with greater financial service choices.

Serving as an intermediary between susu customers and formal financial institutions, the Ghana Co-operative Susu Collectors Association (GCSCA) was created to regulate the collection activities of these moneyguards. With operations supervised by the Bank of Ghana, GCSCA is viewed as a "non-banking microfinance financial institution in Ghana, Africa, and the world" (Ghana Co-operative Susu Collectors Association, 2015). A related effort involved susu collectors in Ghana, in which Barclays Bank attempted to address the financial needs of small traders and micro-entrepreneurs with a program to enhance opportunities for business expansion among this target audience (Osei, 2008).

Despite cost and profitability concerns, programs to merge savings groups into the formal financial system have been undertaken. Westley and Palomas (2010), working with two MFIs, ADOPEM in the Dominican Republic and Centenary Bank in Uganda, reported that operating costs can be covered from revenue generated by a portfolio of financial services. This conclusion overcame previously reported annual marginal operating costs of over 200% for the deposit balances of small savers.

Financial connections between informal entrepreneurs and formal business organizations are also using innovative business models. While Kistruck et al. (2011) report various operational and sustainability challenges, social benefits and additional adaptations of *microfranchising* are suggested for underserved communities to meet local market needs. *Microconsignment* programs provide funding for local entrepreneurs to sell products such as eyeglasses, solar lamps, stoves, and water filters, while *microleasing* allows financing of revenue-generating capital investment items such as machinery or a dairy cow. In each situation, funds are made available through loans or other financial schemes to promote creation and operation of microenterprises.

Potential topics of investigation related to organizational issues for informal financial services might include:

- What types of lending models (individual versus trust group) best serve varied informal financial service settings?
- What factors create the basis for effective informal-formal connections among financial service providers, such as CARE facilitating the VSLA model?
- What models for horizontal linkages of financial service providers can be extended into other informal economic settings?
- How might the benefits of vertical linkages be assessed for the participants involved in this informal-formal collaboration?
- What types of regulatory actions and cooperative efforts with trade associations facilitate effective informal-formal collaborations?
- What potential drawbacks and exploitation might occur as informal-formal financial service linkages are implemented?
- In what ways could the use of microfranchising, microconsignment, and microleasing for delivery of financial services result in a scalable business model?
- What strategies might be the basis for successful replication and scalability of microinsurance programs?
- What types of disruptive technology and cell phone banking systems are creating opportunities and connections for those in need of financial services?

Stakeholder Theory and Ethical Issues

McGahan (2012) reiterates the notion of others as to who should be included and who should be excluded in a stakeholder analysis. By their very nature, participants in the informal economy are excluded from most research and analysis. However, an expanded research agenda regarding stakeholders creates the potential for enhanced inclusion and improved economic benefits for those previously excluded. Creating *shared value* among underserved and underrepresented populations has the potential of improved business development and enhanced quality of life (Porter & Kramer, 2011).

Potential exploitation and fraud is an ongoing concern for small business owners and consumers in unregulated markets, such as loan sharks, 5–6 moneylenders in the Philippines, and high-fee susu collectors in Ghana. In addition, as microinsurance expands in China, illegal insurance schemes have surfaced in a subversive insurance market. Customers are attracted with offers of high rates of return on life insurance products. However, consumers have no recourse when trying to collect since the companies violate Chinese regulations and evade taxes (Li & Hsu, 2009). This situation is just one example of unscrupulous financial service marketplace activities. Also of concern is over-indebtedness among credit customers. Promoting transparency, responsible pricing, and client privacy in the microfinance industry, the Smart Campaign (www.smartcampaign.org) is a global cooperative effort to develop and implement client-protection standards.

Fundamental to the preceding discussion is the exclusion from adequate banking services for millions of people. Many organizations and governments are investigating financial market strategies that include underserved populations and the extreme poor. *Financial inclusion* initiatives address these concerns, attempting to enhance economic growth and stability for emerging markets. The Center for Financial Inclusion (www.centerforfinancialinclusion.org), launched by ACCION International, and the Consultative Group to Assist the Poor (www.cgap.org), an initiative of the World Bank, are clearinghouses for financial inclusion research, policy development, and advocacy.

With regard to ethical aspects of informal financial services, researchers might consider these topics:

- What actions can effectively blend informal and formal business activities to create shared-value models for mutual financial and social benefits of stakeholders ?
- How might unethical and illegal financial service practices be identified and minimized in an attempt to avoid personal and social costs associated with fraudulent activities?
- What financial protection outcomes are desired through informal-formal financial service linkages?
- What approaches to financial inclusion are best suited to the informal economic environment?

CONCLUDING COMMENT

Financial, economic, and political stability are needed for improved business development and enhanced quality of life. The extensive number of people living, working, and doing business in the informal economy, especially in rural and impoverished areas, require financial services. With limited access to formal financial institutions, enterprising individuals and entrepreneurs have implemented a variety of informal, unregistered banking activities. Very limited attention has been given to management scholarship for these alternative financial services. A vast array of research opportunities exists with regard to areas of environmental influences, organizational structure, stakeholder theory, and ethical issues. With great variations in the organization, operation, and regulation of these alternative financial services, all involved in global business development require an ability to recognize and adapt to these cross-cultural banking activities.

REFERENCES

Adams, D. W., & Fitchett, D. A. (Eds.). 1992. *Informal finance in low-income countries.* Boulder: Westview Press.

Allen, H., & Panetta D. 2010. *Savings groups: What are they?* Washington, DC: The SEEP Network Savings-Led Financial Services Working Group.

Anyango, E., Esipisu E., Opoku, L., Johnson S., Malkamaki, M., & Musoke, C. 2007. Village savings and loan associations–Experience from Zanzibar. *Small Enterprise Development*, 18(1): 11–24.

Ardener, S., & Burman, S. (Eds.). 1996. *Money-go-rounds: The importance of ROSCAs for women.* Oxford: Berg Publishers.

Barboza, D. 2011. In cooling China, loan sharks come knocking. *New York Times*, October 13. http://www.nytimes.com/2011/10/14/business/global/as-chinas-economy-cools-loan-sharks-come-knocking.html?_r=0.

Bouman, F. 1995. ROSCA: On the origin of the species. *Savings and Development*, XIX(2): 129.

Bruton, G.D., Ireland, R.D., & Ketchen, D.K., Jr. 2012. Toward a research agenda on the informal economy. *Academy of Management Perspectives*, 26(3): 1–11.

Burns, T., & Stalker, G. M. 1961. *The management of innovation.* London: Tavistock.

Chipeta, C. 2011. *Money and credit in an indigenous African context.* Ekwendeni, Malawi: Imbabili Indigenous Knowledge Publications.

Collins, D., Morduch, J., Rutherford, S., & Ruthven, O. 2009. *Portfolios of the poor: How the world's poor live on $2 a day.* Princeton, NJ: Princeton University Press.

Dlabay, L.R., & Reger, G. 2007. *A regional comparison of informal foreign exchange activities: A qualitative analysis.* Paper presented at the annual meeting of the Midwest Chapter, Academy of International Business, Chicago, IL.

Etchu-Njang, M. 2007. *Tontines (aka Njangis) in Cameroon.* Personal essay.

Faith, D. C. 2011. The hawala system. *Global Security Studies*, 2(1): 23–33.

Food and Agriculture Organization of the United Nations. 2002. *The group savings resource book: A practical guide to help groups mobilize and manage their savings.* http://www.fao.org/docrep/005/y4094E/y4094e00.htm.

Ghana Co-operative Susu Collectors' Association. 2015. About Us. http://ghana-susu.com, January 12.

Ghate, P. 1992. *Informal finance: Some findings from Asia.* Oxford: Asian Development Bank Press.

Isern, J., Deshpande, R., & Van Doorn, J. 2005. *Crafting a money transfers strategy: guidance for pro-poor financial service providers.* CGAP Occasional Paper 10. Washington: The World Bank.

Kistruck, G. M., Webb, J. W., Sutter, C. J., & Ireland, R. D. 2011. MicroFranchising in base-of-the-pyramid markets: Institutional challenges and adaptations to the franchise model. *Entrepreneurship Theory and Practice*, 35: 503–531.

Kondo, M. 2003. The Bombay 5–6: Last resource informal financiers for Philippine micro-enterprises. *Kyoto Review of Southeast Asia.* http://kyotoreview.org/issue-4/the-bombay-5–6-last-resource-informal-financiers-for-philippine-micro-enterprises/.

Lawrence, P.R. & Lorsch, J.W. (1967). *Organization and environment: managing differentiation and integration.* Boston: Harvard University Press.

Ledgerwood, J. (Ed.). 2013. *The new microfinance handbook: A financial market system perspective.* Washington: The World Bank.

Li, J., & Hsu, S. 2009. *Informal finance in China: American and Chinese perspectives.* Oxford: Oxford University Press.

Mas, I., & Radcliffe, D. 2010. *Mobile payments go viral: M-PESA in Kenya.* http://siteresources.worldbank.org/AFRICAEXT/Resources/258643-1271798012256/M-PESA_Kenya.pdf.

McGahan, A. 2012. Challenges of the informal economy for the field of management. *Academy of Management Perspectives*, 26(3): 12–21.

Mercy Corps Nepal. 2008. *Mercy Corps Nepal microfinance assessment: Scope of meso-level technical service provision to MFIs in Nepal.* http://nepal.mercycorps.org/pdf/MercyCorpsNepalMicroFinanceAssessmentScopeofMesoLevelTechnicalServiceProvisiontoMFIsinNepal.pdf.

Micro Finance Regulatory Council in South Africa. 2015. *Loan sharks.* http://www.mfrc.co.za/loan-sharks, January 12.

Mohammad, G. & Yunaningsih, R. 2014. *Lessons from informal financial systems: Indonesian perspective.* http://blog.microsave.net/lessons-from-informal-financial-systems-indonesian-perspective/.

Nokia Research Center. 2015. *Merry go round: A study of informal self-help groups in Kenya.* http://liberationtechnologydcourse.pbworks.com/f/Self-help+Groups+Report.pdf, January 12.

Opportunity International. 2015. *Trust groups.* http://opportunity.org/what-we-do/unique-offerings/trust-groups, January 12.

Osei, R. D. 2008. *Linking traditional banking with modern finance: Barclays microbanking-susu collectors initiative.* http://www.growinginclusivemarkets.org/media/cases/Ghana_Susu%20Collectors_2008.pdf.

Pagura, M., & Kirsten, M. 2009. *Formal-informal financial linkages: Lessons from developing countries.* http://www.bwtp.org/pdfs/arcm/Pagura.pdf.

Porter, M. E., & Kramer, M. R. 2011. Creating shared value. *Harvard Business Review*, 89(1): 62–77.

Quiros, R., & Gonzalez-Vega, C. 2007. *Strategic alliances for scale and scope economies: Lessons from FADES in Bolivia.* http://www.ruralfinance.org/fileadmin/templates/rflc/documents/1188985642636_FADES_Bolivia.pdf.

Rippey, P., & Fowler, B. 2011. *Beyond financial services: A synthesis of studies on the integration of savings groups and other developmental activities.* Geneva, Switzerland: Aga Khan Foundation.

Ritchie, A. 2015. *Typology of microfinance service providers version 1.31.* World Bank. http://siteresources.worldbank.org/INTCDD/Resources/mftype.pdf, January 12.

Roenigk, E. 2015. *Savings for life: Financial opportunity for the world's most vulnerable.* http://worldrelief.org/recent-stories/savings-for-life-kenya, January 12.

Rutherford, S., & Arora, S. S. 2009. *The poor and their money: Microfinance from a twenty-first century consumer's perspective.* Warwickshire: Practical Action Publishing.

Singh, S. 2013. *Globalization and money: A global south perspective.* Lanham, MD: Rowman & Littlefield Publishers.

Sinha, F. 2010. *Microfinance self-help groups in India: Living up to their promise?* Warwickshire: Practical Action Publishing.

Srinivas, H. 2015a. *A typology of informal credit suppliers: Moneylenders.* http://www.gdrc.org/icm/suppliers/typ-ml.html, January 12.

Srinivas, H. 2015b. *A typology of informal credit suppliers: Pawn Brokers.* http://www.gdrc.org/icm/suppliers/typ-pawn.html, January 12.

Thai Intel ASEAN News. 2015. *No solution in sight for Thailand's estimated US$3 billion loan shark business.* https://aseaneconomist.wordpress.com/2012/12/18/no-solution-in-sight-for-thailands-conservative-estimated-us3-billion-loan-shark-business/, January 12.

Tsai, K. S. 2004. *Back-alley banking: Private entrepreneurs in China.* Ithaca: Cornell University Press.

Thompson, N. A. 2014. Short-term loans and long-term benefits: Tandas are "no-interest, short-term loans that can help Latina entrepreneurs and job-creators. *Latin Post*, April 10. http://www.latinpost.com/articles/10321/20140410/short-term-loans-benefits-latinas-tandas-no-interest-loans-latina-entrepreneurs-job-creators.htm.

US AID. 2008. *Nepal inclusive economic growth assessment: Microenterprise development.* http://pdf.usaid.gov/pdf_docs/PNADN015.pdf, January 12.

Westley, G. D., & Palomas, X. M. 2010. *Is there a business case for small savers?* Occasional Paper 18. Washington, DC: CGAP. https://www.cgap.org/sites/default/files/CGAP-Brief-Is-There-a-Business-Case-for-Small-Savers-Jan-2011.pdf.

World Relief. 2012. *World Relief Malawi empowering rural women and men to save and loan.* http://www.standforafrica.org/pdf/wr-malawi-press-release.pdf.

World Relief. 2015. *Rwanda Gahanga group.* http://worldrelief.org/Page.aspx?pid=1969, January 12.

Contributors

Garry Bruton—Garry D. Bruton is a Professor at Texas Christian University. He has published or has forthcoming over 100 academic articles in leading academic journals. He is currently the general editor of the *Journal of Management Studies* and associate editor of the Strategic Management Journal, the past president of the *Asia Academy of Management*, and the former editor of the *Academy of Management Perspectives*.

Les Dlabay—Les Dlabay is Professor of Business at Lake Forest College. He has authored or has adaptations of 40 textbooks in the United States, Canada, India, and Singapore. Dlabay serves on the boards of Bright Hope International and Andean Aid. His research emphasis involves alternative financial services in informal economic settings.

Gibb Dyer—W. Gibb Dyer is the O. Leslie Stone Professor of Entrepreneurship and the Academic Director of the Center for Economic Self-Reliance in the Marriott School of Management at Brigham Young University. He received his BS and MBA degrees from Brigham Young University and his PhD in management philosophy from the Massachusetts Institute of Technology. He has previously served as Chair of the Department of Organizational Behavior at Brigham Young University. In 2007 he was given the faculty teaching award from Brigham Young University's division of continuing education, and in 2008 was given the outstanding faculty award from the Marriott School of Management. He is currently an associate editor of the Family Business Review.

John Ginther—John Ginther is a Research Associate with the T-HOPE team at the University of Toronto and Consultant with the World Bank. He specializes in private sector development and healthcare and holds an MBA and Master of Global Affairs from the University of Toronto.

Müge Haseki—Müge Haseki (MA, University of Wisconsin-Milwaukee, 2008) is a doctoral candidate in the School of Communication and Information at Rutgers University. Her research focuses on information and communication technology use for development with an interest in information seeking and social networks.

Duane Ireland—R. Duane Ireland is a University Distinguished Professor and holds the Conn Chair in New Ventures Leadership in the Mays Business School at Texas A&M University. He is a former editor of *Academy of Management Journal*, former President of the Academy of Management, and a Fellow in the Academy of Management.

Urs Jäger—Urs Jäger is Associate Professor at INCAE Business School and Associate Professor (Privatdozent) at the University of St. Gallen. He has published a number of articles in leading journals for third sector research and five books, including *Managing Social Businesses: Mission, Governance, Strategy and Accountability* (Palgrave Macmillan, 2010).

Robb Jensen—Robert Jensen is an Associate Professor at BYU. He researches knowledge replication with special attention on bottom-of-the-pyramid markets. Robert has published 17 articles in top strategy and international journals such as *SMJ*, *JIBS*, *Management Science*, and *Organization Science*. He is currently on the *JIBS* editorial review board.

Joe Mahoney—Joseph T. Mahoney earned his doctorate in Business Economics from the Wharton School of Business. He joined the College of Business of the University of Illinois at Urbana-Champaign in 1988 and is currently Professor of Strategy & Entrepreneurship, Caterpillar Chair of Business, and Director of Research for the Department of Business Administration.

Anita McGahan—Anita M. McGahan is Associate Dean of Research, PhD Director, Professor and Rotman Chair in Management at the Rotman School of Management at the University of Toronto. She is cross appointed to the Munk School of Global Affairs; is a Senior Associate at the Institute for Strategy and Competitiveness at Harvard University; and is Chief Economist at the Massachusetts General Hospital Division for Global Health and Human Rights. In 2013, she was elected by the Academy of Management's membership to the Board of Governors and into the Presidency rotation.

Vijay Sathe—Vijay Sathe is the C.S. & D.J. Davidson Chair and Professor of Management in the Drucker School at Claremont Graduate University, California. He has published numerous articles and six books, including (co-edited with Urs Jäger) Strategy & Competitiveness in Latin American Markets: The Sustainability Frontier (Edward Elgar, 2014).

Bill Schulze—William (Bill) Schulze is a David Eccles Professor of Business at the David Eccles School of Business at the University of Utah. His current research focuses on family enterprises, governance in private and closely held firms, new venture formation and growth, and, of course, the alleviation of poverty.

Craig R. Scott—Craig R. Scott is a Professor in the Department of Communication at Rutgers University. His research is primarily focused on organizational communication, where he examines issues of anonymity and identity/identification. His current work examines hidden organizations—when an organization and/or its members conceal parts of their identity from various audiences.

Brad Skousen—Bradley R. Skousen is a PhD candidate in Business Administration at the University of Illinois at Urbana-Champaign and a graduate of Columbia University's School of International and Public Affairs. Bradley's research focuses on the intersection of institutions and entrepreneurship with a particular interest in the context of nascent entrepreneurship.

Justin W. Webb—Justin W. Webb is the Belk Endowed Scholar in Business Innovation in the Belk College of Business at The University of North Carolina at Charlotte. His research interests include understanding the contextual and individual influences on the entrepreneurship process, market-based solutions to poverty in base-of-the-pyramid markets, and the informal economy.

Xiaodong Yu—Xiaodong Yu is a doctoral student at Renmin University of China and a visiting scholar in the Neeley Business School of Texas Christian University. His research field includes informal economy, family business, and corporate governance.

Index

Note: Italicized page numbers indicate a figure on the corresponding page. Page numbers in bold indicate a table on the corresponding page.